PRAISE FOR

EICHMANN IN MY HANDS

"A great historic event rates a great historic book. Alas, it seldom happens. But it happens here. And something more happens, something incredible. Humanity sings out of these pages. And this is the purest vengeance, it leaves the hangman in the dust. Peter Malkin, who grabbed Eichmann by the throat on a lonely street in Buenos Aires thirty years ago, now takes us in his hands—and delivers us from evil."

—**Sidney Zion, author of** *Markers* **and** *The Autobiography of Roy Cohn*

"In EICHMANN IN MY HANDS one relives the dramatic apprehension of Adolf Eichmann in Argentina. . . . The details of the entire secret operation are fascinating. . . . Intriguing, too, are the conversations in the aftermath as the captured murderer attempts to justify himself to his Jewish captor. Fiction can only strive for such effects. This is the real thing."

—**Abraham H. Foxman**
National Director
Anti-Defamation League

EICHMANN
IN MY HANDS
Peter Z. Malkin
& Harry Stein

*TO SAM MIRKIN
WITH LOVE
Peter Z. Malkin
11/11/01*

WARNER BOOKS

A Warner Communications Company

Warner Books, Inc., 666 Fifth Avenue, New York, NY 10103
A Warner Communications Company

Printed in the United States of America
First Printing: May 1990
10 9 8 7 6 5 4 3 2 1

Library of Congress Cataloging-in-Publication Data

Malkin, Peter Z.
    Eichmann in my hands/Peter Malkin and Harry Stein.
      p.   cm.
    Includes bibliographical references.
    ISBN 0-446-51418-7
    1. Eichmann, Adolf, 1906–1962.   2. Malkin, Peter Z.   3. Secret
service—Israel.   4. War criminals—Germany—Biography.
5. Holocaust, Jewish (1939–1945)   I. Stein, Harry.   II. Title.
DD247.E5M35   1990
364.1'38'092—dc20
[B]
                                                          89-40464
                                                          CIP

All photos except that of Haasi Eichmann
from the collection of Peter Z. Malkin

Photo of Haasi Eichmann by
Francisco Vera, Life *Magazine*
© 1960 Time Inc.

Book design: H. Roberts

For Fruma

ACKNOWLEDGMENTS

Many hands and hearts went into the making of this book.

For their perseverance and unflagging support, we thank Roni, Priscilla, Omer, Tamar, and Adi.

For the special quality of their friendship we thank Saul and Robert Steinberg. For their generosity and understanding we thank Uri Dan, Steve and Marina Kaufman, and Professor Wolf Kirsh and Marie Kirsh.

Howard and Judith Steinberg were never not there.

Larry Kirshbaum and Jay Acton believed in this project from the start. Jamie Raab and Ellen Herrick were free with their time and counsel. Susan Suffes was an extraordinarily thoughtful and sensitive editorial voice.

Joshua Morgenthau, Sadie and Charlie Stein, and Adam Zion served as a particular source of inspiration; living evidence that, for all the horrors of the past, there is a future in which to believe.

With the exception of Peter Z. Malkin, Isser Harel, and Amos Manor, the names of all individuals involved in operations described in the book have been changed for security reasons.

The narrative voice throughout the book is that of Peter Z. Malkin.

CONTENTS

PREFACE

The Holocaust occurred a mere fifty years ago; tens of millions remember it firsthand, and survivors still wander among us. Yet, to an almost uncanny degree, it has already begun to recede into history. For many of the young in particular, the unspeakable events of those years seem increasingly to carry little more emotional weight than the Boer War or the assassination of Julius Caesar.

Even for many alive at the time, names and places intimately bound up with the Nazi program of genocide have grown indistinct, familiar yet stripped of specific meaning. Names like Heydrich and Streicher. Places like Babi Yar, Sobibor, the ghettoes of Lodz and Vilna and Warsaw.

In one important sense Adolf Eichmann stands as an exception to that rule. Thirty years after his execution his name still rings notorious; he was the number-one war criminal hunted down in the postwar era. Yet tellingly, the lessons of even the Eichmann case have grown hazy, the general impression somehow being that the notorious SS

Obersturmführer was merely an important cog in a vast and impersonal machine, and, more, that Nazism itself was an aberration, and we will never see its like again.

We understand as well as anyone why the full import of Eichmann as a moral example so often fails to register. By the measures usually applied to such things, he was not an obviously cruel or thoughtless man. Were he living among us today and, say, running a shoe factory, he would probably be regarded with quiet respect; a steady husband and father, producing excellent shoes at a fair price, a pride to his community.

Yet this is precisely what ought to make the Eichmann story continually unsettling, and never more so than in times as ethically ambiguous as our own. For it is not just about the unspeakable evil perpetrated by the agents of Nazism—where we are comfortably able to identify with the victims—but about the astonishing capacity of those not wholly unlike ourselves for self-justification; the ease with which, in the interest of ideology or simple ambition, seemingly normal souls escape their better selves.

History has appropriately branded Adolf Eichmann a monster, a man oblivious to every impulse—compassion, remorse, respect for the sanctity of life—by which we ought to define our humanity. Still, if we look closely, the most shocking thing is that he seems so very familiar.

—*Peter Z. Malkin and Harry Stein*

EICHMANN
IN MY HANDS

INTRODUCTION

A little past midday on a sweltering day in July 1961, I joined a long line snaking around a large, low building in central Jerusalem. Formerly a community center known as the Beit Hamm (the House of the People), it had lately been converted into a courtroom, one vast enough to accommodate 750 spectators, including reporters from forty countries, an elevated bank of TV and newsreel cameras, and, where ordinarily the defendant would sit, a spacious booth of bulletproof glass.

The booth was widely recognized as a major innovation in personal security, but already it had also come to stand for something else: the isolation of Adolf Eichmann from the rest of humanity.

As I waited, I made note of the security outside the building as well. A ten-foot fence of steel mesh had been erected around the entire structure. Border policemen patrolled its roof and grounds, submachine guns at the ready.

Even now, at lunch hour, the building was bathed in flood-lights, making the temperature almost unbearable.

Within twenty minutes my shirt was soaked through; within forty-five my head was starting to pound. Up and down the line, people were complaining: What was going on here; when were they going to open the doors? Even the group of Yemeni schoolchildren, brought here by their teacher to witness history in the making, had grown listless.

The heat did little for my disposition. History was the furthest thing from my mind; I had come only reluctantly, to honor a commitment. Now, as the minutes passed in that blast-furnace heat, I was more persuaded than ever that the errand was pointless. More than a year had passed. Surely Eichmann himself no longer remembered that exchange back in Buenos Aires.

Nor were my spirits much raised when the line at last began edging forward and I found myself obliged to enter a cubicle in the building lobby and submit to a rigorous body search: a reminder, as if any were needed, that even on my native soil I was without identity or standing, the very nature of my work a state secret. *Hell, if I'd wanted to KILL the sonofabitch, I'd have done it then!*

All of which has a lot to do with why, another twenty minutes later, I was so surprised by my own excitement as an urgent murmur passed over the crowd. I strained forward in my seat, above the judges' bench and a little to the left. There he was, being led into his booth.

The sight was staggering. Though doctors had dismissed his lawyers' claim that he had suffered two heart attacks in the three months since the start of the trial (the condition was diagnosed as functional arrhythmia), neither they nor the photos had suggested the extent of the man's physical deterioration. Fifteen pounds lighter than when I had last seen him, his cheeks deep shadows and the blue suit made for him by an Israeli tailor limp on a narrow frame, his skin had gone a waxy yellow. Seeing him, it was easy to believe, as Eichmann's associate counsel had recently claimed, that the fifty-five-year-old defendant had become obsessed with a prediction made years before by an Argentine gypsy that he would not live past his fifty-seventh birthday.

And yet he didn't *carry* himself like a beaten man. Taking a seat at the desk within his cage, oblivious to the blue-uniformed policemen on either side (like all of Eichmann's guards, of *non*-European origin), he immediately began organizing his papers into neat piles before him. As one observer had it, he was turning the glass booth into "a tiny island of fussy bureaucracy."

And, moments later, when he began to speak, I knew for certain he had not changed. Instantly it all came back with full force: the man's astonishing self-control, his sense of certainty, his maddening, almost unbelievable, moral obtuseness.

Eichmann was in the midst of his eighth day of cross-examination, and the subject before the court, carried over from the morning session, was responsibility for the eradication of a group of one hundred Jewish children. From Lidice, the Czech village obliterated in 1942 in reprisal for the assassination by partisans of Eichmann's immediate SS superior Reinhard Heydrich, the children were dispatched *en masse* to the gas chambers at Chelmo.

Yes, Eichmann allowed drily, rising in his booth to respond to the sharp question put to him by prosecutor Gideon Hausner, he recalled the events in question, at least the assassination. "But the affair of the children I do not remember." After all, he added, he occupied himself with questions of transport, not those of life and death.

Eichmann seemed to have been born knowing that bland makes for excellent protective coloring. Indeed, even at the height of his personal power, the months and years when he traversed Europe going about his grisly work with a zeal and relish that stunned even some of his most committed contemporaries, he had often taken refuge behind a bureaucratic cloak.

But Hausner, the Israeli attorney general, bored in. Citing prior testimony to the effect that Eichmann had personally marked the Lidice children for "special treatment" —a favorite Nazi euphemism for immediate extermination—he waved a letter written to the defendant at the time by a subordinate seeking confirmation of the order that they be sent forthwith to the death camp.

Eichmann sat for a long moment listening to the translation.

"Look here!" demanded Hausner, brandishing the letter. "Do you mean to say that Krumy [the subordinate] did not know who was competent to deal with this matter?"

In his booth Eichmann slowly rose to his feet. Though steady, he betrayed his anxiety by gnawing on his lower lip. "Maybe he wrote to another department, could not get a reply, and then wrote to me," he offered.

"But the children had nothing to do with the transport question! Why did Krumy contact you? Why YOU?"

"Krumy's in prison in Germany," came back Eichmann evenly. "Ask him."

None of this was surprising, of course. Through almost three months of eyewitness testimony, some of it so gruesome as to challenge the very capacity for comprehension, the government had painstakingly described the Nazis' highly organized systems of terror and barbarity and then tied specific acts directly to the commands of the defendant. The world had learned that it was Eichmann who had commissioned the design of the first gas chambers; Eichmann who had instituted the campaign of deceit to encourage the victims' compliance, denying them their dignity even as they were led to the slaughter; Eichmann who, in his single-minded pursuit of the National Socialist agenda, dispatched to the ovens even those Jews whom his superiors were ready to spare. In fact, it was Eichmann who even at the very end, when others were looking to save their skins, ignored explicit orders from the top that the liquidation be halted. This was a man who, on hearing a conscience-stricken subordinate exclaim, "God grant that our enemies never have a chance to do the same to the German people!" replied with cool contempt, "Don't be sentimental . . ."

Nor was there anything unexpected in Eichmann's line of defense. It was the standard one, that he had only been following orders, an argument which, carried to its logical conclusion, would hold that no one in the Third Reich besides Adolf Hitler was guilty of anything at all; indeed, that the very concept of personal responsibility had no meaning.

Still, watching now, there was something disturbing in the way Hausner was going after him. Striding the courtroom in his black robes like a balding, bespectacled bat, now raging, now full of mocking contempt, incessantly waving an accusing finger or pounding a fist, exasperated by even the legitimate objections of Eichmann's attorney, the rotund Dr. Robert Servatius, this was a man out to enhance his reputation. Did the fact that we had been victims give *us* license to be less than just?

Indeed, not content to convict Eichmann of the unspeakable crimes for which he bore clear responsibility, Hausner had also set out to make the case, with little documentary evidence, that in 1944 he had killed with his own hands a Jewish boy caught stealing a piece of fruit on the grounds of his Budapest residence. It was, as anyone familiar with Eichmann knew (and the three justices would eventually conclude), a charge that strained credulity. Certainly the man murdered without mercy or conscience, but only at a distance. Like SS chief Heinrich Himmler, he was sickened by the sight of blood.

But in the portrayal of Eichmann merely as a bloodthirsty executioner, truth was being done an even more fundamental disservice. It was far more complex than that and, in a real sense, more chilling. For even as he sat in that booth, he truly did not *understand* that he had done wrong.

The fact is that Eichmann believed himself a man of honor. Yes, he was cruel when he had to be, and remorseless—this he admitted—but never indiscriminately so.

Even now, listening with equanimity to accusations of mass murder, he bridled at any suggestion that he had been anything other than "correct" in his one-to-one dealings with the Jewish leaders he had so masterfully used to his horrifying ends.

To him this was the heart of the matter. The *content* of his beliefs, the acts themselves, were secondary.

Just a couple of weeks earlier, flipping through the papers, I had been keenly reminded of this side of the man. His own version of his capture had just appeared for the first time in a London tabloid, and according to the account I read, he had gone out of his way to compliment those of us who had carried it out, terming the operation "an elegant job," handled "impeccably and with precision." Immediately I recognized this as a gesture aimed at me.

In fact, characteristically, Eichmann didn't have a clue. He knew little more of what had gone on behind the scenes than those in the Israeli popular press who for a year had been touting us as heroes, or those abroad who imagined us some Israeli version of grim, faceless men in trenchcoats. The bringing of Eichmann to justice had been, in the end, less a model of crisp, military precision than a seat-of-the-pants adventure.

Above all, what Eichmann himself could not grasp—given who he was, would never have been capable of understanding—was that we had regarded the operation as a task of almost biblical moral weight. And that some of us had been transformed by it.

Though as a Jew I myself had come to age with the understanding of how readily those untethered by conscience can turn into monsters, always before it had been theoretical. I was among those many who, in the wake of the Holocaust, had come to see the very gentleness of spirit and abhorrence of injustice that for centuries had helped sustain us as a people as naive, impractical, the mentality of oppression. Moreover, like so many whose lives had been ravaged by loss, I had grown accustomed to keeping certain

thoughts and feelings at bay. Emotionally incomplete, perhaps, but at least far from pain, I was one of those people
reflexively uncomfortable at the thought of earnestness, let
alone self-examination.

But my brush with Eichmann had started to change all
that. In the guise of professional responsibility I had been
forced to face myself. Long an accomplished agent, I was at
last becoming a complete human being.

Now, in the courtroom, I watched closely as, head
bowed, listening to the translation, the defendant formed
the answer to another question. Only this time, when he
raised his eyes, he happened to glance in my direction.

He abruptly stopped, registering surprise, then a kind
of bewilderment. For a long moment our eyes remained
locked.

"Accused!" shouted Hausner into the stillness. "You
are required to answer the question!"

Eichmann turned toward him and began speaking.

I listened a moment longer, then rose and headed for
the exit. I had seen who I came to see, the only soul in that
vast, historic assemblage who had the slightest idea of who
I was.

ONE

Resistance of the Powerless

AMONG the pivotal figures in my life—certainly in this story—is someone I hardly recall at all. I was only four and a half in 1933 when the rest of the family left our village in eastern Poland for Palestine, leaving our sister, Fruma, behind. Exit visas were in desperately short supply. At twenty-three, Fruma had a husband and children of her own. Somehow she would join us later.

It was the first time any of us had been apart for more than a couple of days. My parents had four children, but to me, as the youngest, it had always seemed there were just two of us and four doting grown-ups. Jacob was just two years older than me, but there was a fifteen-year jump up to Yechiel, already old enough to work beside our father, buying wheat from farmers in the outlying districts for sale to the local mills. And Fruma, living next door, constantly in and out of the house, was more like a second mother, as nurturing as our own and less intimidating.

I recall only fragments of those early years: the look of

certain faces, the sense of being in particular places, random moments so extraordinarily vivid that it sometimes seems I must have made them up. But, too, I recall a feeling of warmth and security I have never known since.

Fruma is at the center of the most persistent of those memories. It is late afternoon and, playing behind the house with Jacob and her son Takele, our best friend, I take a hard fall, banging my head. Almost instantly Fruma is holding me tight in her arms, rocking me back and forth, singing softly. Looking up through my tears, I see large blue eyes and, from beneath a maroon kerchief, wisps of blond hair.

Another memory. Moshele, my sister's brother-in-law, the village dandy in his elegant tunic and polished boots, is in our house late one winter night, telling stories. All the grown-ups are laughing. Though he is a little hard to follow, since he is using a different voice for each character, our parents encourage us to stay up until the end. My sister stands with her back to the warmth of the oven wall, her eyes glowing, the most beautiful woman I have ever seen.

And another. Straying from my mother and Fruma, I am drawn to the village church. Inside, it is such a contrast to our drab wooden synagogue. I am most fascinated by the statue of the naked, bloody man on the cross. When they find me, my mother is furious; back on the street, she shakes me violently, tells me I'll end up like Piatnik the Thief. It is my sister who takes me home, explaining once again about the Poles and the Jews, and telling the story of Piatnik.

Strange as it sounds, in later years I would not even remember the name of our village; partly because, in Palestine, my parents would so seldom talk about it; partly because, when they did, I would refuse to listen. But I would never forget my almost mystical connection to Piatnik the Thief. In a time and place where such superstitions were taken very seriously, I had been born at the very moment he lay dying alongside the well in the center of town, two long stab wounds in his chest.

For Jews, being afraid of the Poles was a way of life. It

was understood we were at their mercy. Indeed, our very speech was full of code and double meaning. We would never refer to the taxman but to "the one with the papers"; we would say "yellow" when we meant gold. The resistance of the powerless. One never knew when "they" would lash out, or why. As a grown-up my brother Yechiel would still bear scars from the time he was beaten unconscious by a Polish peasant with a club for being too slow in pulling his cart to the side of a dusty road to let him pass. At the time Yechiel was eleven years old.

A last Polish memory. One evening, walking home with Jacob from our *cheder*, the tiny school where we studied Hebrew and the Holy Books, we are suddenly aware of a brilliant orange sky. When we reach the center of town, we see our synagogue is in flames. One of our neighbors, Baruch the candy seller, has been killed.

But that is almost secondary. What I recall most clearly of that evening is my parents fighting. They never fought. My parents were as devoted to one another as any man and woman I have ever known. Though she was capable of wicked sarcasm, my mother never turned it on my father; she always got her way through gentle persistence. In the end my father, allowed to maintain the delusion that he was in charge, could deny her nothing. But on this night my mother is screaming. He can stay, she cries, and she will take us by herself. My father, controlled at first, starts yelling back; then he storms out of the house.

Huddled together in bed, terrified, disbelieving, Jacob and I take it all in.

In memory it seems only a split second later. But knowing what I do now, it must have been at least a couple of months after that that Jacob and I found ourselves at the rail of a ship, pushed and jostled by those behind, as we squinted toward Palestine in the distance. Those larger people crowded around us seemed to have lost all control, shouting with joy, breaking into song; but I felt only confusion. Staring at the landscape through the shimmering midday heat, I could see only *brown:* stony tan hills, occasionally relieved by a dusty stone house or a twisted dry tree. Where were the lush jungles and tropical forests? Where were the fantastic birds? Where was the milk and honey?

Now, as we drew closer, we began to pick up activity in the harbor: Arab porters, barefoot with trousers rolled to their knees, running in all directions, the peddlers of oranges and dates, countless others on heaven knows what business engaging in vigorous disputation. We might as well have been going to live on another planet.

"Jacob," I said softly, taking his hand, "I don't like it here. I want to go home."

My brother must have found the prospect of this new existence even more frightening than I did. Sweet-natured Jacob was one of those boys, so prized in the land we were leaving behind, already recognized as intellectually gifted. His great passion was the study of the Holy Books.

"Quiet, Peter," he gently soothed. "Have faith in God."

Then there were the other questions. Why had Jacob and I been told to answer to a different last name? Why was my father having to pretend to be a rabbi? Above all, where were Fruma and her children?

I would begin to learn the answers only when I became acquainted with this new land and its history. The British, in control of Palestine under the terms of the mandate granted after the First World War, were vigorously limiting Jewish immigration. Indeed, it was only through incredible resourcefulness—and more than a little subterfuge—that our mother had managed to secure exit certificates; and even at that, she could only get five. Somehow she would find a way for Fruma and her family to join us later.

I saw my first British police within the hour, when a half dozen boarded our ship from a launch. I was amazed to see these grown men wearing *shorts.* It soon became clear, however, that they were the opposite of pleasantly informal.

On shore, as we made our way through the chaos of the harbor into the narrow streets of Haifa, our bags atop a hired donkey, policemen pushed and beat their way through the crowd with their short clubs.

"What's the difference?" muttered my father. "Are these any better than the ones in Poland?"

We were heading for the eastern slope of Mt. Carmel. My father had some distant relatives living there and my mother had written them of our impending arrival. We were therefore more shocked by what happened next than anything that had come before. Arriving at the tiny building of concrete and stone after a grueling three-hour walk through the heat and desolation, we were greeted by the woman of the house, a certain cousin Ruchele, tight-lipped and severe, wire-rimmed glasses perched on a sharp nose. Having come to Palestine some twenty years before on her own, Ruchele and her husband had chosen to live in this place with their baby through their commitment to Socialist Zionism, and she could hardly inform us soon enough of her contempt for all we represented: We were in the land of Israel now, there was a country to be built. Here there was no place for parasites.

When she stopped her harangue, she led us into the house, installing us in a room perhaps seventy feet square. Three beds had been crammed in for the five of us and the heat was oppressive. Ruchele had warned us not to speak above a whisper so as not to wake her baby.

For a long moment we sat on the beds, staring at one another in silence. Then my father rose to his feet, terrible pain on his face. "I'm going for a walk," he said.

Wordlessly I scurried after him.

My father was hardly the most communicative of men. I am not sure he ever spoke the words "I love you" in his entire life. But now he took my small hand and gave it a gentle squeeze. It meant the same thing.

We walked for ten minutes in silence, our worn shoes making crunching sounds on the baked soil. Finally he took a seat on a large stone. "We've got to get out of here," he said, his gaze taking in the entire mountain, if not the country itself.

I stared at him, waiting for more. There was nothing.

"Papa," I said softly, "what will we do here?"

"We'll work." He snorted. "It's like Ruchele says, we'll work."

"What about Fruma?"

"They'll join us soon enough. With God's help they'll come."

"Will I work too? And Jacob?"

"Don't worry, Peter, you'll do fine. You're braver than you think." He paused and offered a small smile. "Remember Piatnik the Thief."

I thought about it. What did he know that I didn't? I didn't think of myself as brave at all. I was only a little boy.

My father pulled a cigarette from his pocket and lit it with a long-wicked Polish lighter.

"Papa, tell me about Piatnik the Thief."

"He was a nobleman, Piatnik the Thief. I knew his father a little."

"But why did they kill him? He wasn't a Jew."

He took a long drag on his cigarette. "He was friendly with the Jews. He was a good and very brave man. He would warn us of what was coming."

"He helped us?"

He nodded. "If Piatnik were still alive, they wouldn't have been able to burn the synagogue." He paused, looking around at our barren surroundings, then at me. "He gave his life trying to do what was right. It is something worth trying to live up to."

TWO

The Seeds of Power

*I*N 1933, *an obscure twenty-seven-year-old SS sergeant named Adolf Eichmann, having just completed his formal military training, was about to begin a spectacular rise through the Nazi hierarchy.*

Eichmann was born in 1906 in Solingen, Germany, the first of five children. When he was eight, his accountant father moved the family to Linz, Austria, to become a commercial manager at the electric works. A remote figure, stern and deeply devout, for many years an honorary elder of the town's Evangelical congregation, Karl Eichmann ran an austere and loveless household. Above all else, it nurtured respect for thrift and order.

His eldest child was uncertain and withdrawn. A mediocre student, Adolf Eichmann made little impression on his peers in Linz, home to the young Hitler a generation earlier.

The one great serious disruption in the young Eichmann's childhood would appear to be the death of his mother in 1916, when he was ten. Yet, revealingly, by his own subsequent account, it affected him hardly at all. He noted simply that in short order his father remarried and life continued as before. More than forty years later, Israeli interrogators would be struck by the undercurrent of resentment with which he still spoke of his father, and by so extreme a hostility to the religion in which he had been raised that, pliable as he otherwise tended to be, he refused even to consider taking the oath on a Bible in court.

In the years after the German-Austrian defeat in World War I, his evident sense of powerless rage began to find expression as extreme militaristic posturing. Though only a teenager, he contrived to march alongside battle-tried former soldiers in parade formation, and tried to insinuate himself into the tradition-bound, quasi-military fencing club at a local university, another cauldron of jingoistic discontent.

One of his history teachers during this period was a certain Dr. Leopold Poetsch, whose rabid nationalism had once stirred the young Hitler. Now Poetsch fueled in Eichmann the conviction, increasingly widespread among the alienated young of the era, that Germany had lost the recent war not on the battlefield but behind the lines, cheated of victory by treacherous leftists and greedy Jews.

Eichmann's anti-Semitism undoubtedly started more as a theoretical position than as anything visceral. His closest childhood friend was a Jew named Harry Selbar.

But as his political fervor intensified, so did his enthusiasm for the program of National Socialism. Though the Nazis' brand of racism was not only crude but wildly inconsistent—before working-class audiences, Jews were described as "capitalist bloodsuckers"; before the wealthy, as Communists and revolutionaries—by the late twenties Eichmann accepted it whole, without question. For, of course, according to Nazi doctrine, doubt itself was intolerable, and the restoration of German greatness demanded the elimination of such "weak" character traits as compassion or a commitment to honesty.

Almost immediately, party work became the central focus of Eichmann's life. When, as the Depression worsened, he lost his job as a salesman of service station products for an oil company, he seized the opportunity to leave Austria and join a regiment of the Nazi military arm, the SS, based outside the town of Dachau in southern Germany. He lied to his father, saying that he had been fired by a Jewish inspector because of his party activities. Though the SS training was brutal, Eichmann flourished. Throughout the rest of his life he would show off the scars on his elbows and knees, the result of drills in which he was obliged to crawl over barbed wire, boasting how in that year he rid himself of all susceptibility to pain.

His training complete, Eichmann volunteered for the SD, the security service of the SS, where he was assigned the relatively modest rank of Scharführer, roughly the equivalent of sergeant. But by now Hitler had ascended to power, and in those early, heady, chaotic days of the Third Reich, anything was possible for an ambitious young man unburdened by conscience. Early in 1935 a subordinate of SS chief Himmler, casting about for a candidate to direct a proposed "Jewish Museum," a euphemism for a new bureau that was to collect data on the holdings of German Jews, found his way to Eichmann. Accepting the position eagerly, the young SS man launched himself into the study of Jewish history and culture. In astonishingly short order, he was known in high Nazi circles as an expert on the Jews.

More than that, Eichmann was already beginning to show the kind of surprising creativity and zeal for which, as the campaign against the Jews escalated, he would become known, and which, on the record, would be a greater source of personal satisfaction than any he had ever known.

Among other things, he visited Palestine in 1937, arriving with a very specific agenda: to establish contacts with the violently anti-Semitic grand mufti of Jerusalem,

Haj Amin el-Husseini, and to learn firsthand about the Jewish community in the Holy Land, with which, as the Nazis' resident "expert on Jewish questions," it was assumed he would one day have to deal.

"I was not just a recipient of orders," as he put it years later, in response to the familiar suggestion that he might have been more administrator than initiator. "Had I been that, I would have been an imbecile. I was an idealist."

THREE

Out of the Old Testament

I myself was eight years old in 1937 and living in a state of quiet turmoil. Having lived in Palestine three years, I certainly gave every appearance of having adjusted to circumstances there; indeed, I had begun to carry myself with a decided swagger, cocky and apparently fearless. Yet, within, I very much remained the naive and sensitive child of the *shtetl* I had been before.

My posture was a simple matter of adjustment to circumstances. It had not taken long to grasp how harsh this new world was going to be—or what it would take to survive it. Just a few weeks after our arrival, my mother took Jacob and me to the Haifa construction site where my father and Yechiel had landed jobs making bricks. It was backbreaking labor: fifteen-hour days under a brutal sun hauling sand, breaking stones, mixing cement, with pay not by the hour, but by the brick, a horrifying scene out of the Old Testament with my own father in the middle of it. But even more shocking was the behavior of the boss. Large and red-faced, sweating like a pig, he drove the workers with continual abuse. When at long last one of the men to whom he was particularly harsh dared to answer back, the foreman sent him to the ground with a vicious blow to the face. "I'm the boss here, you lazy bastard!" he screamed. "Don't you dare contradict me!"

I stood there, gaping. A Jew hitting another Jew! How could it be? What kind of place was this?

Soon enough, of course, the realities of this new environment were reflected even in the life of my own family. Shortly afterwards we moved to a small apartment in Haifa, and my mother, too, had to go to work to help pay for it, selling delicatessen out of a tiny storefront near the Arab market. Always, my life had revolved around the home and the *cheder*. Suddenly, Jacob and I found ourselves with virtually no adult supervision from midafternoon, when school got out, until nine in the evening.

This didn't change things all that much for my brother, at least at first. Each day he would dutifully return to the empty apartment, contentedly passing the hours in study of the Talmud. But for me the streets were irresistible.

For what streets they were! Our neighborhood in the Old City, a historical treasure trove where successive cultures had built one upon the other through the length of recorded history—beneath the Turks were the Arabs; beneath them, remnants of the Crusaders, and on and on back to the Romans and the Greeks and beyond—likely boasted more blind alleyways, abandoned wells, and underground passages than any other couple of square miles on the face of the earth.

Before long, I attached myself to a group, roaming the winding passageways every day after school, scaling ancient walls and exploring abandoned basements and storerooms, playing pirates and cowboys and soccer on cobblestoned streets beneath a thick canopy of hung laundry. These guys liked to regard themselves as tough, and, though younger and smaller, I was determined to keep up with them. If we didn't have money for candy, we would simply swipe it from an outdoor stand, or else lower one of our number into a marketplace basement to appropriate empty sacks and then resell to the merchant who owned them.

For me, always a *good* boy, such behavior demanded a fair amount of rationalizing. I knew stealing was wrong, but then, again, it didn't seem to much bother anyone else; besides which, being small and quick and wily, I happened to have a real talent for it.

When I finally did put my foot down, even temporarily, it was only because I had been pushed into a corner. One day the unofficial leader of the gang, so regarded because of his skill at soccer, decided that as the youngest and smallest, I could remain with them only if I passed a test. Using a long stick with five or six nails driven into the end, I was to steal a chocolate bar from a candy seller known for her vigilance. I did as I was told but midway into the act she grabbed the stick and pulled me toward her. Nabbed.

Except, far from the rage I expected, her face showed a kind of sorrow. Why had I done it? she wanted to know. If I wanted it so badly, why hadn't I just asked her? And she handed me the candy bar.

It turned out she was a recent emigrant from Poland herself and that I reminded her of the son she had lost to diphtheria.

Still, when I reported this to the boy who had given me the order, he was unmoved. "Do it again," he said.

"Why should I? She'll give it to me."

He considered briefly. "Then you can't be in the gang. And don't talk to any of us."

I lay up most of that night in torment: I couldn't be in the gang. I couldn't even *talk* to any of them! Then it occurred to me: Why couldn't I?

The next day after school, I walked right up to the leader and said hello.

"I told you not to talk to me," he said.

"I'll talk if I want to. You don't have to answer."

That did it. I was back in.

It was useful to know that no one can ever make you keep your mouth shut. It was early evidence that, no matter what they say, remaining true to one's principles breeds the respect of others.

Indeed, from that day forth I was quietly regarded as something of a leader myself, my opinion accorded special weight, my skills readily acknowledged.

By ten, among my growing claims to others' esteem was my reckless unpredictability. I loved testing myself. Sometimes, just for the hell of it, I would dream up something I would claim I could do—say, run to the top of Mt. Carmel and back in three hours, or eat an entire roast chicken, plus its eyeballs, in five minutes—and then proceed to take bets. If it was a matter of persistence, or will, or just dumb stubbornness, I knew I couldn't be beaten.

If my capacity for introspection had faded, so too had any trace of self-doubt.

About the only one to whom I still ever showed my other side was Jacob. Late at night in the room we shared, watching him scrunched up in his bed reading the Bible by candlelight, I would feel an intensity of love beyond expression and an abiding respect. Yet it bothered me that he always seemed to look so sad.

"Jacob," I put it to him one night, "aren't there any happy stories in the Bible?"

"Of course. Everything is in the Bible."

"Ones that make you laugh?"

That got a small smile, anyway. "Even that. Now go to sleep, Peter."

There was little in the climate that encouraged gentleness or moderation. Here even school was another trial to be gotten through. My old *cheder*, cramped and dark, with only one door and one window, had seemed suffused with light. Now, looking around at the vast school building with its hundreds of windows, it struck me that even if God wanted to come in, he wouldn't know where to enter. The new teachers, offering instruction in geography and world history, may have been sophisticated in comparison to our gentle and soft-spoken *malamed*, with his tales of the Messiah appearing on a white horse to bring justice to the world, but none commanded remotely the same level of respect. And some could be needlessly cruel. One afternoon when a friend and I could not stop giggling in class, we were led to the principal's office. The principal was one of those grim and self-righteous types who were always making children's lives miserable in Dickens's stories. Without so much as bothering to ask what had happened, he pulled off his belt, yanked down my friend's pants, and started beating him furiously.

It was less the sight of the angry red welts that upset me than the sense of calculated humiliation. Without a moment's forethought I scrambled up on the window ledge and edged close to the third-story window.

"Stop!" I shouted. "Stop now, or I'll jump."

He paused in midswing. "You get down from there."

I moved even closer to the open window, looked down at the traffic below. "I mean it." I did, too; suddenly the idea seemed oddly plausible. I didn't even think I would be hurt.

The principal's face began to lose its color. He put down his belt. "All right. I was finished anyway."

"And you won't touch me either."

"No. All right. Just get down."

"*Ever*. You won't touch me *ever*."

"I won't. I swear on my honor."

And whether out of fear for my safety or, more likely, for his job, he never did.

I always had trouble blindly accepting authority. It simply seemed to me that respect ought to be earned. Show me a smart and able superior, preferably one with a sense of humor, and I'll follow him anywhere. But almost always, someone who relishes power for its own sake is merely hiding his own insecurities behind the cloak of authority. Reflexively I'll question every word out of his mouth.

Not, as I would also come to discover, that such a policy was without its drawbacks. Those in charge generally find ways to get even. Though bright and intensely curious, I soon found myself locked into the role of class clown, finding approval more through wisecracks and an ability to walk to school on my hands than through any kind of academic achievement.

My parents, for their part, seemed to have almost no idea about any of this. They weren't around enough. Dropping into bed every night exhausted, not even knowing whether or not I had done my homework, they moved in and out of our lives like well-meaning strangers.

It was just the way it was, and not only in my family.

Thus, by default, it fell to me to deal with what was happening to Jacob. Friendless, existing in almost total isolation, he had grown increasingly withdrawn. Utterly misunderstood by those around him, his rich inner life taken for indolence, he was subjected to almost daily abuse by his contemporaries.

Far worse—indeed, the circumstances that instantly made the problem inescapable—was that our older brother, Yechiel, more and more openly agreed with them. When I returned to the apartment early one evening, where ordinarily I would have spent another several hours in the streets, I was shocked to find Yechiel in a full-blown rage. He had stopped by the house for a quick snack in the midst of a fifteen-hour workday, and the sight of his brother quietly reading had been too much to bear. Jacob only took, he accused; Jacob had no responsibilities to anyone but himself. Hell—he pointed at me—even little Peter sometimes brought home a few pounds.

Sitting there, his book open before him, Jacob offered no defense, just gazed up at him with large, sad eyes.

The very next day I took Jacob and a borrowed wagon

with me to the Arab marketplace. My plan was to offer our services as delivery boys. Hardly the easiest way to secure cash I knew of, but with Jacob anything illicit was unthinkable. In fact, he viewed even this scheme with trepidation. As he trailed after me through the hubbub, I was struck by how dramatically our roles had changed.

Alas, the enterprise proved a fiasco. What I hadn't counted on was that we would be regarded by local Arab boys as unwanted competition. That, and how utterly useless my brother would be in a fight. We ended that day *owing* money, for the wagon had been smashed against a wall.

I don't know what I had been thinking. Already, Jews and Arabs were living in tenuous coexistence. My own gang had early on included as many as half a dozen Arab boys. But it seemed that every casual disagreement soon turned into a fight, and every fight immediately got ugly, with harsh words giving way to fists and then, far too often, to stones.

In Palestine no one was allowed to forget, even for a moment, who was who. We belonged to cultures that seemed almost fated to misunderstand each other; one in which sharp verbal give-and-take is an old and honored tradition, the other in which every perceived slight is taken seriously, demanding a face-saving response.

After that I made a point of trying to be in the apartment whenever our older brother was apt to stop by, and so happened to walk in on the most gruesome scene of all.

"Parasite," Yechiel was raging. "You're nothing but a parasite!"

It was the first time I had heard the word since that time with Ruchele. "Yechiel," I pleaded, "stop. Leave him be."

He ignored me. "Say something," he sneered at Jacob. "Don't you think I deserve an answer?"

"You're right, Yechiel," he replied softly.

This seemed to infuriate Yechiel even more. "Don't

you think *I'd* rather relax all day, too? What am I, an animal?"

Suddenly looming over Jacob, he grabbed his Bible and flung it against the wall. Then he began pummeling him, sending him to the ground.

I don't know which of them was more surprised. Jacob reached up tentatively and touched his bloody lip. Then he bolted out the door.

Tears streaming down my face, I followed him all the way down to the beach. From a distance, by moonlight, I watched him undress, then run into the surf. He swam vigorously past the fishing boats silhouetted on the calm bay straight out to sea.

Twenty minutes passed. Thirty. I knew I would never see him again. Then, suddenly, he was struggling out of the water and collapsing on the sand.

"It's all right, Jacob," I said, crying, embracing him, stroking his hair. "Everything will be all right."

He just lay there. "No," he said. "No, it won't."

It is a measure of how little I understood that I believed my parents were oblivious even to this, the disintegration of their home.

Indeed, it seemed to me that my mother had never been happier. Having always been recognized in her own tiny circle as sharply opinionated and full of humor, as deft with a canny observation or a glib put-down as a practiced comedian, for the first time she was now showing herself to the outside world; wheedling and bantering with her customers, amusing them with her imitations of this or that rabbi or politician, or parodies of how they themselves walked or whined or cursed the fates. My father proudly claimed that she had the most loyal clientele in the Old City.

And if I was vaguely aware that whenever she had a free hour, she spent it at some government office or private refugee agency, to a young boy's eyes that was just one of her routines, no more meaningful than her frenzied shopping for the Sabbath.

How could I know that those pilgrimages to the offices of those in a position to help Fruma and her family were increasingly desperate? How could I even begin to grasp my parents' apprehension and crushing sense of helplessness?

It was 1938. The news from Europe was of "peace in our time." How could I have known the tragedy we were all about to live?

FOUR

Out of the Bureaucratic Shadows

ACCORDING to a report prepared by the Nazi statistician Dr. Richard Korherr, just before World War II there were a total of 10.3 million Jews in the world. By the dictates of National Socialist ideology, every one of them a biological enemy of the German people and nation. It was the business of Eichmann's department in the SD to formulate plans to "neutralize" them permanently.

Into the late thirties the New Order's campaign against the Jews was held at least somewhat in check. Though the Nuremberg decrees of 1935 effectively stripped German Jews of their basic rights, denying them participation in the economy and outlawing social contact with Aryans, though Jewish children had been dropped from school roles and signs were posted outside many towns announcing JEWS NOT WANTED HERE, Hitler remained conscious of international opinion. Germany was not yet at war; certain pretenses had to be at least marginally maintained.

Thus it was that during this period, while still earning

regular promotions, including one in 1937 in which his immediate superior lauded his "comprehensive knowledge of the organizational methods and ideology of Jewry, the enemy," Eichmann generally went about his work far behind the scenes.

His work at this time, he recalled, "was often of a confidential and embarrassing nature, as when I established that the Führer's diet cook, who was at one time his mistress, was one thirty-second Jewish. My immediate superior, Lieutenant General Heinrich Müller, quickly classified the report as Top Secret."

It was only with the Anschluss, the German annexation of Austria in March 1938, that Eichmann emerged from the bureaucratic shadows. Four days after German stormtroopers marched into Austria, the thirty-two-year-old SS man appeared in Vienna, assigned to render his former country judenrein, literally, "Jew-free." Within days he had devised a program of action: a combination of calculated brutality and brazen duplicity. First he moved to have the Gestapo terrorize the capital's Jewish population, numbering 183,000. Men and women were dragged from their homes and shops and viciously beaten; rabbis were seized, their heads shorn before jeering mobs; synagogues were razed, Jewish property seized or destroyed. In a couple of weeks, more than a thousand Jews were murdered; dozens of others took their own lives. Then it suddenly stopped. Eichmann, the very picture of reason, now offered the council of Jewish leaders he had assembled his assurance that, if the Jews would only trust him and cooperate, conditions would improve. Indeed, he actually managed to persuade some of his victims of his sympathy for their plight. On one occasion he astonished a roomful of Jewish functionaries by reciting by heart a page from a contemporary volume on the history of Zionism.

Eichmann began meeting regularly with highly placed Jewish officials, setting up a system that accomplished several Nazi ends simultaneously. Still more than a year before the outbreak of war, the Nazi aim in Austria was not annihilation but expulsion. Granted limited administrative control over their own affairs, but with all funds in the community frozen and the SS otherwise overseeing financial matters, the desperate Jews were thus made to cooperate in their own undoing. The final stage of Eichmann's process ensured that no one escaped before being robbed, not just of his property, but of his self-respect. ("A Jew would enter the [emigration] office," as prosecutor Hausner would later describe it, "and he was still somebody, having a job or a shop, an apartment to live in, some property or cash in the bank, his child still registered at school. As he proceeded from window to window he was stripped of these things one by one. When he finally left the building he was jobless, his property had been requisitioned, his child crossed off the school roll, and his passport taken away. All he had now was a passport with the letter 'J,' valid for two weeks. It was his task to find a foreign visa. He was expressly told that if he were found in Austria after the passport expired, it would be valid, but only for a single, one-way journey: to a concentration camp!")

During Eichmann's tenure in Austria, a new camp had to be built in Mauthausen. Dachau and Buchenwald were full.

Those who had known Eichmann earlier were now often struck by the change in the man. Living and working in what had been the Rothschild mansion, chauffeured about Vienna in the Rothschild limousine, always meticulously outfitted in full SS regalia, he now carried himself with a conqueror's hauteur. Married for only three years and about to be a father for the second time, he took on an elegant mistress, the first of no fewer than nine whom, by war's end, he would have arrayed through the capitals of Europe. Always fond of good food and wine, he now dined in ostentatious splendor and unstintingly indulged in the finest vintages.

But, above all, it was his professional style that had changed. Capable of smoothness, even charm, he would fly into a fury when he perceived himself to have been crossed. The Jews with whom he dealt lived in abject fear of these mood swings. On meeting one important Jewish leader for the first time, he suddenly began raging and slapped him in the face, screaming that it was his intention to "rehabilitate the Jews" and demanding the man's unconditional cooperation. On another occasion, tongue-lashing an elderly Jewish leader for showing insufficient enthusiasm for his methods, he snapped, "You have been too long out of the concentration camp."

What his victims could not know was that most such outbursts were at least partly calculated. As he would later boast, the Jews with whom he dealt were terrified of him, never knowing what he would do next. They "thought I was really a kind of a king."

In the wake of his overwhelming success in Austria, he secured the lofty rank of Obersturmführer. But even the promotion failed to indicate the extent of his rising power. Now directly accountable to only one man—Reinhard Heydrich, the brutal, calculating head of the SD, soon to be notorious as Europe's "Hangman"—he was now in a position to shape policy in his field of expertise almost single-handedly. "Eichmann," as his recommendation for promotion succinctly had it, "directs the entire Jewish emigration."

It is hardly coincidence that the main file in his Berlin headquarters bore a new heading: FINAL SOLUTION. He had hit upon the term himself.

FIVE

The War Begins

IN the spring of 1939, I joined the Haganah, the underground army fighting for the establishment of a Jewish state in Palestine; or, more precisely, I was selected for their ranks. They had been watching me, said the young teacher who had called me into a back room after school; they thought I had what it took.

My arm needed no twisting. The English, supposedly neutral in the worsening struggle between the Jews and the Arabs, had lately been increasingly pro-Arab in their behavior, so much so that the unofficial slogan of the rising "Arab Revolt" became the triumphant *Ad-dowlahma'anah!* ("The government is with us!"). English soldiers, routinely slow to react to Arab attacks on outlying kibbutzim, were firm in cutting off Jewish pursuit of the attackers. Captured Jewish activists expected to be treated harshly by the courts, their Arab counterparts with often extraordinary leniency. Arab snipers seemed able to return to one particularly strategic point, above the highway near Bab el Wad, virtually at will.

There was no question that the occupying forces didn't like us, but there was more to the pro-Arab tilt than mere anti-Semitism; indeed, they didn't like the Arabs much better. To them we were all "colonials," and expected to accept our status as such. Rather, it was a clear policy decision. Though the Balfour Declaration of 1917 had guaranteed the creation of a Jewish state in Palestine, and Britain's mandate over the territory had been granted by the League of Nations to prepare for such an eventuality, the English had quickly come to regard the Holy Land as a piece of the empire. It made sense that a difficult situation should be handled the same way such situations had often been handled in India or Ireland: by keeping the locals at one another's throats, with the occupiers above the fray, nudging it this way or that. At the moment the Jews, animated by the dream of a homeland, desperately pressing for mass immigration from Eastern Europe, clearly posed the greater threat.

Not that many of us in Palestine yet understood the full extent of English duplicity. Throughout the thirties mainstream Jewish authorities, including most of those who would eventually guide Israel to independence, were inclined to accept British assurances that their policies were in our interest.

In part their acquiescence was due to the entirely reasonable assumption that any effort to take on the world's great colonial power was doomed to fail. But, too, it was grounded in something far more disturbing: our own view of ourselves. Having survived the centuries through accommodation and retreat; having, moreover, come to regard those who made their way in the world by force of arms with a curious mixture of awe and disdain, most Jews were simply not emotionally prepared, even on the eve of cataclysm, to regard armed conflict as a serious option.

In deference to British policy, even the Haganah had initially operated strictly as a defense force. Only with the formation of the Irgun, in 1937, had anti-Jewish violence

begun to prompt Jewish reprisal; and even then, respectable
Jewish authorities routinely joined the British in condemning the Irgunists as terrorists, often cooperating in their
capture.

I had begun to find myself in the middle of all this, in
a direct and personal way, one late afternoon about a year
before. Heading down Hertzl Street in the general direction
of home, I paused to read an Irgun poster that had just been
slapped up on a wall when an English armored car turned
the corner. Out of the turret popped a soldier in one of those
flat helmets, "anemones" we called them, after the flowers.

"Hey, you, what you doin'?" he demanded in what I
even then recognized as a cockney accent.

I hesitated, petrified. "Peeing," I said finally.

The first soldier was joined in the turret by another. A
moment later he climbed down, walked over to me, and
examined the wall. "You a Jew, boy?"

I nodded my head.

That was enough. Suddenly he kicked me hard in the
stomach. I fell to the ground and looked up at him in pain
and confusion, just in time to see the boot coming at me
again. Now the other joined him, the blows coming so
quickly they registered not individually but as a single prolonged agony. Still, I could scarcely believe what was happening. What were they doing? I was a child! Would they
kill me in broad daylight, so close to the Central Synagogue?

By the time they finally left and passersby led me home,
bleeding profusely, they had made an enemy for life.

Indeed, had I been given the choice, I would have chosen
to join the radical Irgun over the moderate Haganah. Which
is not to say I treated the honor lightly. I took the oath that
very day at school, swearing on the Bible not to reveal my
membership in the organization to anyone.

I never did, not even to my parents.

The Haganah's obsession with secrecy was such that,
in years of sitting side by side, I never learned which of my

classmates were in the organization. I didn't even know about my own brothers. The only ones I was sure about were those in my own small group, with whom I trained.

Our training forays, generally to the hills, were passed off as youthful outings, a local version of Cub Scouts. Too young to study weapons, we were given instruction in communications, which in its way was just as vital. The organization depended on an extraordinarily well organized system of communications; one that could instantly spread the alert in case of danger and mobilize hundreds of men, later thousands, in less than an hour. We kids of nine and ten were expected to master every important technique then in use: how to convey messages in code, by flag, by signal light at night; how to hide messages on the body and how to dispose of them when trapped; the nooks in walls that made the best drop-off spots; the shortest routes to almost everywhere.

The English knew a great deal about the Haganah, but they didn't appear to much worry about us. Even if we were perceived as a threat, at that juncture they had far more important things to worry about.

So, of course, did we. The coming of war in Europe swept everything else aside. Even the Irgun called a truce. From the start, virtually every Jew understood that our very future was in question. The Nazis had never been shy about their feelings.

That is not to say anyone imagined what was about to occur. Yes, as the Germans moved through Poland and then swept through the countries in the west, we began to hear reports that Jews were being rounded up and sent to mass gathering places; and, yes, we understood that under these terrible circumstances, some were probably dying. But how could we fathom anything more?

Certainly there was a desperate, willful blindness in this. As early in 1942, stories began appearing in reputable publications, including *Time* and *Newsweek*, that told of mass slaughter in Poland. We had access to such reports. But, then, if Americans had trouble accepting them as credible—according to a Gallup poll as late as November 1944, a vast majority considered the atrocity stories wildly exaggerated, a variation on the "bloodthirsty Hun" propaganda of World War I—we, with so much more at stake, needed to dismiss them out of hand. My sister and her children were there, literally dozens of other family and friends, decent, well-meaning souls. Even the Nazis could not be so insane as to slaughter such people.

(After the war, American Supreme Court justice Felix Frankfurter, himself a Jew, recounted a story I very much understood. He told of listening in 1942 to the account of a Pole who had escaped from the Belzec death camp, desperately trying to sound the alarm in the West. When the man finished, Frankfurter told him he could not believe him. The Pole started to protest vehemently. "You don't understand," Frankfurter cut him off, "I know you are telling the truth. But I cannot believe you.")

Indeed, my mother carried on precisely as before, writing letters to the same addresses. When we got no answers, we simply told ourselves that the war had disrupted communications. It made sense, after all.

Ironically, given our extraordinary powers of denial, never had we read the newspapers more closely or listened more regularly to the Voice of Palestine on our ancient set, trying to pick up sound through the ocean of static. But all we got was war news. They almost never talked about the Jews, just about this or that Allied bombing or the movement of armies.

Not that the war was all that remote. The Italians twice attacked Haifa, aiming for the British oil refineries. Worse, for a time we were threatened by General Erwin Rommel's advance in North Africa. If he succeeded in overwhelming the British in Egypt, there was little question that the former grand mufti of Jerusalem, once viewed as a comic-opera figure with his flowing red beard and bright green turban, would personally organize a massive pogrom. As Hitler's guest in Berlin he had spoken of "the Jewish cancer eating the flesh of the world"; and it would shortly come to light that, in 1943 and 1944, accompanied by Eichmann, he had secretly inspected Treblinka, Majdanek, and Auschwitz, closely questioning his guides on the workings of the facilities.

Among ourselves, we children used to speculate on the grim possibilities; we knew as well as our parents that there was no place left to escape to.

That is why, when the Irgun announced shortly after the Allied victory at El Alamein in October 1942 that it was resuming operations against the British, so many of their fellow Jews reacted with shocked outrage. The Irgun rationale—that the dream of a Jewish homeland could no longer be deferred; that, if recent history had established nothing else, it was that even those purporting to be our friends would not extend themselves on our behalf—was readily brushed aside. Yes, it was conceded, in the desperate years before the war, country after country had closed its borders. Even ships laden with refugees from Nazi Germany, unwelcome in every free country, had been forced to return to German ports. And, yes, no one had been more intransigent than the British in Palestine. *But that was then and this is now.* Nothing, *nothing,* could be allowed to subvert the war effort. The goal now, the only goal, had to be the eradication of Hitlerism.

It was only years after the war that the Irgun position was somewhat vindicated. In fact, for all the noble talk, the British had been doing almost nothing on behalf of Europe's doomed Jews. Even as the various factions were arguing the point in Palestine, Jewish leaders, increasingly aware of the horrifying facts, were strenuously urging that the RAF begin bombing the rail lines leading to Auschwitz. It was an eminently achievable task, since English planes were already bombing Warsaw, two hundred miles farther from their base. The English leadership refused without explanation. It does not take much of a cynic to guess that they saw an advantage in cutting down the possible number of postwar Jewish refugees to Palestine.

In the history books, of course, World War II continues to stand as Great Britain's finest hour, and there is much to that. The heroism of her civilan population was virtually without precedent. (Years later, when I visited England for the first time, I was genuinely taken aback to discover that, in fact, the people there *were* all the things the newsreels said they were, warm and plucky and generous spirited. Not one of the Englishmen *I* had ever met was like that.)

Then again, that was part of the lesson, at once seductive and very dangerous, that we in Palestine were yet to learn: that those in charge generally have posterity their own way.

SIX

The Eichmann Authority

*L*ESS than a month after the German invasion of Poland that launched World War II, a new department, IV-D-4, was created within the SD. For all the months of planning that had preceded the attack, few plans were in place for dealing with Poland's vast and highly diverse Jewish population, a tenth of the country's total. Department IV-D-4, with Adolf Eichmann as its head, was now charged with responsibility for "deportations and emigration." In time, the department would come to be known simply as Dienststelle Eichmann (the Eichmann Authority).

With his customary zeal, Eichmann set about his first task: trying to ensure that all Jews were idenitified and under tight supervision. In a matter of days, regulations had been issued mandating that a yellow Star of David be worn at all times by all Jews over the age of six. The yellow stars had already proven effective in Germany itself, not only, as Eichmann later explained, in isolating Jews but in

*warning off Gentiles who might have been otherwise in-
clined to take their side. "We wanted Germans to feel embarrassed, to feel afraid of having any contact with Jews."
Simultaneously the process was begun of herding Jews into
specially designated areas (ghettoes) which they were forbidden to leave under penalty of death.*

*As always, Eichmann was keenly aware that these
measures would also have a severely debilitating effect
upon the morale of the Jews, breaking them psychologi-
cally, limiting the possibility of widespread resistance to
the imposition of more stringent measures later on. "Eichmann was very cynical in his attitude toward the Jewish
question," his subordinate Dieter Wisliceny would later
explain. "He gave no indication of human feeling toward
these people. He was not immoral; he was amoral and
completely ice-cold in his attitude."*

*Particularly in the larger cities, conditions in the ghet-
toes, teeming with people and cut off from food and fresh
water, were desperate. Within months tens of thousands
succumbed to starvation and disease. SS major Rolf Heinz
Hoepner, presiding over the huge Lodz ghetto, was actually
moved to write his superior Eichmann that, under the circumstances, "it is seriously to be considered whether it
will not be more humane to settle it with them through a
quick-working medium, especially with those who are unable to work. This will be pleasanter than watching them
starve to death."*

*Eichmann did not disagree. He had already engaged
in high-level discussions on more efficient approaches to
the Final Solution. By early 1941 he and Heydrich were
ready to institute one "quick-working medium" on a vast
scale: special SS units called* Einsatzgruppen *that would
enter newly occupied areas right behind frontline troops.
Eichmann was present when their commanders were
briefed just before they were sent into service, in the wake
of the invasion of Russia. The Jewish population was to be
"totally exterminated."*

Now, even bureaucratically, all pretense of "emigration" was dropped, as the functions of Department IV-D-4 were redefined to comprise responsibility for "Jewish affairs and deportations." Shortly after the program began, Eichmann traveled east to witness personally an Einsatzgruppe in action. The one arranged for him outside Minsk was a model of efficiency. Having been assured they were merely to be transported elsewhere, the several hundred Jews had marched from the city carrying suitcases. As Eichmann watched, soldiers ordered them to leave these behind, marched them quickly to a long, freshly dug trench, and shouted for them to kneel before it. Then, moving along the line, the soldiers fired point-blank into the backs of their heads and, in a move they had practiced, sent each victim pitching forward with a sharp thrust of a boot. "I can still see a woman with a child," Eichmann would recall later, dispassionately. "She was shot and then the baby in her arms. His brains splattered all around, also over my leather overcoat. My driver helped me remove them."

Over the following year Eichmann charted the results of the program closely, tabulating numbers at his Berlin office as the totals ran into the tens, then the hundreds of thousands, and finally into the millions. He was much impressed, too, about the value of the property—cash, jewelry, household effects, even clothing—"confiscated" from the Jews.

But, like other Nazi leaders, he recognized that shooting had certain drawbacks. It was inefficient; ever cost-conscious, he viewed it as a frightful waste of ammunition. Then, too, the process seemed to be having a negative impact on the morale of some of the men. Witnessing the aftermath of one Einsatzgruppen action during the course of an official visit, Himmler was so taken aback at the sight of bloody figures in a pit, covered by a thin layer of dirt, some of them still moving, that he nearly fainted.

Indeed, a few Germans present seemed almost to sympathize with the victims. "A family of about eight persons passed by,"—a civilian engineer recalled in the safety of the postwar a massacre he witnessed outside the town of Rowno,—"a man and a woman, both about fifty, with their children of about eight and ten and two grown-up daughters of twenty and twenty-four. An old woman with snow white hair was holding a one-year-old child in her arms, singing to it and tickling it. The child was cooing with delight. The couple were looking on with tears in their eyes. The father was holding the hand of the ten-year-old boy and speaking to him softly; the boy was fighting back his tears. The father pointed to the sky, stroked his head, and seemed to explain something to him. At that moment the SS man at the pit shouted something to his comrade. The latter counted off about twenty persons and instructed them to go behind the pit. Among them was the family I mentioned. A girl, slim, with black hair, pointed to herself as she passed by me and said, 'Twenty-three years.' "

The need, as one leading Nazi put it, for German soldiers to "be spared all these bloodbaths" led directly to the search for new killing techniques. Eichmann was initially enthusiastic about the possibilities of pumping exhaust into the sealed interiors of moving trucks; it had already been tried on mental patients, and after inspecting a model of one proposed advance on the form—an airtight chamber disguised as a Polish peasant hut, the exhaust to be supplied by a Russian U-boat motor—he marveled that he'd never imagined such a thing technically possible. But after lengthy trials this also proved less than entirely satisfactory. The gas killed slowly and removing the corpses was often a gruesome business. Worse, the gas sometimes sickened the SS men; Eichmann was obliged to set up a school to instruct drivers in proper gassing technique and a doctor had to be assigned to each unit to safeguard their health.

Still there were problems. "The men of the special commandoes complained to me about headaches after each unloading," wrote one SS doctor in his report. "The application of the gas is usually not undertaken correctly. In order to come to an end as fast as possible, the driver presses the accelerator to the fullest extent. Thus the persons excuted die by suffocation and not dozing off as planned."

In 1942, after witnessing the operation of the new Belzec camp in Poland, whose primitive gas chambers could dispatch up to fifteen thousand people a day, Eichmann became a wholehearted supporter of large stationary killing centers. With the introduction of a gas called Zyklon B, previously used as an insecticide, they became more effective still. Moreover, such camps readily lent themselves to the kind of merciless manipulations at which he had become so adept. It was at Eichmann's initiative that the newer camps were set up far from population centers, and that, in many, the gas chambers were surrounded by flower beds and disguised as showers. Nor was he intent on hoodwinking only Jews. When officials in the relatively autonomous German satellite of Slovakia began making inquiries about the fate of local Jews sent away on "labor assignments," he arranged for a Nazi journalist to visit a number of the "happy settlers" at their new home and report in print that "I saw only laughing faces around me in Auschwitz"; and when that failed to allay Slovak suspicions, letters and postcards began arriving by the hundreds from the camps, all describing excellent living conditions. Often as not, they were dead before the mail was delivered.

By now, with Heydrich having been assassinated in the spring of 1942, Eichmann was operating largely as a free agent, his vast energies devoted to the immense logistical problems at hand. As he himself laughingly put it, once he had been a traveling oil salesman, now he was "a traveling salesman for the Gestapo."

The business of moving vast numbers of human beings to their deaths without arousing appreciable resistance required enormous powers of persuasion, great tactical skill, and perseverance; so, too, in the midst of the war effort did the wresting of the physical resources, notably the railway facilities, he considered essential to the task.

It was during these years that in the Jewish communities of occupied Europe, Eichmann became the stuff of horrific legend. Openly contemptuous of what he viewed as bureaucratic obstacles, hostile even to other Nazis whom he regarded as insufficiently commited to his mission, he brushed aside opposition with increasing imperiousness. "Could you relinquish some of your trains for us?" he was once asked by the functionary in charge of dealing with the insane. "I thought then," Eichmann recalled, "here I am in the most important place in the Reich, from where all I did was being watched, day and night, and here this fellow asks me for a few trains so he can heat the stove with some idiots!"

Quite simply, Eichmann saw his mission, the elimination of Jews from the face of the earth, as a priority at least equal to that of winning the war. Nothing could be allowed to impede it. Traveling the Continent, from France in the west, north to Denmark, then down to middle Europe and the Balkans, meeting with SS authorities and officials of the local police, urging them to greater efforts, he allowed no exceptions to the Final Solution. When in 1943 there arose some question as to the racial origins of the Krimchaks in the Crimea, he decreed that, for safety's sake, they had to be eliminated. Where others argued that Mischlinge (the offspring of Aryan-Jewish marriages) ought merely to be sterilized, thereby preserving their useful qualities for the Reich while eliminating any chance of their handing down undesirable traits, he succeeded in having most of them sent to the camps. When friendly embassies issued pleas on behalf of this or that Jew who in the past had rendered a great service, or who had highly placed friends, always they were refused. "Any exception will create a precedent which would impede the dejudaization measures," he brusquely dismissed one such plea.

Even as the war began to go badly and others sought ways to put a better face on their activities, Eichmann adamantly opposed the deals with outsiders, supported by some of his more pragmatic colleagues, in which Jewish lives were to be bartered for desperately needed trucks or clothing. It thus came as a considerable surprise to his colleagues when in late 1944 he finally relented, agreeing to the departure of seventeen hundred Hungarian Jews for Spain. But, hardly for the first time, others had under-estimated the man. At the last minute the train was diverted to Bergen-Belsen.

Hungary would prove Eichmann's crowning achievement. Through a unique combination of circumstances— her status as a German ally, the acute awareness on the part of her leaders of the possibility of Allied victory, the strength and independence of her regent, Miklós Horthy— Hungary's 800,000 Jews had remained beyond Nazi reach through almost five years of war, persecuted and stripped of property but permitted to stay where they were.

It was a state of affairs that Eichmann increasingly took as a personal affront. At last freed of political con-straints—"Send down to Hungary the master in person," went Himmler's order in the early spring of 1944—he had hurried to Budapest with all of his principal lieutenants.

Following the scenario that was now almost an art form, he assembled the leaders of the Jewish community and demanded their cooperation. "I am not an adherent of violence," he told them, "but any opposition will be broken. If you think of joining the partisans or applying their methods, I shall have you mercilessly slaughtered. After the war the Jews will be free; all the Jewish measures will be abandoned and the Germans will be good-natured, as before. You tell me if anyone harms you and I will protect you; but I warn you not to try to mislead me. I know all about Jews. I have been dealing with Jewish affairs since 1934; I know Hebrew better than you do. I will visit your museum soon, because I am interested in Jewish cultural affairs. You can trust me and talk freely to me. As you see, I am quite frank with you."

The next day he sent his railway specialist to Vienna to finalize details of the transport of Hungarian Jewry to Auschwitz.

In mid-May, six weeks after his arrival in the country, mass deportations from the provinces began, thereafter proceeding with astonishing speed. According to Nazi records, by July 11, 437,402 individuals had been deported and, Budapest excepted, the country was "free of Jews."

But now, with the Russians advancing steadily in the east, Horthy ordered the deportations halted. In desperate military straits Hitler was unable to risk crossing his ally, and Eichmann, who had already formulated plans for a roundup of all four hundred thousand Jews in the capital in a single day, was obliged to withdraw from the country.

But he waited. On October 14, when Horthy announced Hungary's withdrawal from the war, Germany moved to occupy Budapest, and Eichmann returned with the first of the German occupying forces. Russian troops were now driving on the capital, and Allied bombing had cut rail lines. Racing the clock, overcoming obstacles on all sides, including the determined opposition of the Swedish diplomat Raoul Wallenberg, Eichmann began a forced march of civilians to the west. It succeeded to an appalling degree. By the time he fled Budapest on Christmas Eve, more than three hundred thousand Jews had been evacuated. "I wanted to show these Allies my hand," he would boast later, "to tell them as it were: 'Nothing will help. Even if you bomb and destroy, I still have a way to the Reich.' "

Now Eichmann made his way back to Berlin. In the months that followed, as the Reich collapsed around him, he pressed vigorously for the destruction of those Jews remaining in the camps, regularly issuing orders designed to circumvent the ones issued by suddenly prudent German *higher-ups. His subordinates later reported that in the general gloom he often seemed a man curiously content.*

In April, as the Allies closed in, Eichmann hastily formulated a plan to lead a unit into the Austrian Alps he knew so well from earlier days, there to fight on as guerrillas. But almost immediately after they entered the mountains, they received orders to lay down their arms: Germany had surrendered unconditionally. Heeding the entreaties of the others, who had no wish to be captured in the presence of so notorious a figure, Eichmann agreed to move off on his own.

They watched him leave, making his way down a mountain trail, lightly armed and carrying a couple of days' provisions.

For years afterward, that was the last the world would see of him.

SEVEN

A New Army

AT the war's end, there was an eerie silence. All of us waited to hear from loved ones.

Nothing.

Then the reports began to come in, the ones from legitimate news sources, followed almost immediately by the first newsreels from the camps. The enormity of what had occurred began to register. They had been murdered. Not by the thousands or even hundreds of thousands, but *millions* of them. Whole communities. Entire populations. A rich and flourishing culture, our past, had been obliterated. At the time, barbarity on such a scale seemed too great to ever absorb. *Six million.*

And the details! The sight of the corpses on film! The *ways* they died! Babies dashed against walls. People packed so tightly into gas chambers that when the doors were opened they tumbled out like cordwood, stiff, reeking of sweat and excrement, their faces reflecting the terror of those last moments, all to be dumped into mass graves and forgotten.

The Final Solution to the Jewish Question.

Even those accustomed to the numberless cruelties of war looked on in horrified disbelief. General George Patton became physically ill while inspecting the newly liberated camp at Ohrdruf. Supreme Allied commander Dwight Eisenhower, deeply shaken, noted soberly, "We are told the American soldier does not know what he is fighting for. Now, at least, he will know what he is fighting *against.*" And he ordered all camps under his jurisdiction thrown open to the world's press.

At least they could take some action. For us, there was only bottomless sorrow and unassuageable guilt.

In our house descended a crushing silence. We avoided one another's eyes. Jacob virtually lived in the synagogue, saying Kaddish for the dead for days on end.

Even now, my mother did not stop hoping. There was so much confusion, there always remained the possibility: Maybe, maybe, one of them had escaped.

Sometimes it actually happened. Miraculously someone would appear. The daughter of an elderly couple just across the street from us turned out to have been hidden by Polish peasant neighbors. The uncle of one of my classmates had fought with the partisans. Letters came; a brother, a cousin, a friend had survived the camps.

But it never happened for us.

How does one deal with that? How to start to talk about it, console one another?

My own reaction was to shut off. At sixteen I just didn't want to face the grief, the camps, anything at all. Numb, I kept living as best I could and stayed away from the house.

One early evening, after perhaps six months, I couldn't get around it. There was my mother, sitting at the kitchen table, head in hands, sobbing. I was the only other person home.

"Mama . . ."

She didn't look up.

"Mama, please . . ."

Suddenly I, too, felt something welling up within. I might have cried, but managed to rein it in.

"Mama . . ." I laid a hand on her shoulder. "Mama, I just want to tell you. I'm going to kill three Germans. I promise. One for each child."

It was during this period that one first started hearing the name Adolf Eichmann. *He* was one the survivors talked about the most, more than Himmler, or Hermann Göring, more even than Hitler; the most bloodthirsty of them all. Newspaper articles appeared. Eyewitness accounts were recorded. In the public mind he soon began to take on mythic proportions of evil, a contemporary satan, the one who had organized it all.

In January 1946, one witness testified at Nuremberg to hearing his horrific boast: "I will leap into my grave laughing, because the feeling I have 5 million human beings on my conscience is for me a source of extraordinary satisfaction."

And then there were the rumors: that he was in Egypt, helping to lead the new war on the Jews; that, with his knowledge of Hebrew and Yiddish, he was actually living among us, in Palestine, *as a Jew*. With Eichmann, no malice, no deception, seemed too farfetched.

In subsequent years, traveling abroad, I would be startled to discover he was so less well known than he was in Israel. In some places few people had even heard of him. They talked about other Nazis, the political leaders, the policymakers, the military chiefs. We Jews talked about the killers.

And Eichmann was the one who had escaped.

Jacob, my gentle, fragile older brother, never recovered. In June 1949 he was hit by a car and died en route to the hospital. Witnesses reported he never looked up from the book in his hand.

Only those in the immediate family knew how profoundly my father had changed. He ate less, he smoked more. He seemed to sleep hardly at all. Always an amusing and easily amused man, he never laughed anymore. A couple of years later his heart gave out on the job.

Suddenly what had always been a large family, immediate and extended, was only three of us: my mother, Yechiel, and me.

No one offered any sympathy. We were in no way unique. As never before had there been murder on the scale of the Holocaust, never had there been so many souls simultaneously in mourning; an immense community grappling with grief, struggling to make sense of the inexplicable, looking for new meaning in lives empty but for pain.

Thus it was that in those terrible days the dream of independence was everywhere embraced with such desperate fervor. The logic was as compellilng as ever: We needed a place of our own; the English had proven themselves unworthy of trust. But more than ever, logic was beside the point.

By the end of 1945 the Haganah had joined the Irgun and the equally militant Stern gang in pitched battle against the occupying forces. Virtually every Jew in Palestine saw himself as party to that war.

Having entered a technical high school in 1944 to study engineering, I continued to go to school. That was my public life. My real one was lived mostly at night. Suddenly my intimate familiarity with the back alleys and underground passageways of the Old City was proving more useful than it had in a decade; and, too, I had found wondrous new uses for my skills as a thief. Instead of candy, I went for guns and ammunition.

Yet, oddly enough, in its way, it remained what it had always been: terrific fun, a game full of excitement and risk, a distraction. We rarely thought about getting caught, let alone the very real possibility of being killed or hanged. Half a world away, our contemporaries were staging panty raids. Instead, we were raiding British installations.

Within the organization our small group began to acquire a bit of a reputation. One particularly memorable night, dressed in black, face smeared with burnt cork, I made my way on crepe-soled shoes into the Haifa harbor police station, picked the lock of a second-story storeroom, filled a sack with pistols and ammunition and, making my way onto the roof, tossed it to a colleague waiting below. By now the alarm had sounded. Hurriedly I tied a rope to an outcropping, threw it over the edge, and having forgotten gloves, took half the skin off my hands sliding down. A moment later, with my friend Edna at the wheel, we roared off in a small panel truck. The duty officer started to chase us on foot, then turned and ran back into the station to warn the guards at the gates to the harbor; fortunately my other friend, Yehuda, had sliced the telephone line. Within two hours the weapons were hidden on Mt. Carmel, and the truck, changed from black to gray, bore new license plates.

Not that all of my brushes with the police ended so well. At least a dozen times I was pulled in without cause; or, more exactly, because I was a Jewish teenager. Once, savagely beaten, I suffered three lost teeth and a broken rib. When I was taken home, my mother became hysterical. That got to me. I was living now as much for her as for myself.

Still, I understood why it had happened. Earlier in the day there had been an attack on the central police station downtown. The English were even more frustrated than usual. They needed to see Jewish blood.

Of course, that was the point, to convince them that their position was untenable, that victory could be achieved only at an intolerable cost. Even getting kicked around had its strategic value.

This, in a real sense, was my generation's reaction to the Holocaust: a fearlessness born of the certainty it would never happen to us. We would be strong and self-reliant; if we went, it would be the opposite of passively. Indeed, a case can be made that we became too free of fear. Few outsiders have a full understanding of how much, even today, Israeli policy remains a visceral reaction to the specter of our loved ones being herded into the ovens.

In 1947, shortly after graduating from high school, I was selected for intensive training in explosives.

There were five in our group. Every day for three months we met in the desolate hills outside Haifa, learning all there was to know about fuses, detonators, primers; Molotov cocktails, explosives with a 360-degree impact, and those intended to launch other objects; foot mines and anti-tank mines, assorted booby traps, and bridge demolition.

It was a wonderful collection of characters, the sort normally thrown together in a screenwriter's imagination. And doing what we were doing, depending upon one another for our very survival, we became extraordinarily close.

There was Green, a squat, muscular set of walking contradictions. Unbelievably stoic, impervious not simply to pain, but to all surrounding stimuli, he would never fail to get upset about one thing: cooked carrots. Inordinately concerned about his appearance, he not only polished his boots to a high shine and wore pressed puttees even in the most miserable heat, but shaved five and six times a day. Yet he almost never closed his fly.

"Why, Green?" I asked him one day. "What's the point?"

He ran a hand over his smooth face and shrugged. "Why bother?"

Joshua, tall and reed-thin, sensitive and hyperromantic, would have seemed far more at home studying the violin than the instruments of death with which we were becoming so adept. At first put off by his impatience with banter and his anger at being teased, even when it was merited, the rest of us soon recognized him as a remarkably steadfast and generous friend.

Josef, born on a kibbutz in the Negev, was perhaps the most gifted of us all in the use of explosives. His fertile mind never left the subject. He spent hours alone in our makeshift laboratory. During breaks from training, he would often sit on the ground, stick in hand. Afterward there would be a design for an ingenious new booby trap in the dirt.

Of the bunch, Armoni was my particular soulmate; odd, because we were so very different in temperament. While I was deeply, incurably happy-go-lucky, seeing no reason to be entirely serious about anything except my work, he was as intense as anyone I had ever known, his dark Yemenite eyes apt to flash in anger at the slightest provocation. What we shared was a passion for the arts. I had lately begun drawing and writing journals. He poured his soul into poetry, and into long letters to his fiancée. These he would endlessly rewrite, showing me each new version, soliciting suggestions as to how it might be improved. This he did with more than an eye toward his literary reputation than any regard for the fiancée. He made no secret of his intention to eventually have them published.

Aside from all the rest, the five of us had in common a thorough contempt for Mr. Mark, our instructor. A career military type, Mark operated on about a dozen catchphrases. Anyone dealing with explosives, went one, can make only one mistake in his life. Not exactly big news, but he repeated it at least three times a day. I hated it even more when he told us that the country couldn't afford to waste money on soldiers who would be killed on their first mission. I was positive he had picked it up from a movie. Worst of all was when he began chiding that something had happened because we hadn't listened to him. There was not the slightest doubt in any of our minds that if one of us were on the ground bleeding to death, he'd get in at least three or four I-told-you-so's before calling an ambulance.

When the British finally pulled out, in May 1948, it briefly seemed as if all the bitterness and pain of the past ten years had suddenly been wiped away. Everywhere there was joyous exultation, mixed with dazed wonderment: After two thousand years, the dream of statehood had actually been realized!

For those of us who danced for hours in the streets, or struck up sudden friendships with strangers, or found ourselves in the huge crowd spontaneously breaking into our haunting national anthem, "Hatikva," as David Ben-Gurion read the official proclamation of independence, the memory of those days remains precious and indelible. With the birth of our nation, *we* were being reborn.

Even then, we knew what probably lay ahead. For months, ever since the British declaration of their intention to withdraw and the passage of the United Nations partition plan, the intention of the surrounding Arab states to "push the Jews into the sea" had been made abundantly clear.

Still, no one expected the conflict to come quite so quickly or with such intensity.

There was still dancing in the streets when the first shots rang out. The Arab uprising in the cities had been coordinated with full-scale attacks at the frontier by Syria from the north, Egypt from the south, Jordan and Iraq from the east. In literally minutes the entire nation was a front.

In Haifa the shooting began in the Old City, our neighborhood, principally Arab but with a fair sprinkling of Jewish homes. The snipers, some undoubtedly people I had known for a decade, seemed to be everywhere. Dozens of people died in the confusion. That evening I found three bullets lodged in my living room wall.

There was no question about what to do. We had rehearsed it often enough. After getting my mother to the safety of a friend's house in the predominantly Jewish New City, I made my way to our designated gathering place, my old high school, and was issued orders. My team of five, armed with pistols, grenades, and ancient Italian rifles, was to silence the snipers in our neighborhood.

Our strategy over the next couple of weeks was not fancy. Basically we laid low until dark, then, as I began making my way toward the building where the sniper we had targeted was holed up, the others started shooting like crazy. When I got close enough, I would blow up the whole place and everything in it. One by one, we got every one of them.

Our task was made easier by enemy overconfidence. In the war's first hours Arab radio broadcasts had begun urging those sympathetic to the cause to abandon their homes, that they would be able to return as soon as the Jews had been dealt with. By the tens of thousands they complied, leaving certain streets in Haifa and elsewhere all but empty, isolating the Arab fighters, giving us freer rein not only with traditional explosives but with some improbable new weapons jerry-built by soldiers in the field. We relied particularly on something we called the Rolling Bomb, a large ball of corrugated iron packed with powder and a finger of nitroglycerin. Since in Haifa, as in most towns, the Jews were on the heights and the Arabs controlled the old cities below, we simply set the things rolling and covered our ears. They didn't do much damage, but the A-bomb itself couldn't have made a more terrifying sound. The Rolling Bomb sent more than a few battle-hardened soldiers fleeing to the hills in panic.

Then there was the Davidka, a primitive mortar named for the engineer who invented it. Quite effective at short range, it also had a tendency to blow up in the faces of its operators. Only the nerveless Green approached it without terror. The rest of us would set the charge and beat the hell out of there. Still, to any army almost totally without heavy weapons, it was a godsend.

And by the time the cities were cleared of the enemy, an army is what we suddenly began to find ourselves—a surprisingly confident one. For that initial victory was not merely over the adversary, we had also defeated something in ourselves. If the world was stunned to see Jews fighting with such courage and skill against so numerically superior a force, so, too, were many of us.

Still, the war continued to rage in the countryside. Our explosives team was soon assigned the task of clearing mine fields to facilitate troop movements, unappealing work under the best of circumstances, but in this war a bona fide nightmare. The problem was the Arabs' utter disorganization. Mine fields normally display specific characteristics. Especially on their home ground, armies typically lay only one type of device in a given field. It makes things easier later on when the fields have to be cleared. But the Arabs seemed always to place mines totally at random, one German, the next English, the one after that Swedish, all of different design and quality. Moreover, some were brand-new, others so rusty they were liable to go off on their own.

All in all, I was profoundly grateful when our little group was called to the front lines.

Over the course of the next year, we fought in all parts of our infant country. Any of us who might have still believed that war was anything like a romantic adventure quickly set the fantasy aside. Often I was made physically ill by what I saw.

Still, we had each other, and that was considerable consolation. Moving this way and that like so many volunteer fire fighters—from Acre and Naharia in the north, to Tyre, to the Druse villages of Osha and Kasaya, to the Syrian and then the Lebanese borders—we actually began to view ourselves as charmed. All around us, every day, others were falling. We remained untouched.

But one day, outside the village of Janine near Jordan, the attack was anything but routine. Throughout the afternoon the enemy repeatedly assaulted our position in waves. We were forced to seize every lull to try and burrow into the stubborn, stony ground with our pitiful field shovels. By midafternoon I had Jacob's Bible out of my knapsack and within reach. Low on ammunition, we had to make it to nightfall (the Arabs didn't attack at night) and then hope for reinforcements.

Just before dusk, they began one last, furious attack. I glanced over at Green, crouched behind a rock perhaps twenty yards away. He was shaving.

"Green, are you mad?"

"I haven't shaved all day."

With someone else this would have been bravura. Green was entirely serious. "Hey," I called, "how's your fly?"

He glanced down. "Open."

We held on. At last the raw, moonless night came on. The cries of coyotes in the surrounding hills mingled with the moans of the wounded. Now there was only sporadic incoming fire, a waste of bullets, since they couldn't see a thing.

I wolfed down a K ration and resumed my digging.

After a couple of hours I heard someone crawling toward me.

"Get out of the foxhole."

It was Mark, my former instructor. I ignored him and kept working.

"Out. That's an order."

"If you want a hole," I hissed, "go dig one yourself."

"I could have you court-marshaled, Peter!"

"Get out of here before I beat the shit out of you!"

The bastard crawled off.

A court-marshal! In *this* army? Fat chance!

A few minutes later another figure came my way, stumbling forward in the blackness. Green. "That's the way it is in life, isn't it?" he said, sitting down heavily. "There's always someone wanting your foxhole."

"You, too?"

"I gave it to him. He needs it more than me." He paused. "What were they screaming during that last attack?"

"The same as the Germans, only in Arabic: 'Slaughter the Jews.' "

He laughed. The man would laugh at *anything*.

Green settled in near me. From the sound I could tell he was laying out his grenades in neat rows on the ground. It was something he liked to do.

"Where's Armoni?" I asked.

"Up the hill. I just had a nice visit with him."

As the night went on, it grew colder and the sniper fire increased. "Not the best of situations," observed Green mildly into the darkness.

"I think most of Company 24 was destroyed."

"I think so, too."

Suddenly he got to his feet and started walking. "I left my K rations up there."

He hadn't gone more than three paces when he came crashing down. He made a gurgling sound, his breathing labored.

I crawled beside him. When I touched his face to give him water from my canteen, it was wet with blood.

"Green, can you hear me?"

"I don't feel my hand."

"It's your head, not your hand." I tore off material from my shirt and wrapped it around his head, trying to stop the bleeding.

"My head is okay."

"Relax. Try to save your energy."

But he was right and I was wrong. An hour later the first light showed that most of his left hand was gone.

"You see?" he said, smiling. "You thought I was crazy."

"At least you'll live," I said, "if we can stop the bleeding."

"Maybe, but now I'll never be a concert pianist."

Around noon, when the shooting finally subsided, I

crawled over to Armoni to give him the news. He was curled up in the fetal position, asleep.

"Armoni, wake up."

When I got beside him, I saw that he was clutching the bullet hole in his stomach. His mouth was open, and white worms were crawling out.

Nearby, beside the flashlight he had been using, lay his open journal.

EIGHT

A New Life

BEFORE the war, I had assumed I would become an engineer. It was something I was good at. I had attended a technical high school. It was what someone in my position *ought* to do.

Returning from the army in 1950, I had no plans at all. No one I knew seemed to have any either. After everything we'd been through, it was simply impossible to look at the old plans—so eminently practical, so pleasing to parents—with the same eyes we once had.

Heaven knows the problem wasn't lack of choice. There we suddenly found ourselves, starting life in a brand-new country, one that needed *everything:* farmers, workers, business people, bureaucrats, artists, shopkeepers. For a young man on the move, no situation could have been more ideal. If I had chosen to become a professional clown, I would have had an excellent shot at soon becoming the best clown in Israel.

So what I did, like almost everyone else I knew, was

nothing. I went out with friends, I caught up on my sleep, I got used to my mother's cooking again, and to hearing her speculate on the growing likelihood I would never pass a productive moment again.

One afternoon a couple of months into this period, I happened to run into a guy I knew from the army at a café. It struck me as odd, because he lived and worked across town, and he didn't drink.

"Listen," he said after a couple of minutes of conversation, "you ever consider joining the Defense Ministry?"

I shrugged. "What could I do there?"

"You're a good mechanic, right? They need mechanics. I've got a friend there if you're interested."

"Why not?"

A week or so later I got a call telling me to come down immediately. When I arrived, I was ushered into a hot, unadorned office. A tall man in pressed, short-sleeved khakis was reading a report. For a couple of minutes I wasn't sure he knew I was there.

"I understand you're very good with explosives," he said, looking up suddenly.

I nodded. "That's my training."

"People say you've got a lot of nerve."

"Really? Who?"

He glanced at the report. "A high school teacher of yours who was a commander in the Haganah. Your friend Shaul Kaminovich. Others who know you from the army."

"Shaul? He's working in the income tax office."

He gave a short, dry laugh. "No, Shaul is here with us." He paused. "We've got a test for you, if you're interested. It might be a little dangerous."

Fifteen minutes later I was wedged in the front seat of a pale blue Chevrolet between this guy (his name turned out to be Morris) and, at the wheel, a short fellow in civilian dress with thick glasses and a bandage wound tightly around his head.

"A bullet wound?" I asked him.

He shook his head, smiling. "Shrapnel. Every six months they take one piece out of my head and one out of my foot. All my vacations are planned in advance."

Though we had not been introduced, I recognized the guy from the army. His name was Uzi. Eventually I would come to regard him as my closet professional associate.

We were heading toward the Syrian border. En route Morris described the assignment. There was a safe inside a house that had been occupied by a prominent terrorist, killed in a shoot-out a few days before. They needed it opened and its contents removed. There was every possibility that both the house and the safe were booby-trapped.

The temperature at our arrival, just before noon, was already above 100 degrees. The house was much like the others in this sunbaked region: one story, of stone and mortar, surrounded by a low stone wall. A dozen of our soldiers stood perhaps two hundred yards from the house, rifles in hand, watching.

"Who's going in with me?" I asked Morris.

He indicated a young man nearby. "He's done some explosives work."

A few minutes later the two of us were slowly making our way toward the house, searching for mines as we went. When we reached it, I entered alone through one of the windows—there was no sense in both of us risking our lives just yet—and located the door leading to a back room. A check of the door frame with a strip of celluloid indicated two barriers, a Dom lock, and a Yale lock. Easy; in a couple of minutes they clicked open. Very slowly I pushed open the door a crack, peering within with a pencil flashlight. Attached to the interior handle was a string, its other end affixed to a mine in the center of the room. There was a lot of slack, a good sign. Evidently the person who set it had been nervous.

After cutting the string, I radioed to have my companion enter the house. Together, we examined the safe in the corner.

It was English-made, a Mosler, just a couple of years old. There were no wires leading in from the outside. Also good. We were safe at least until the thing was opened, and then I'd have the same working room to disarm any device that the guy who put it there had had to set it up. I could only hope he was as much of a coward as he appeared to be.

My experience cracking safes was limited, just a few days of instruction and several trial runs. But from the start I had shown a real aptitude for it. Working a safe is all touch, a literal feeling for the subtle relationship between the three discs within. One searches for the weakness in the lock, the numbers that will leave the wheels in parallel formation, allowing the hammer to fall into the slot.

Gently I began manipulating the dials, straining for the sense of a pin being pulled. As I worked, my helper held the light and jotted down the numbers as I softly spoke them.

"Ten and a quarter.

"Fourteen and a quarter.

"Twenty-seven and a half."

It took more than three hours to find the combination. Both sweat-soaked, we took a break to share a peach and then opened the door a crack, searching with our light for wires. Seeing nothing, I opened it a tiny bit further, then further still. I had some concern about light-sensitive explosives, in their infancy as a terrorist tool. But at this point I had no alternative but to trust in my late adversary's regard for his own health.

At last wide open, the safe's contents were revealed: several pistols and revolvers; thick wads of Israeli, Syrian, and Egyptian currency; a foot-high pile of documents.

Touching nothing, I used a pocket mirror to search the sides of the safe, then behind the pile. *There* it was, beneath the documents. The mine would be set off when the paper was lifted, relieving the pressure.

Quickly I had the other guy fetch a heavy rock from

outside. Then, keeping the pressure on the pile constant with one hand, I began removing pages, a few dozen at a time, with the other. In ten minutes we had them all. Thirty seconds after that, we were out through the window, the rock sitting in place atop the mine.

Before we left the scene, I blew the whole house to kingdom come.

First thing the next morning, I was awakened by a call from my new pal Uzi. "Turn on the radio," he said.

I did. There was a news report about a group of saboteurs in Jerusalem who had been arrested, with a large cache of weapons and explosives, based on information in important newly discovered documents.

"I think you're in," said Uzi, "if you want to be."

Not that it proved quite so simple. When I filled out the formal application several days later to join the department of internal security, the Shin Beth, I pondered over how to respond to "Reason for Applying," finally settling on "I like adventure."

Such a response was not only unorthodox but deemed quite inappropriate.

"Look," I put it to Morris, "you saw what I can do. Just because I like adventure, it doesn't mean I'm not serious. What was Christopher Columbus, an office drudge?"

The more specific objection, I was told, was that, unlike almost everyone else, I hadn't written about a sense of obligation to the country.

Of course I loved the country, I objected, and I felt I had already shown that. But there was absolutely no contradiction between love of country and what I was after. I believed excessive patriotism was exactly the *wrong* reason to get into security work. If you believe it's a good thing to die for your country, you will.

Eventually, because they wanted me, they found a way not to disagree. My hand was shaken and I was welcomed aboard at a monthly salary of forty dollars.

*   *   *

In organization and structure, above all in spirit, the Israeli secret services in those early years were unlike any the world had ever known. Under the leadership of Isser Harel—under five feet tall, but as commanding a figure as any I have ever encountered—we were a model of democracy in action. There were no prima donnas in our midst, no sense that any task was ever trivial. Everyone did some of everything. Isser himself answered phones and took messages. Secretaries were called upon to act as operatives. The assumption was that in every sense we were a team.

Nor, at the start, was there anything like the subsequent rigid distinction between domestic and foreign activity. Though technically I was attached to Shin Beth, responsible for internal security, in short order I was traveling extensively abroad.

My principal assignment was to train Israeli embassy personnel, primarily in Eastern Europe, in the detection and disarming of letter bombs, which were then being addressed with alarming regularity to various Israeli governmental figures. While there, I was usually charged with examining our security arrangements in those locales in general.

This often involved a stay of some duration in what for me were very odd places, usually (in the interest of anonymity) on my own. I would spend long days wandering the streets or sitting in cafés and darkened movie houses, trying to get a fix on how people behaved locally, on how they thought and what they believed. With an eye to counterintelligence, I periodically changed not only hotels but identities, switching from an English to a French businessman, though at the time my command of neither language was absolute, all the while probing, probing, trying to figure how I, as a terrorist, might contrive to breach local Israeli defenses.

It was great fun, especially at the beginning. Having always been fascinated by people, their habits and idiosyncrasies, the ways in which their future actions can be anticipated on the basis of past behavior, I found it endlessly intriguing to note the ways in which entire cultures, too, embrace specific attitudes and modes of behavior.

It did not take long to grasp how little real undercover work has to do with the fictional version. A good agent survives on hard work and brains. The use of force invariably means a serious problem; the very thought that one might have to resort to it is an admission of self-doubt. After leaving the army, I never carried a gun.

In some respects surveillance is a skill that can be learned and mastered. Not attracting attention to oneself is very much a matter of technique. I recall a time early in my career when a couple of us were on a crowded street in downtown Athens (no parking was allowed, so no possibility of a two-way mirror in a van existed) assigned to watch a building where an important terrorist was believed to be hiding. What to do? What conceivable excuse is there for sitting on a bench with a newspaper for six hours? Out of necessity, the two of us designed a surveillance based on the simple truth that the casual eye takes less notice of someone moving than of someone who stays in place. For the next three days we walked the area in a coordinated pattern, each of us periodically changing his gait or subtly altering his appearance, but being always certain that one of us had the doorway in sight, until finally we spotted our man.

But, too, like just about everything else in the business, there is a commonsense aspect to undercover work that cannot be taught. One fellow I knew, otherwise a perfectly competent agent, actually made a hobby of collecting matchbooks from the restaurants he visited, potentially a fatal error. So, for example, and far more common, is not knowing when to ease off a surveillance and lie low.

All in all, the work was not far from what I had had in mind when I answered that question on the application. And it also had other, unexpected compensations. Even while functioning as a productive agent, I had plenty of time to become accomplished as a painter, to master the art of disguise, to fill wide gaps in my spotty education with regular visits to many of the world's finest museums and libraries.

Yet—and I see this clearly now, only in retrospect— the life took a devastating toll. An agent spends his life keeping things to himself, covering up as a matter of course, not only with strangers but among friends, family, lovers, everyone who is not a part of his tiny circle of professional intimates. You lie so often that invariably you start to contradict yourself, forgetting the lies you've already told. Even after decades of marriage, the most revered agent of us all —Isser Harel—rarely told his wife what he was up to; and she knew never to ask.

But, then, without question that is what attracts the best agents to work in the first place: We don't *want* to open up. Fearless in the pursuit of abstract national goals, we find terrible risk in showing ourselves to another soul in the privacy of a quiet room.

In my case the feeling surely had to do with what I had seen in my own family, the sense that profound love and commitment lead only to loss and pain.

When asked, I would always say that I expected someday to marry and have children, and at that moment I always more or less meant it. Yet into my late twenties, watching as one by one most of the men I knew settled down, it was something I could not imagine for myself. Who needed that kind of headache? Why take the risk?

I was just fine as I was. In my position how could I even think of chancing more than the occasional fling? After all, the lies came so much more easily when they didn't matter.

NINE

A "Good" German

*I*N *the astonishingly chaotic days and weeks following the collapse of the Third Reich, with the occupying forces struggling to impose some semblance of order on devastated central Europe, with hunger rampant and untold thousands of refugees on the move, it would seem to have been a relatively simple matter for a man to disappear.*

But for Adolf Eichmann there was danger everywhere. Near the top of every Allied wanted list, he was also among those most vigorously hunted by an array of partisan groups. One such group in the Lublin area of Poland, headed by a Jew named Yechiel Grienschpan, had formed a ten-man team specifically to track down the notorious Obersturmführer *Eichmann. Already, too, other commando units made up of veterans of the Jewish Brigade (recruits from Palestine who had fought with the British) had targeted Eichmann for summary justice; and working independently but with enormous resourcefulness and tenacity, such camp survivors as Simon Wiesenthal and Tuvia Fried-*

man were launching what would become lifelong efforts to see justice done by combing records, interviewing sources, following up on even the most unlikely leads.

But the pursuers were operating under one severe handicap. Though Eichmann's name was somewhat known, only those in his circle of acquaintance knew him by sight. This was no matter of happenstance. For years Eichmann had refused to pose for any photos other than those essential for official purposes, even then seeing to it that the negatives were destroyed and keeping tabs on every print. Frustrated investigators found that even in group shots he had managed to obscure his face, positioning himself in the last row behind larger men.

In fact, it would be almost a year before his pursuers would lay their hands on a usable recent shot, obtained from a onetime mistress of the former SS man. And by then the trail would be cold.

It appears that only after Eichmann was forced from their ranks by his uneasy companions did the extraordinary desperation of his situation fully register. Making his way down from the Austrian mountain retreat of Alt Aussee, accompanied by his adjutant Rudolf Jaenisch, Eichmann, by his own subsequent account, carried a cyanide capsule that he was apparently prepared to use.

But his crisis of confidence quickly passed. Changing into the uniform of a Luftwaffe corporal, he began hitchhiking with Jaenisch in the direction of Bavaria.

The Americans were everywhere. In the Ulm region they ran into a patrol from Patton's 3rd Army and were arrested. Dispatched to the POW holding camp at Berndorf, Eichmann identified himself as airman Adolf Barth (after the family's grocer in Berlin) and claimed his papers had been destroyed.

Fortunately for him, his captors were considerably less than rigorous. Transferred to a second camp at Rosenheim,

Eichmann actually managed to have himself assigned to be a driver for the sergeant in charge of the motor pool. In short order, he escaped on board a truck headed for Munich.

A mere two days later he was captured again. Having worried from the outset that he could be betrayed by the SS number tattooed beneath his right arm, Eichmann now presented himself as a lieutenant in the Waffen SS; and on the chance that a fellow prisoner might recognize him and address him by his real name, he called himself Otto Eckmann, reasoning it was close enough for American ears. Knowing that public records in Silesia had been destroyed by bombing, he gave his place of birth as Solingen-Breslau.

Again, Eichmann had been lucky. In some camps, discipline was stringent and the interrogators were pointed in their questioning of prisoners, particularly SS men. In one not far away, Jewish German-born soldiers, refugees from Hitlerism assigned duty as interrogators and translators, aware of who they had and dissatisfied with the pace of justice, simply handed certain prisoners over to the Russians and listed them as escaped.

But life at the Oberdachstetten camp was relatively easy. The several times Eichmann was questioned his story was never challenged. Still, in January 1946, aware that his name was being mentioned with increasing frequency at the war crimes trial in Nuremberg—even by those he considered friends—Eichmann determined to escape. Two days after particularly damaging testimony by his former associate Dieter Wisliceny, after whom he had named his middle son, he and another prisoner walked away from the road crew. Eichmann headed north in the direction of the isolated and heavily wooded Celle district; a fellow prisoner had given him a letter of introduction to his brother, a forest ranger near the village of Everson.

Now calling himself Otto Heninger, with the help of his friend's brother Eichmann soon secured work as a lumberjack. For a man who had performed little manual labor since adolescence, he proved surprisingly adept. Eichmann remained in the area nearly four years, supplementing his modest income by raising chickens and selling the eggs.

Still, on German soil he had to be ever alert to the possibility of being recognized. At last, in 1950, at the age of forty-four, he made contact with a branch of the far-flung Nazi underground. Supplying him with a full set of documents in the name of Ricardo Klement, they spirited him through Austria to Genoa, Italy, where a Franciscan monk secured for him a Vatican refugee passport.

Eichmann arrived in Buenos Aires in mid-July 1950 aboard the Italian ship Giovanna C., *and took a room at a boardinghouse. Within a few days he had found work as a mechanic at a metallurgical firm.*

He stayed at the job only a couple of months. Indeed, over the course of the next decade, relocating frequently, Eichmann held a startling variety of jobs. A job as a surveyor for a construction company in rural Tucumán was followed by one in a fruit juice factory. Then he ran a laundry, managed an angora rabbit farm outside the capital, worked as a mechanic, clerked in an auto parts shop, and became foreman of a truck farm. Briefly he was even a gaucho.

By now, Eichmann spoke excellent Spanish with only a slight accent. But he had always felt himself distant from the local culture, listening almost exclusively to German music, reading only German books. Having socialized little since his arrival in Argentina, regarded by his coworkers as diffident and frugal if not precisely unfriendly, these were among his few obvious pleasures. During the war his work had allowed him little time for light reading; now he read continually, particularly in the sciences and history. When he felt something strongly, he would stop to make notes in the margins. One volume in his collection, **The Last Days of the Reich's Chancellery,** *by a disillusioned ex-Nazi named Gerhard Boldt, is especially well marked. "The* author of this book is an ass," reads one typical notation, "dumb as a sow. . . . The author ought to be flogged for his vileness. With scoundrels like this the war had to be lost!"

Eichmann had been joined in Argentina by his wife and sons in 1952, two years after his arrival. In 1956 Vera Eichmann officially registered under her maiden name of Lieble but soon known as Catalina Klement, gave birth to a fourth son, Ricardo Francisco, nicknamed Haasi. Soon thereafter, Eichmann moved the family to a small rented house at 4261 Chucabuco Street, in the lower-middle-class Buenos Aires suburb of Olivos. In 1959 he bought a modest parcel of land on Garibaldi Street in San Fernando, an undeveloped district northwest of the capital. With the help of his sons he began constructing a home there.

Around the same time, he found work on the assembly line of the Mercedes-Benz factory in Suareze San Jarosto, just outside Buenos Aires. The plant was managed by Germans. Always a good worker, conscientious and eager to please, Eichmann soon worked himself up to a position as an administrative clerk.

It was in this period, too, that he began sitting down with Dutch Nazi journalist Willem Antonius Maria Sassen, a tape recorder spinning on the table between them. Intending to provide a Nazi interpretation to the Holocaust, Eichmann would later charge that his interviewer had taken unfair advantage of him during these sessions, leading him on, always keeping sure his wineglass was full. But he never denied speaking the words attributed to him. The transcript reflects a man frankly, even boastfully, unrepentant, yet also one who, after almost fifteen years on the run, seems nearly spent.

"I have slowly wearied of living as an anonymous wanderer between the worlds," it ruefully concludes. "The voice of my heart, which no human being can escape, has kept whispering to me to seek peace. Even with my former opponents I would like to be at peace. . . . Despite consci-

entious self-examination, I have to conclude in my own defense that I was neither a murderer nor a mass murderer. . . . I carried out with a clear conscience and faithful heart the duty imposed upon me. I was always a good German, I am today a good German, and I shall always be a good German!"

TEN

Spy

I T is hardly a secret that innumerable German scientists, formerly engaged in research for the Third Reich, played a decisive role in the rocket programs of the United States and the Soviet Union. What remains largely unknown even today is that others, including more than a few rabid and unrepentant Nazis, were brought into the employ of the Arab states, most notably Nasser's Egypt, to fight Israel. But *we* knew, and that intelligence was a source of acute concern at the highest levels of our government and military.

According to our sources, a former SS colonel named Ferdinand Brandner, a gifted aeronautics engineer, had been tapped by the Egyptians with an eye to seeking out former colleagues. Among his early enlistees were: Dr. Eugen Sanger, who had spent the last year of the war helping to develop a revolutionary "rocket plane," and Wolfgang Pilz, one of those behind the weapon that had so terrorized London, the V-2.

It was evident that the problems could not be dealt with through diplomatic channels. Confronted with our intelligence reports, the West German government had professed what seemed genuine sympathy for Israeli concerns —Chancellor Konrad Adenauer and Prime Minister Ben-Gurion were on excellent terms—but took the position that its hands were tied. Technically the scientists were being sought out not by a foreign government, but by private concerns. No laws had been broken.

Thus it was that, quite early on, the matter was turned over to the secret services.

My assignment was Pilz and the group he led. Heading up a clandestine team, I was to learn all there was to know about what they were up to.

I accepted the challenge as the privilege it was, but not without reservations. The fact of having to spend so much time in Germany, where Pilz was based, possibly more than a year, was particularly unsettling.

On my first visit there, five or six years before, my apprehension had been tempered by real curiosity. I have always tried to take people individually. My attitude is that in context almost all behavior is understandable. Indeed, in my business the ability to empathize is vital; a good agent must be able to discern motives for actions that strike others as incomprehensible. So I figured that now, at long last, I would begin to find satisfactory answers to one of the compelling questions of the age: How could it have happened? How could a people with so rich a culture and historical legacy have *let* it happen?

Then, too, how would they react to me? Knowing I was a Jew, would they be embarrassed? Contrite? Hostile?

To say I was disappointed would not begin to express it. What I found was an appalling level of indifference. Less than ten years after the Holocaust, there was infinitely less shame or sorrow over what had happened than clear regret that the war had not been won, less concern with moral responsibility than annoyance that the matter was still being raised at all.

It began to prey on me in ways I did not like. Seeing a man of thirty-five or forty, I would suddenly find myself wondering: Was he SS or merely Wehrmacht? Had he personally participated in the killing, perhaps as one of the thousands to have served in an *Einsatzgruppen* unit, or merely countenanced it? Walking down a street, hearing someone laugh in a café, the thought would suddenly return with a rush: These people were behind the Holocaust, and they don't give a damn!

As to answers, the only one I managed to come up with was a cliché, the one having to do with the way Germans view authority and personal responsibility. Which is not to say it is invalid. Beyond question, certain traits do tend to predominate in certain cultures. Most are neither good nor bad by definition: The same brooding romanticism routinely observed in Hitler helped shape Beethoven and Goethe; the same veneration for efficiency that made it possible for the Nazis to slaughter on so massive a scale has given rise to five generations of automotive engineers. There is little doubt that the particular brand of cruelty that flourished in the Third Reich, and the broad, unswerving allegiance to a madman that made it possible, were at least as much a matter of German as of human nature.

It did not take me very long to figure this out. One afternoon, just a few days after my arrival, I went to a movie. Noting that the theater was two-thirds empty, and wanting the freedom to spread my legs and chomp on my snacks loudly, I took a seat off by myself. Almost immediately somebody sat down on one side of me, then someone else on the other. I moved and the same thing happened again; then again. It finally dawned on me that they were filling in the spaces. In the collective obsession with efficiency they couldn't stand to waste a row!

Now the lights dimmed and a newsreel came on. It was

about a German fighter pilot from the war who had lost a
leg and overcome his adversity to become a champion alpine
climber. The guy was fantastic, a truly admirable character.
Suddenly there came a shot of him falling in the snow and
then sliding awkwardly down the mountain. There was a
pause, and then someone began to laugh. And—I will never
forget it—in an instant most of the audience joined him.
The next time he fell the whole place erupted in riotous
laughter.

The German scientists operation was to be most complex, and it called for an especially capable team of individuals blessed with a degree of patience and perseverance
rare even by the usual standards of the business. Before we
would be able to get what we were after—definitive proof
of the Pilz group's plans and a clear idea of how far they
had already gone in realizing them—there would be months
of painstaking surveillance work. After identifying every
member of the group, we would have to acquaint ourselves
with the specifics of their professional functions and personal lives, their idiosyncrasies and daily routines. Only
then would we be in a position to know how best to get
our hands on the research data, and, even more so, which
of it was most likely to be of significance. Time consuming
and tedious though it may be, banal as it sounds, dogged
effort remains almost always the key to success.

Indeed, *over*preparation was the only way I knew how
to work. The notion of embarking on any operation, let
alone one of this importance, without feeling as fully in
control as humanly possible was enough to make me physically ill. It was not luck that had made me successful in
the field, let alone anything as fuzzy as mere guts or instinct;
it was the incessant awareness of the astonishing number
of ways things could go wrong and the maniacal deter-
mination to constantly nudge the odds in my direction. I
aimed to leave no detail unattended to, to have a solution

at the ready to every conceivable problem, and an alternative solution, and alternatives to the alternative.

Fortunately we were working under optimal conditions: not only plenty of time but enough trained personnel to do the job on our own terms. Our policy would be one of extreme caution. No operative would spend more than a few hours on a given subject at a stretch, and afterward would lay off that subject for at least several days.

Of course, such a system placed even greater emphasis on the human side of the equation. With all the downtime, we would be spending a good deal more time together than most families. Without access to many of the usual distractions, I needed people who would not drive one another crazy.

The first selection was a snap. Meir was a mechanical genius, capable of fixing everything from car engines to submachine guns to the most sophisticated cameras, and of improvising almost anything he could not. Within the secret services his false suitcase bottoms were the stuff of legend, and some of his locks baffled even me. At six-two, his head shaved clean, he could also be called upon as an intimidator. A veteran of the Jewish Brigade, Meir had been part of a team that after the war hunted down particularly notorious SS men and, after an informal trial, generally dispatched quick justice.

But Meir's looks were deceptive. In fact, he was gentle and full of good humor, one of those people aroused to violence only by extreme provocation, a sort of smarter version of Lenny in *Of Mice and Men*. He was the only guy I had ever encountered in the secret services who refused to take personally even the infamous one-on-one, no-holds-barred battles that had been instituted as part of our physical training. Leaving the building after one such session, during which we had been pitted against one another for fifteen grueling minutes, I was so racked with pain I could scarcely step from the street to the curb, but was still so seething with rage I wanted to keep going then and there. All Meir wanted was to take me to a restaurant he had discovered up the coast that specialized in the Russian cuisine he'd know as a boy. Though all we could do was suck up some borscht—even chewing was an effort—before long he had me in a mood as good as his, as blow by blow, gouge by gouge, he lovingly re-created the battle.

The choice of team driver was almost as easy. Since the job involved serving as the team tactician—being dispatched to new locales before the others in order to master local traffic patterns and taking responsibility for choosing the approaches to targets and the best escape routes—the pressures involved were enormous. But where after a few weeks in the job some others developed personalities frighteningly reminiscent of veteran New York cabbies, Jack seemed not to know the meaning of either aggravation or discourtesy. Indeed, he was so reserved, he often seemed not to be around at all. This was the next best thing, in the eyes of a fellow agent who has had a particularly rough day, to being invisible.

It was the final two choices that gave me trouble. For the front man—the guy we needed to rent safe houses, cars, and equipment or to pose as the tenant of an apartment where we were operating, keeping the others in food and cigarettes and maintaining contact with the outside world—I finally settled on a Frenchman named Jean-Claude. It was a pragmatic choice: The rest of us were supposed to be French, at least to begin with. And I knew from experience that Jean-Claude was as dedicated as they come.

Still, I made the move only after enormous hesitation. For I also knew far better than most what a colossal pain in the ass this tall and courtly Frenchman could be. On a prior assignment together, in Greece, the first few days were total confusion. I would give him specific orders, he would nod and then proceed to ignore me. Or, worse, he would do something else entirely and then insist *that was* what I had told him.

One morning it reached a head. I sent him out to pay a parking fine and he returned with a pair of airline tickets to Vienna.

"You're impossible," I screamed at him. "You're an idiot!"

He looked terribly hurt. "You *told* me to get the tickets."

"I said *pay* a ticket! How could anyone confuse the two?!"

One of our colleagues cornered me that night after dinner. "Didn't you know? He has a hearing problem."

"He does? He never said a word."

"He doesn't like to talk about it. He's vain." He shrugged. "He's French."

So I made the appropriate adjustments. When he got things straight, he was fine, if still more than occasionally temperamental. The trick with Jean-Claude was to stay on his good side, then double- and triple-check every move he made.

The final decision was the hardest of all. Almost every such operation included a woman. In those pre-women's liberation days, she generally doubled as an operational secretary and an agent, most often assuming the role of a wife or girlfriend of one or another of the men as the need arose.

It was no simple task, harder, in its way, than anything any of the rest of us had to do. If we men were living highly unnatural lives, in our enforced isolation and endless wariness unable even to speak our native language in public, at least we had each other for companionship. If we understood that there could be no public recognition for a job well done, we could at least be sure of the esteem of our peers.

Looking back on it, a woman on a team was isolated in ways the rest of us couldn't even fathom. To us it seemed altogether normal that conversations on certain subjects abruptly ceased when she entered a room, and it went without saying that in our view no woman, however capable, was ever indispensable to the success of a project. Or, at any rate, couldn't be replaced by someone just as good.

Then, too, there was her characteristically close working relationship with the group leader. Since among other things, the female operative was usually charged with coordinating contact between the leader and the rest of the team, the two of them often shared the same hotel, apart from the others. Yet, if there existed the merest suggestion of anything other than a strictly professional relationship between them, the resentment of the less senior men could threaten the unity of the team, a calamity of immense proportions, potentially compromising the entire operation.

Going in, I had a list of qualities I wanted in my operational secretary. She had to be fluent in French, German, English, and Italian, French in appearance and style and accustomed to pressured situations. The woman I eventually chose was a sabra named Hannah. Twenty-six years old, the daughter of a French mother and a German father, she had been an ambulance driver in the Sinai campaign before joining the secret services. Her qualifications were above challenge by even the most suspicious mind.

And if I could not help but note that she was also someone whose face I wouldn't mind seeing first thing every morning—she had black hair and blue eyes, my favorite combination—I kept that part to myself.

At the outset the investigation proceeded with extreme caution. The Pilz group was spread out over three German cities, and it took us more than two months simply to identify all its members, then another six weeks to get a rough fix on their schedules.

But, too, the pace was dictated by the recognition that we required an adjustment period. We all had powerful, intensely personal feelings about this project. Living in Germany, tracking unregenerate Nazis, was not something for which any of us could have ever been fully prepared. If the job was to be properly done, it would be necessary more than ever before to keep vital aspects of our true selves under wraps.

I was surprised by those who had the hardest time. I could not but be impressed by how rarely Hannah and, of all people, Jean-Claude lost their composure. But Meir, who as a soldier had been among the first inside the camps, reacted to much of what he saw around him with a depth of passion of which I had never before even suspected him capable. Sometimes, after returning after a day's work, he would rage against something he had seen or overheard on the streets. Then there was Jack, who had lost much of his family to the Nazis. His gentle nature sometimes now gave way to a desire for retribution that was almost physical.

Naturally I understood; but the point, as I knew from personal experience, was to learn to control those impulses, to harness that emotion in service of the project at hand.

Increasingly close to these people, no older than most (in the case of Meir, five years younger), I also had to be aware of the need to establish a certain distance. We were friends, but I was also their commander. It is a distinction easier to maintain in wartime, where combat situations demand a steady stream of decisive orders, than in a situation as relatively unstructured as ours. I wanted to give my people some free rein, feeling strongly that the capacity for independent thought and action is as vital to the success of such an operation as competent command, but they also had to know who was in charge.

It was a balancing act that, all in all, I think I handled damn well, especially given the behavioral excesses to which I am sometimes prone. Never one to bark out orders or demand anyone's respect, I talked softly and tried to earn it in increments. If nothing else, they knew I was fair, that I was against heroism for its own sake; that the risks I took were at least as great as those I asked of anyone else.

They also knew—and this I am as proud of as anything else—that I was eager, if at all possible, to give them an outlet for relaxation. One thing I did insist upon was that the team, as a unit, go on regular outings to museums and galleries. In fact, within the secret services we soon acquired a certain reputation as intellectuals, and under my tutelage, and that of another part-time artist, a gifted forger named Danny who periodically joined the operation from his base in Paris to provide us with fresh documents, Jack and Hannah eventually took up painting.

The only one who ever made me long to crack the whip was Jean-Claude. The latest problem was his extraordinary devotion to my well-being. Every time I turned around, he'd be cleaning my room, straightening up the shelves, dusting the furniture. The man was like my mother.

Then he took to bugging me about my attaché case. I shouldn't take it out with me so often, he would warn. I was going to lose it. I should buy *another* case so that I would only have to carry out the documents I needed for that appointment.

"You're *worse* than my mother!" I would scream. "Let me breathe. I don't care if I lose it."

He would just stand there, shaking his head. "Oh, absolutely, you say that now."

One afternoon, ten minutes after we walked out of the restaurant in the Zurich train station, he suddenly realized I *had* left it behind.

"Oh, God," I exclaimed, "you're right!"

"Oh, no, oh, no," he wailed, desperation warring with delight, "I told you this would happen!"

"You did, I know you did. We've got to go back."

"How could you do it? Why wouldn't you listen?"

"I don't know, I don't know." I paused. "Wait a minute, there's something important in my pocket. Could you get it?"

He gave me an odd look and fished out a note. "Schmuck," it read, "stop saying 'I told you so.' The case is in a locker."

It got him off my back for maybe all of two days.

But soon I found myself having to come to grips with

a potentially far more serious problem. One early July evening, simply in the normal course of things, Hannah and I were on a surveillance together, posing as a couple. It seemed appropriate to hold hands as we strolled, so we did. Pausing in a doorway, it seemed the absolutely correct move to kiss, so we did that, too.

"Peter," she suddenly whispered, *"on partage une chambre ce soir?"* (Why don't we share a room tonight?)

I was thunderstruck. *"C'est pas Peter,"* I whispered back sharply. (Don't call me Peter.)

A couple of minutes later, sitting on a deserted bench, my arm around her, my loins beginning to ache, I explained what she already knew: It was impossible.

But she wouldn't accept it, and back at our hotel the discussion continued into the night. She was lonely, she told me, she liked me a lot. Didn't I care for her at all?

In fact, I was extremely attracted to her. Though not classically beautiful (as a matter of policy, the secret services never hired anyone liable to attract unnecessary attention), she carried herself with the particular grace born of self-confidence. I also loved to hear her talk, and, maybe even more, watch her listen. So few Israelis know how to listen.

But it just couldn't be, I told her again. In the space of ten years the secret services had moved from the equivalent of a mom-and-pop operation to a giant corporation, with all the attendant backbiting and political maneuvering. Even if the mission itself were not in any way jeopardized—and of course that was the overwhelming consideration—once the rumors got started, and they would, we would be ripped apart within the organization itself.

I knew what I was talking about. I told her of an episode that had occurred just the previous year. One morning I was called before the new director of internal security in the Haifa office, a young, intensely ambitious fellow. He announced that he had some bad news. "It's something that concerns not only you personally," he said, "but the service.

I must inform you that your wife has been sleeping with another man in your apartment. Other men, in fact."

For a long moment I was literally speechless. "How does that affect the service?" I finally asked.

"There are pictures on the wall of you with Isser Harel and others."

In feigned fury I insisted he immediately accompany me to my place. We would confront her together. As I expected, we found the Yemeni cleaning girl going about her tasks. I asked her point-blank if she had been using my apartment to turn tricks while I was abroad.

She at least had the good grace to be embarrassed and beg my forgiveness. The security man had so obviously viewed the story as a weapon against a potential adversary that, even confronted with the truth, he seemed reluctant to give it up.

"Don't you understand?" I confronted him finally. "*I'm not married!*"

"We'll have to look into this in light of the new evidence," was all he would allow.

"The point," I concluded to Hannah, "is that you don't take that kind of chance. You never compromise the integrity of the team, and you never give easy ammunition to anyone out to get you."

Even I didn't expect her to take it quite so much to heart. Whatever ideas she had been entertaining of a romance between us seemed to be dead before the conversation was over. Indeed, in the days and weeks that followed, her entire manner began to change dramatically, her spontaneity and lively good humor giving way to an intense seriousness of purpose. Nothing, she made it clear in a dozen ways, nothing at all, must ever be allowed to interfere with the mission.

It is a measure of how far we strayed from that moment in the doorway—indeed, of how bizarre was this existence we were leading—that now, if she watched me at all, it was less with longing of a secret lover than the wary gaze of a mother.

Another mother.

Things probably reached their low point a few months later during Oktoberfest. Hannah, Meir, and myself were sitting one Sunday afternoon in the vast Munich beer hall renowned as the starting place of Hitler's 1923 *Putsch*. It may have been that which got to me, or just the sight of so many towheaded, red-cheeked, lederhosen-garbed locals in one spot, raising their steins in raucous song, a picture-postcard tableau that was also a personal nightmare. Whatever it was, I couldn't restrain myself, even if it meant violating my own rules. Spotting eight or ten young men at an adjacent table about to begin a beer-drinking contest, I leaned over and bragged that I could outdrink them all.

"Jean-Jacques," said Hannah sharply, using the name on the passport I was carrying at the moment, "stop it. This is stupid."

I knew at once she was right. This was hardly inconspicuous behavior, but I quickly rationalized that they were drunk, wouldn't remember much, and probably did this sort of thing all the time anyway. Indeed, I had to borrow cash from my two companions to cover my bet. At that moment I cared only about humiliating those Germans.

The waitresses fetched the largest steins I had ever laid eyes on, two liters apiece, and driven by sheer will and Meir's loud encouragement, making certain to take in only liquid and not air, I chugged them both down in less than a minute. The Germans, surly and resentful, were miserable losers, but casting glances at Meir, they paid up.

It was Hannah who gave me real trouble. "You're mad," she raged as we left the place. "You're completely out of your mind."

"I am," I slurred, leaning heavily on Meir's shoulder, "maybe I am. But it felt *wonderful!*"

ELEVEN

Israelis in Germany

IN those days a rather odd concept of rest and relaxation existed in the secret services. Home for a month was supposed to be a breather. However, one was apt to work harder than ever, since there were all the debriefings and strategy sessions and so much catching up to do around the office.

Then there was the physical training. It was bureaucratic gospel that a prolonged stretch in the field may be even harder on an agent's strength, agility, and reaction time than on his psyche. I may have disagreed in principle, but given the obvious effects of my fondness for German beer and pastry, I kept my mouth shut.

Thus it was that one morning I found myself in a dimly lit gymnasium in shorts and sneakers, ringed by twenty or so men, as Meir, teeth clenched and eyes narrow, warily approached. The decision to call us back at the same time, leaving Jack in charge of a skeleton crew in Cologne, was a strategic one—temporarily relaxing surveillance in a long-term operation can be useful in keeping an adversary's guard down—but at that moment I could not have been sorrier about it. Though my friend, too, showed a lot of flab where once there had been only muscle, he remained capable of inflicting enormous physical harm.

He kept plodding toward me, I kept circling, strength against speed. I was vaguely aware of the others shouting out frenzied encouragement; there was always a lot of betting when we fought. The only voice I picked up clearly was that of Herschel, our instructor. His speech was a distinctive slur, the result of a knife wound fighting with the partisans in his native Czechoslovakia that had left half his face paralyzed.

"Look," he said evenly, "search out a weak point."

All at once, Meir made a desperate lunge. Catching him off balance, I flipped him to the floor. As I moved to press my advantage, driving a knee into his gut, he grabbed my chin and tried to push me away. I drove the knee in harder. Grunting, he countered with a hard shot to the ribs.

"The balls," ordered Herschel's impassive voice.

Suddenly Meir had my testicles in a vice grip. Never had I experienced such sudden excruciating pain. I was later told my face went from red to sheet white.

Squeezing even harder, Meir flipped me onto my back. Seeing bright lights, I felt I was about to faint.

"The neck is open," I heard Herschel point out.

The neck was Herschel's specialty, his favorite point of vulnerability. Sometimes he greeted the class with what he called the "knockout push," moving down the line, jabbing a thumb into the quarter inch beneath our Adam's apples, watching us fall in turn like so many ninepins.

Now, summoning up what strength I could, I drove both thumbs into Meir's throat. Eyes bulging, he made a gurgling sound. It occurred to me that I was killing him, but he wasn't relaxing the pressure, so neither did I.

Finally he let go. There came a quick pounding on the mat, the sign of surrender.

A couple of afternoons later I was sitting at my desk in the office, opposite a young woman who had come in to be interviewed about an opening in our department for a secretary.

"How did you happen to hear about the job?" I asked, a pro forma question. It wasn't the sort of thing that was advertised in the newspapers.

"A friend in the Defense Department told me," she said. She produced a folder. "I've brought my résumé and references."

Already I could see that she was acceptable physically. Of medium height and nicely shaped, with medium-length black hair and a long angular face, like a Modigliani. She was attractive but not a head-turner. I glanced at the résumé. Her name was Gila.

"What languages do you speak?"

"English, French, Arabic. A little Russian. I type eighty words a minute."

"Do you have any experience with undercover work?"

She hesitated. "No."

"What did you do in the army?"

"I assisted in a medical unit. Nothing special."

"Have you done any acting, anything in the theater?"

She gazed at me quizzically. "What difference does that make?"

"Well, everyone here is called upon to do some of everything." I smiled; actually she was quite pretty.

"I'm not sure I understand you."

Incredibly, she really seemed not to.

"You do know where you are? This is the headquarters of Shin Beth."

"I know that. But I was told the position was secretarial."

"What I am saying is that a secretary is sometimes expected to perform other tasks. Is keeping secrets a problem for you?"

"Yes, I think it would be."

The response was so straightforward, I was momentarily at a loss. Over the years, in innumerable similar situations, I had grown used to hearing people say *anything* to be accepted within the secret services. One time a young man sat down and, before I even had a chance to pose a question, announced that there was no act he was unwilling to perform on behalf of his country.

"What exactly did you have in mind?" I asked him.

"Anything," he repeated forcefully.

"Fine," I offered. "What would you do if, say, you were traveling on a false passport and a customs inspector suspected there was something wrong with it?"

"I'd grab it from him and eat it," he answered instantly.

"You'd eat it?"

"Absolutely."

So I produced a German passport. They are particularly thick. "Show me."

I'll never forget his expression as he fingered it. "This is *really* big," he said finally.

Which is what I initially found so intriguing about this Gila. If bravura could be a fatal liability in my business, her brand of honesty could be turned into a virtue. It is important to know that one's fellow operatives have not only sharp minds but functioning consciences.

"Why is keeping secrets so hard?"

"It's just not something I'm used to doing."

"Even if it were necessary?"

"I just can't see myself lying to people I care about."

"That's not how it works," I said. "If you've got a husband or boyfriend, they soon get used to not asking. Do you tell everyone everything now?"

"That's crazy," she insisted. "I'm not Mata Hari! I'd *want* to tell them."

I paused, exhaled slowly, gave up. "Look, there are departments here where you wouldn't have to lie. Let me look into it."

She nodded. "Fine. All right."

I hesitated. "By the way, *do* you have a boyfriend?"

Half an hour later we were sitting in the coffeeshop across the street and she was asking the questions, mostly variations on a single theme: How did I deal with the issues involved in such work?

I shifted in my seat. No one had ever asked me to think about it before. "It's not really something I concern myself with."

"You seem like a sensitive person. How can you go through life like that?"

"Look," I said too sharply, "these just aren't questions I ask. The work has value, so I make the appropriate sacrifices. That's all."

Soon I managed to steer the conversation back to safer ground. It turned out she was a sabra; her family had been in Palestine for two generations already. It explained her sense of openness which, to someone from my background, was altogether alien. A skilled potter—she had a studio in the home she shared with her mother and brother in the New City—she had had exhibitions at several galleries. But she was not driven by ambition; more than anything else, she looked forward to a family.

I don't think I'd ever been so instantly at ease with anyone, certainly not with a woman. We spent most of the rest of the afternoon in the coffeeshop, then headed to a restaurant to continue talking over dinner.

Late that evening, parked on a bluff off the coast road high above the Mediterranean, we began kissing. Soon I started running my fingers over her thigh, sharply defined beneath the thin fabric of her peasant dress, and she made no effort to stop me.

Yet the more aroused I became, the more vivid became the memory of my encounter with Meir in the gym.

I finally gave up. "I'm sorry, I can't now."

But a couple of days later I could. And by the time I left, two weeks later, we considered ourselves a pair.

Still, I gave her no hint of where I was going or what I would be doing when I got there.

In the letters I wrote over the following months (all of them postmarked, as required by regulations, in Israel, so that more than once she received letters from me that had been mailed blocks from her house) I dealt only with approved subjects. I talked about the books I had been reading or historical figures I admired, my views on art, philosophy, religion, my boyhood in Haifa and all we would do when we were next together, the past and the future, if not the present. More and more as time went on, she responded the same way, so that eventually the very nature of the correspondence in one sense served to strengthen the bond between us. We were dealing with things that most young lovers, in mutual self-absorption and the blur of daily goings-on, tend not to get around to for a long time.

Yet, too, of course, it also threatened it. I had fallen in love with this woman. For the first time, I felt inclined to make a life with someone. Yet, from my end, so much could simply not be shared.

The operation was at its crucial stage. Having meticulously monitored our quarry for months, having ascertained not only when they went to bed and got up but with whom, not merely how often they dined with which colleagues but what they like to eat, not only how they traveled to work but, even more important, where they journeyed when they left town and for how long, now it was time to zero in on their work.

Already, I had surreptitiously visited the apartments of two of the scientists, including Pilz himself, but to little avail. The documents I discovered and photographed, phony passports and other fake ID, proved nothing at all, except possibly that their owners were paranoid. I carried the same with me all the time.

The question was, Which of their workplaces should we try to penetrate? Our team had established the existence of no fewer than four research facilities in different parts of the country, and our undercover people in Egypt had targeted potential operational sites there as well.

For me, the answer was clear. I lobbied hard for the Pilz group's laboratory in Cologne. If there were files to be had on German soil, I was persuaded that this conventional second-story apartment was where we would find them. I felt so strongly about it that more than six months before, I had decided to risk one of Isser's famous tirades about money foolishly spent by renting a third-floor apartment diagonally across the enclosed courtyard.

Eventually I made my point.

Thus it was that on a nearly moonless January evening I stepped from the courtyard window of our apartment onto a narrow ledge and began inching my way toward the target, moving on my haunches below window level. We had waited more than a week for this night. Pilz was out of town, on one of his monthly visits to Zurich, where he did his banking, and we also knew that most of his colleagues had tickets to Wagner's *Tannhäuser* at the local opera house. As we suspected, no light shined from the laboratory window. A steady snow had been falling for an hour, which I regarded as a piece of luck. I brushed it off the path before me as I went. Should anyone suspect the laboratory had been penetrated, there would be a blanket of white, unmarked by even a single footprint, to set the suspicion to rest.

Indeed, after all the debate and planning, the actual break-in was an anticlimax. I had done this sort of thing many times before.

The French window I used to reenter the building was identical to the one through which I had exited. In five seconds I jimmied it and stepped into a pitch-black public hallway, then crept down the steps, keeping close to the wall so they wouldn't creak, and felt my way round a corner. Then I momentarily switched on my pen flashlight. Before me were the double glass doors that led into the laboratory.

What a laugh. They were secured by no more than a simple Yale lock, probably the one already in place when they rented the space. I took out a strip of celluloid from my pocket to flick it open. But suddenly something came crashing against the doors from within.

Stunned by the force of the blow and unable to see a thing in the darkness, I was overcome by dread. I knew I was going to die.

Then I heard barking. A dog! Now it was hurling itself against the glass again, so hard I thought it would break, making a terrible racket. I had to get out of there.

But I forced myself to hold my ground a moment longer and turned my flashlight on the thing. It stopped and stared. Black and tan, it was a huge Doberman with immense bared fangs and ebony eyes that shone as if lit from within. Then I got the hell out of there.

The next day I was back in Tel Aviv for consultation. It seemed like such a ridiculous problem, yet no one had any idea how to proceed. My next stop was Paris. We had an operative in a suburb north of the French capital, an elderly woman who had survived the camps. She trained dogs professionally.

Mme. Messmer listened to my story with an odd mix of sympathy and amusement. "You're sure it was a Doberman?" she asked finally.

"I'm not absolutely sure, I think so." I paused. "I can tell you that it was as big as a horse and it wanted to kill me."

She rose to her feet and pulled on a bulky sweater over her stained white laboratory coat. A tiny woman, she barely came up to my shoulder. "If you had opened those doors, it would have. Well, let's go see."

Behind her house was an extensive kennel. The sound of all the barking made me hold back just a little.

Mme. Messmer noticed. "Don't worry." She laughed, revealing stubby yellow teeth. "These are *my* children. They speak French, not German."

We first passed a number of cages housing German shepherds. "Gibor," she said, addressing one particularly handsome animal in French-accented Hebrew, "be still."

I looked down at her in surprise.

"I just speak a few words," she explained. "We're training fifty shepherds for blind soldiers in Israel."

"How do dogs like these do in a fight against a Doberman?" I asked.

"Obviously these here aren't bred for aggression. But in a fight to the death, almost no dog will best a Doberman." She paused. "Why?"

"I've been thinking about something, that's all."

"Though," she added, "aside from another Doberman, a well-trained shepherd might do as well as any other. Or a Rottweiler."

"Do you have any Dobermans here?"

She took my arm and led me around a corner. "There."

I shuddered at the very sight. This one was as big as the other and looked to be just as vicious. It was staring directly at me and, teeth bared, growling hideously.

"Do you have any shepherds trained to fight?" I asked. "Or any of that other kind?"

"Rottweilers? I have a male Rottweiler, one of the best guard dogs I've ever handled. It was starved deliberately to enhance aggression."

"Would it attack me? I'm not so good with dogs."

"Not if I introduce you."

"He'll take on a Doberman?"

She laughed. "*Vous êtes très dangereux, n'est-ce pas!*" (You're a very dangerous man, aren't you?)

Half an hour later in her living room, over cheese and wine, I let her know what I had in mind. I wanted to take the Rottweiler back to Cologne. I would also need an impression of the Doberman's teeth cast in bronze.

She puffed on a Gauloise, nodding. "The cast will take a few days. Use the time to get used to the dog."

Four days later I was back in our safe house in Cologne, and Meir, eyes closed and teeth clenched, had his arm thrust out before me. "Ready?" I asked.

"If you must!"

Taking the cast of the Doberman's bite, hinged so that it opened like a real mouth, I clamped it down on my friend's upper arm, tearing his shirt slightly and drawing blood.

He winced. "You enjoyed that, didn't you?"

I laughed. "Right. My nuts haven't even begun to pay you back. Now, you'd better hurry."

It was a little past 3:00 P.M.

In my absence it had been determined that each afternoon a secretary walked the laboratory Doberman between 3:30 and 4:00. Taking our Rottweiler's leash, Meir hurried out the door.

The Doberman was right on schedule. Rounding a corner, he caught sight of the enemy beast. The Rottweiler tensed momentarily, then made a leap forward, straining at his leash. The Doberman did the same, with even greater force, dragging the hapless woman forward. The two dogs tore into each other with incredible ferocity. Meir, shouting, was caught between them, ending up on the ground, as the animals raged above him.

By the time they were finally pried apart by passersby, he was screaming that he had been bitten by the Doberman. He yanked open his torn sleeve to prove it.

"That looks bad," someone said. "You'd better get to a doctor."

"What about that dog?"

"That dog should be put in quarantine," spoke up one of the passersby, who happened to be Jean-Claude. Others readily agreed. So did the policeman who shortly happened upon the scene.

The dog got forty-eight hours in the clinker, more than enough time for me to stage a return trip to the laboratory.

The only surprise was how much material I found there to photograph. Not only was there a raft of documents and letters but, in a filing cabinet in Pilz's private office, opened by keys discovered in a secretary's drawer, blueprints for liquid-fuel rocket engines.

Meir, Jean-Claude, and I returned to Israel the next morning, our usefulness in Germany temporarily at an end. But in this area and others, the operation against the German scientists would continue into the early sixties, escalating into one of the most complex and difficult episodes in the history of the Israeli secret services.

But that day, in the office, among those few who knew the story, there was only jubilation, and raucous congratulations all around.

TWELVE

Blindman's Buff

*T*HOUGH British foreign secretary Anthony Eden had described the pursuit of war criminals as "the biggest manhunt in history," by the close of 1947 the Western Allies had all but abandoned the hunt. With the onset of the Cold War, attention and resources were turned to the new perceived threat; and even the capture of the most notorious of the escaped Nazis—Eichmann, Martin Bormann, Josef Mengele, and Gestapo chief Heinrich Müller—vital as it remained to civilized opinion, was suddenly a less than urgent matter of national policy. Indeed, in some cases (that of Klaus Barbie, "the butcher of Lyon," is the most notable example) Western intelligence services, viewing former SS men as useful in the covert war against the Russians, knowingly provided them with cover.

In fact, it was not a government at all that most vigorously pursued Adolf Eichmann in those early years, but the Haganah. Having kept a dossier on the murderer since reports on his activities had begun filtering into Palestine early in the war, the clandestine organization in 1946 dispatched a five-man team to Austria to hunt him down. Eventually locating Eichmann's wife in the town of Bad Aussee, they actually managed to infiltrate the household by passing off a fair-haired, blue-eyed female agent as a maid.

But as far as could be determined, Frau Eichmann never gave the slightest indication of her husband's whereabouts. In fact, in 1947 she filed papers with a local court seeking to formally establish that he was dead; killed at the war's end in Prague.

In 1948, on the eve of Israeli independence and with war certain to follow, the team was recalled to Palestine; even the Haganah now had other priorities. Before their departure, the team leader concocted one last plan: to kidnap Frau Eichmann and her sons, making it clear that they would be released only in exchange for the war criminal himself. It was summarily rejected by headquarters.

Now only the handful of free-lance operatives, meagerly funded, encountering frequent bureaucratic obstacles, facing very real threats to their safety, continued to pursue Eichmann ardently. Doggedly through the late forties and into the fifties they kept at it, pursuing every conceivable lead. Occasionally they seemed to make headway. Wiesenthal, in particular, was successful in tracing the financial resources Eichmann seemed to have set aside during the war years. In one overlooked file, he discovered a detailed accounting of the booty appropriated from his victims. It included thirty-one crates of gold, eighteen crates of jewelry, and more than fifty thousand dollars in cash.

But, in the end, none of it led to the man himself. Privately even some of those most utterly obsessed with the hunt began to doubt that he could ever be found.

Meanwhile, in early 1957, unaware of any of this, a blind retiree in the remote Argentine town of Coronel

Suárez, several hundred miles to the southwest of Buenos Aires, began to entertain suspicions about a man he had never met. Of German-Jewish extraction, the blind man had been in the camps; his parents had died there. Yet he bore one of those names that left his ethnic background ambiguous, and his half-Jewish nineteen-year-old daughter possessed what the Nazis had preferred to think of as pure Aryan features. Always interested in his child's activities, he was especially intrigued to one day learn that she had come to know a young man in the capital named Nicolas Eichmann.

The blind man had followed the war crimes trials as best he could. Eichmann. The name seemed to ring a bell.

Yes, his daughter noted, this Eichmann had been quite open about his views, noting, among other things, that he regarded it as tragic that the Germans had been unable to complete the work on the Jewish problem they had undertaken during the war. However, such a view was anything but uncommon in the capital's large and flourishing German population.

The blind man decided to pursue the matter. His pretty daughter encouraged the friendship. When one afternoon the young man happened by the house for a visit, the mother wondered aloud where he had come by such an odd accent, one not distinct to any region. Young Eichmann replied that when he was growing up during the war, his family had lived throughout the Reich in connection with his father's work. By his tone it was clear that the work had been of great importance.

Soon thereafter, the man traveled to Buenos Aires with his daughter. Though Nicolas had not given her his address, requesting that she write him instead through a mutual friend, she asked around and managed to locate the house. It was on Chucabuco Street in the Olivos Quarter.

She knocked at the door and it was answered by a middle-aged woman. Almost immediately a balding middle-aged man in dark-rimmed glasses appeared behind her.

When she asked to see Nicolas, the man answered that he was still at work. "Are you Herr Eichmann?" she asked. He looked uncomfortable and made no reply. She broke the silence, asking instead if he was her friend's father. Hesitantly he acknowledged that he was.

Soon afterward the blind man wrote a letter to Dr. Fritz Bauer, the public prosecutor in Essen. Bauer, too, was Jewish and a survivor of Nazi persecution. A judge in Stuttgart before the rise of Hitler, he had spent three years in prison. Since the war, he had been among Germany's most committed anti-Nazis.

Bauer found the information more than a little intriguing. He wrote the blind man back urging him to continue his inquiry.

Then, dubious about his own government's resolve in such matters, he passed the tip on to the Israeli mission in Cologne.

THIRTEEN

Target

I did not make it easy on Gila. Even the relatively conventional part of my dual existence was nobody's idea of normal. She never had the slightest idea when I was going to be in the country. Yet, when I was, I pretty much assumed she would be there for me. For someone more defiant by nature than quietly yielding, that must have taken a lot of hard swallowing.

Then there was my sense of humor. Gila maintained that one of the things she loved best about me was my unapologetic boyishness, but even this she sometimes clearly found exasperating.

One afternoon, arriving at Tel Aviv's Lod Airport after a flight from Madrid, I called and arranged to meet her that evening in Haifa, at the bus stop down the street from her office. But when she got there, I was nowhere in sight. After waiting, fuming, for forty-five minutes, she began heading home and noticed a middle-aged man matching her stride for stride.

"Were you waiting for someone?" he asked.

"No." She kept walking.

"Listen," he said, "why don't you have dinner with me instead?"

She quickened her pace. "No, thank you."

"What a bum he must be to do this to a woman like you. Why do you put up with it?"

As she wheeled to confront him—"Who do you think . . ."—I took out the false teeth, whipped off the wig, and watched her jaw go slack. Then I had to endure a twenty-minute tirade on what a jerk I was.

Even my friends sympathized with her. One evening when we both were a bit down because I had to go abroad again the next morning, my pal Uzi, nominally my superior, suggested over dinner that what we needed was a long vacation together. "Where do you want to go?" he asked. "I'll set it up."

"Ohhh," said Gila, smiling, "Paris would be nice."

He slapped the table with an open hand. "Done. There's always work to be done in Paris. Maybe I'll come along myself."

I laughed. As head of operations this was something Uzi loved to do, invent wonderful assignments, involving lots of travel and enormous fun. "Oh, yeah?" I asked. "What's there to be done in Paris?"

He paused only momentarily. "We've got to work on our French, don't we? It's in the national interest."

If he could have sent us, he surely would have. Uzi was an undercover version of a Columbo, his fumbling manner and incredibly unkempt appearance (generally featuring a half-open fly and shoes caked with mud) masking a steel-trap mind and a soft heart. Just that afternoon he had visited a spy he had helped put away in prison.

"How can you do that?" I wondered aloud a few minutes later. "A person like that deserves *no* pity. He betrayed his country."

"He did what he did," he said, "but he's also a human being."

As we continued discussing the case—talking about why the guy had done what he had done and Uzi's role in his capture—Gila listened in fascination. She was almost never privy to discussions of our work. But, of course, that investigation was concluded and on the public record. I said nothing about where I would be flying off to the very next day.

In brief, if Gila had allowed herself to believe that the tenor of our relationship was about to change fundamentally, she was learning otherwise. Clearly I was not yet ready for such a commitment. Over the next year I was up to my armpits in work, principally antiespionage and antiterrorist matters. When in Israel, I continued to operate as I always had, going from early morning to past midnight, sometimes pressing on through whole nights and weekends. Nor was I any less likely than before to disappear abruptly for weeks at a stretch.

Matters finally came to a head one Sunday afternoon as we drove from the Haifa suburb of Nesher, where Gila lived, toward Jerusalem.

I was feeling terrific. The wind whistled in my ears as I negotiated the hairpin turns on the narrow road. In the distance the sun shone brilliantly on Acre Bay. Just that morning I had returned from Switzerland, and the bottle of French wine and the hamper of delicacies I brought with me, without having to worry about customs, sat on the back seat. Gila had lately had her black hair cut short, accentuating her cheekbones and eyes. It had taken me by surprise, but now, a half hour later, I found her more appealing than ever. I began singing the folk song "Bab el Wad" and reached over to stroke her leg.

She removed my hand. "Please keep your eyes on the road."

I stopped my singing. "I was just . . ."

"You drive like a madman," she cut me off. "Someday they're going to find your body down in the quarry."

For a good ten minutes we drove in silence.

"What I want to know," she suddenly spoke up again, "is what's going to become of you."

I laughed. "What do you mean? You think I'm going to be killed?" It was not, of course, an entirely misplaced apprehension; it had happened to others in the field, including a couple of friends.

"No, that's not what I meant." She turned toward me. "How are you going to end up? What kind of life are you building?"

"You know what? I don't think about it. Not even once in a while."

"A person's got to think about such things. Peter, you're more than thirty years old."

"I like the life and I like the work. *That's* what matters to me."

It wasn't what she wanted to hear, but it was the truth. She had known who I was from the beginning. Besides which, there seemed to be a contradiction here: She clearly loved me as I was, yet she wanted to change me.

"But what kind of a career is it?" she pressed. "You're so talented, such a wonderful artist. It would be so easy for you to stay in one place, work reasonable hours, raise a family."

I exhaled deeply. "This is supposed to be a nice weekend. Can we talk about it later?"

"Later," she repeated. "That's your constant refrain. No, we're going to talk about it now. Pull over."

I had learned when Gila meant business. I slowed down and edged onto the shoulder of the road. We were a couple of miles from the Druse village of Usfiyya, a shimmering blur in the dusty distance.

"Look," she said, gazing at me intently, "I love you. Very much. I want to marry you. But I need you beside me, free to open up, as a husband does to a wife. If you stay in this business, there's no way it's going to work."

It was only now that it occurred to me that she had been planning this scene for some time.

"I'm happy the way things are. Why do you have to be beside somebody all the time? To me that's not love, it's bondage."

Naturally, on some level, the life she envisioned appealed to me. But what was the big rush?

"Do you know," she continued, "you've never once said 'I love you'?"

"I admit it, I'm not comfortable with those words. But I've said 'I like you.' " I paused. "What's so important about the words?"

She was silent for a few seconds. "You're right," she said. "Let's not talk about it anymore."

We drove on to Jerusalem and checked into a tiny, secluded hotel, where we spent the next day and a half. Rarely had our conversations been so intimate, never had we made such extraordinary love. Then, over breakfast the morning we were to leave, Gila told me she had reached a decision: She wanted to break it off, at least for the time being.

"That's crazy," I said, panic-stricken. "I"—the pause was involuntary—"like you so much."

Despite herself, Gila started to laugh. I joined her.

"Listen," she said, taking my hand, "both of us just have to give it some thought. We'll stay away from each other for a couple of months with no communication at all and then see how we feel."

"You mean that?"

"Yes, I really do."

"Okay." I shrugged. "What can I do?"

I was surprised how hard the separation hit me. Over the days that followed she was constantly on my mind. I went on and on to friends about it, even found myself whining in the office. Several times I picked up the phone to call her. Then, knowing it would lead to nothing, and even give her some satisfaction, I grabbed hold of my self-respect and slammed it down.

One afternoon a couple of weeks into this, I was in the field. There had been terrorist activity in Nazareth, a cause for considerable concern: Nowhere in Israel was an incident such a potential nightmare, which is why I was taken aback by the message that came over the field radio. I was to return to headquarters immediately.

I walked into Uzi's Tel Aviv office about 5:30 P.M. His muddy boots were on his desk atop a pile of clutter, a cigarette dangled from his lips, he had a glass of cognac in his hand. "It's about time," he said, hardly his usual cordial greeting.

"What was I supposed to do, fly? I was in Nazareth," I said, slightly annoyed. Rank had never figured even remotely in our relationship.

He motioned me to sit. "Never mind. Have something to drink." He poured out a cognac, came around the desk, handed it to me, and picked up a pointer. "You ever been to South America?" he asked, slapping it against a map of the world on the wall.

"Uzi, I'm in no mood for this sort of thing now."

"Well, you're going. We both are. We're going to Argentina to bring back Adolf Eichmann."

I knew at once he wasn't joking. Even he wouldn't joke about such a thing.

And yet, for a long moment, I didn't react at all. Eichmann was not so much a man to me as an abstraction, a myth.

In fact, I knew little about the man so widely reviled as the architect of the Holocaust. I had never read a single book dealing with the Nazi death machine; I took care to avoid documentary films on the subject. In the fifteen years since the end of the war, I'm not sure I had even had a detailed conversation on the subject. My imagination was vivid enough.

Now the thoughts came in a jumble, followed closely by a rush of adrenaline. Eichmann! *Actually laying my hands on him!* It was almost too much to grasp.

Not, to someone at my level, that it was any secret we had been looking for him. A thick file on Nazi criminals was kept in our operations department and constantly updated. One fellow worked on it full-time. There were hundreds of names in the file, most wholly unknown, including local or regional Nazi administrators, particularly bloodthirsty camp guards, commanders of *Einsatzgruppen* death squads. When we came up with what looked like a piece of solid information, the general policy was to pass it on to the authorities in the country most directly concerned. Only the previous month we had helped the Dutch get their hands on an SS officer responsible for the execution of scores of Dutch partisans.

But Eichmann was one of the few who fell into a different category: those whose crimes not only cut across national borders but who set the standards for Nazi barbarism. Those we wanted for ourselves.

Indeed, he was at the very top of the list.

Still, like most of my colleagues, I had come to view the matter realistically. Our mission was national security; and it was the Arabs that threatened Israel's existence. We could not allow ourselves to be obsessed with the search, or allocate to it too many resources.

We tried, within reason, to keep tabs on the most notorious criminals' families. If there was a plausible report of a sighting, steps would immediately be taken to check it out. But we recognized that at this juncture it was unlikely such a report would be of value. How, on the entire planet, do you locate a single individual who does want to be found and who will bolt at the merest sign of danger? Almost by definition, such an operation would be hit-and-miss, as much a matter of timing and luck than any kind of preparation.

Indeed, that sense had been confirmed by personal experience. Just a couple of years before, while working in Germany, I had been ordered to Munich by headquarters. It had been learned that the son of former Gestapo chief Müller, due several weeks vacation, had purchased a ticket for Brazil. The son was to be monitored closely.

Thus it was that, posing one morning with my operational secretary as part of a couple, I was surveilling the apartment building where he lived (three stories high, four dwellings per floor) when a middle-aged man strode out the front door into the street. The man wasn't on the list; we had only been given photos of the son, his family, his mother. But from his bearing, from something in his stride, I *knew* this man was SS! As we strolled, we consulted in hurried whispers, then left our post to follow him. He walked briskly toward a shopping district, stopped at a tobacconist, picked up a newspaper. When he boarded a bus for downtown, we elected to return to the son's building.

That night we got a picture of Müller. To this day, others in the secret services are skeptical—some scoff at the very notion—but the two of us are absolutely certain: *It was him!* But he never returned to the building.

Eichmann was an even more elusive target. Over the years, there had not been a single serious report of a sighting. We had no trail to follow, not even a cold one; the man might as well have never existed. Indeed, fifteen years after the fact, there was every possibility he was no longer even alive.

What I had not figured on was the degree to which individuals outside the formal Nazi-hunting network might become involved, people whose interest in the case, and in Jewish well-being generally, was as intense as our own.

Looking back, that was naive of me. Our own department was staffed by as skilled and dedicated a collection of professionals as those in any intelligence agency anywhere, and we employed the very best technology. But, too, we owed our vaunted reputation at least partly to the fact that so many Jews, having grown up as part of a tiny minority within other cultures, often so well integrated as to be indistinguishable from the majority, found themselves uniquely well prepared for the curious business of information gathering. The two most famous spies Israel ever produced—Wolfgang Lotz, whose impersonation of a high-living German aristocrat brought him into the highest circles of the Egyptian elite, providing invaluable material on the German scientists and their rocket program; and Elie Cohen, whose proximity to the highest circles of the Syrian government and military eventually enabled him to produce devastatingly accurate diagrams of Syrian fortifications on the Golan Heights—were both playing out roles to which they had virtually been born. Lotz was the son of a non-Jewish father and Jewish actress mother in Mannheim, Germany, and Cohen was a Jew of Syrian derivation from Alexandria, Egypt. It is not unreasonable to surmise that even more successful Israeli agents similarly played on their backgrounds.

Of course, non-Israeli Jews do not fall into the same category. Their first loyalty is almost always to the country in which they live. However, it is not surprising that such individuals often take a particular interest in matters they perceive as involving a threat to the existence of the Jewish people itself.

This, as Uzi explained it to me, is precisely what had occurred in this instance. The man thought to be Eichmann had been discovered in Argentina by a German-Jewish expatriate in 1957.

I looked at him closely, waited for an explanation. Nineteen fifty-seven was three years ago.

"Well . . . ?" I prompted.

Uzi shook his head. "It was a travesty. We could have lost him."

My friend went on to explain that our people had at

first discounted the information after an investigator, dispatched to Argentina, concluded it was without basis. Meeting the informant, he was put off by what he took to be the blind man's hyperactive imagination. Then, on examining the house on Chucabuco Street, he became convinced that a man of Eichmann's stature could not possibly be living in such a place.

Only the blind man's persistence, and that of Dr. Fritz Bauer, the German-Jewish prosecutor, had finally persuaded Isser, all this time later, to send a second investigator. By now the target, going by the name Ricardo Klement, had left his old house, but he had been readily tracked to a new one in San Fernando, a low-lying working-class district in the outskirts of Buenos Aires. This time the results were extremely promising. Reasonably clear shots of Klement had been taken, and they indicated a resemblance. Moreover, the ages of his wife and two older sons—a much younger one had also been identified—corresponded to those of Vera, Nicolas, and Dieter Eichmann. Most encouraging of all, the Klements had been observed celebrating what would have been the Eichmann's twenty-fifth wedding anniversary.

As I listened, I felt like leaping and shouting. It was true, it had to be!

But I reined it in. "What about the issue of their living conditions?" I asked. "Would a man like Eichmann . . . ?"

He shrugged. "People do what they do to survive."

"Any chance these people suspect anything?"

Uzi sighed. "We hope not. Not yet." He paused. "The job hasn't exactly been neat and clean."

A considerable understatement. My friend went on to describe the recent operation in Buenos Aires. It had been under the direction of a fellow named Hans, a capable interrogator who, however, had little experience as an operative in the field. As I listened I shuddered at the sheer number of openings he and his subordinates had allowed for detection. Aside from very basic procedural errors—

grossly excessive surveillence of the Klement house, asking questions in places where their presence was apt to arouse suspicion, holding important conversations where they might be overheard—they had made some gaffes that seemed almost beyond invention. One evening they actually overturned a jeep on a quiet street only blocks away from the Klement house. Worse, in an effort to work their way closer to the target, they concocted a cover story that would have given even a child trouble. They maintained that they were canvassing the area as representatives of a North American firm interested in building a factory—this despite the fact that there was no central source of water or electricity, and the district had such poor drainage it flooded every winter. At one point they actually approached Klement's own daughter-in-law with this ludicrous tale. When she overheard them speaking English, she switched to that language herself. And since she spoke it better than they did, they were obliged to beat a disorderly retreat.

Even then, they didn't relent. Shortly thereafter, in an effort to get a close-up with a briefcase camera, they approached Klement himself. They got the pictures but then, the coup de grace, sent the priceless film to be developed through a large camera store downtown. This in a city crawling with Nazi sympathizers.

"You want to know the worst part?" concluded Uzi, smiling. "Hans is going back to Argentina with us."

For, incredible as it seemed, in light of the litany I had just heard, the operation remained viable. Klement was still in place. We couldn't worry now about the others' mistakes; our job was to get on with it.

We began the planning right there. It was understood from the start that I would head the operational team that would effect the capture itself.

"Offhand, how many men do you think you'll need?" he asked.

I didn't have to give it a moment's thought. "Just one. Me and myself. Maybe three others as backup."

"You think so?" He smiled. "I thought you might say that."

"So I said it."

"Why? Give me the thinking."

"Look, we'll probably be working at night, in a deserted area. If he sees too many people, a man like this, he could panic. Besides, it's simpler. I'll be able to practice by myself."

"What if he's strong? What if he fights?"

"I'm stronger. And I'll have the element of surprise."

"How? Show me."

I rose to my feet. "How? Walk toward me."

He approached tentatively. Abruptly I grabbed him, spun him around, took a chokehold around his neck, and clamped down on the larynx to shut off speech.

"See?" I released him.

Rubbing his neck, he draped an arm around my shoulder and steered me onto the balcony outside the office. It was a glorious spring evening. One could see the old clock tower of Jaffa illuminated in the distance and, beyond, the Mediterranean lapping against the old harbor wharves.

Uzi was still gently massaging his neck.

"Well?" I asked.

"We're going to bring Adolf Eichmann to trial in Jerusalem," he stated. "And you're going to capture him, Peter. You, personally."

FOURTEEN

The Plan

UZI and I talked so long into that night, it was almost dawn by the time I made it back to my apartment. The Theater Club, the popular nightclub operating from the basement of my building, had closed only an hour before. Except for a sanitation truck rumbling past, all was still. Exhausted, I climbed to my tiny third-floor apartment and collapsed into bed.

But I could not get my mind to stop racing. Over the previous ten hours, we had agreed on the broad outlines of a plan as well as on the makeup of the team that would attempt one of the most difficult operations ever undertaken. Now all we had to do was pull it off.

The question of who was to make up the team was less difficult than one would suspect. In our business, talent was impossible to miss, if not always adequately rewarded. Anonymous in the outside world, everyone in the secret services had a reputation within the organization.

The third name on the list, after Uzi's and mine, belonged to Uzi's second-in-command in the Special Operations Department, Aharon. Swiss-born and rather tight-assed, exacting in his expectations of himself and all others, he was a man with zero patience for mediocrity. "This is worse than criminal," I had heard him say more than once, in an incongruous, Germanic slur that called to mind Peter Lorre, "it's stupid." Not an easy man to warm to, but on a mission like this, reassuring to have on hand.

Aharon's particular responsibility would be logistics and planning. It was safe to assume that he would shortly take on the character of a crazed Yeshiva student, locking himself away, staying up most of every night to pore over street maps of Buenos Aires and its environs, memorizing routes in and out of the operations area.

Next there was Meir, also an obvious choice. His strengths were so great that they more than compensated for what, in anyone else, might have been regarded as liabilities: his difficulty with languages and his problem in general of adjusting to new cultures, especially new foods. In Germany the food had not been an issue, but he left speaking the same high school German he knew before our long service began.

My own feeling was that the language issue was often overstated, that, indeed, not speaking a country's language can sometimes be an advantage. It makes it easier to play dumb, lessening the possibilities of arguments with cab-drivers and waiters. Even if a stranger does offend somebody, it is likely to be written off to ignorance or inadvertence.

This time the question was moot anyway. Few of us would speak Spanish. Of greater concern was that Meir might start gagging in public on some local specialty. Fortunately Meir would be largely out of sight, occupied with setting up the safe house and vehicle maintenance.

Also included on the team was Danny, my Paris forger friend, absolutely the best in the business. Hollow-cheeked and perpetually mournful, a figure out of an El Greco painting, Danny appeared a more likely candidate for a convalescent home than undercover work. Yet somehow he found the stamina to work meticulously hour after hour. Another man we absolutely could not do without.

I did not know any of the others particularly well: the German-born Hans, who had nearly botched the investigation in South America but who was known to be a first-rate interrogator; a fellow named David, who was to function as the front man; a doctor from a Tel Aviv hospital, who would be charged both with the health of the prisoner and, in our total isolation, that of the team; and several others to be determined, including, almost certainly, one woman.

We were as capable a crew as could be assembled within the Israeli secret services. Though all in our late twenties or early thirties, the key operatives—Uzi, Aharon, Meir, Danny, and myself—averaged more than ten years in the field. Just as important, we were on intimate terms with one another's styles and idiosyncrasies. Motivation was even more explicitly a given than usual. Except for Uzi, every one of us had lost immediate family in the camps.

Then, too, there was a final member of the team: Isser Harel himself. Unusual though it was for the supreme commander of a country's secret services to even think of going personally to the field during such an operation, and given the possibility of international repercussions, potentially awkward in the extreme, there was no way Isser was going to miss it, even if it meant that all other work came to a standstill. Having virtually single-handedly molded the Israeli secret services into a potent force, he was maniacally protective of his prerogatives and reputation. But that was hardly Isser's only motive. He had said—I had *heard* him —that he would have given anything to get his hands on Hitler. This was the closest he was ever going to get.

I myself took the information that Isser would be in Buenos Aires as a positive development. It meant that we would get whatever we needed immediately, without having to work long-distance or deal with subordinates: safe houses, vehicles, outlays of cash. Nor would we have to worry about the boss monitoring our activities moment to moment or day to day. He would be living in a hotel, apart from the rest of us. Indeed, he was in the process of devising a curious and highly complex plan for himself, in which he would spend most of his waking hours wandering the cafés of the Argentine capital in a predetermined pattern, occasionally, but not necessarily, intersecting with individuals with whom he needed to transact business.

It was a typically Harelian plan. The man was so in love with the idea of clandestine activity that often, to my mind, he seemed to go out of his way to complicate matters that were essentially simple. He was also a sucker for code names. Already he had dubbed this operation "Attila."

After only a couple of hours of sleep I was back in Uzi's office. Meir and Aharon were on hand for the meeting, too. It struck me that in some unspoken way we were suddenly appraising one another with different eyes. Together, we were about to turn the world upside down. For a minute or two it was as if we hardly knew each other.

Then Uzi broke the ice. "Well, you've all slept on it. Any bright ideas?"

Vintage Uzi. Where Isser was the prototypical lone wolf, always seeking security and secrecy, often reluctant to confide even in his most senior aides, Uzi would sit with his team for hours, reviewing every possible course of action. No matter how important the operation, his style was always to encourage consensus. Though it was a given that in the end the decision would be his, he always conveyed the sense that everyone's ideas were valuable and valued. There was nothing altruistic in this; he valued resourceful operatives and had less than no interest in those who knew only how to follow orders.

"We'd just better hope that this man Klement stays put," spoke up Aharon drily, in his odd Swiss slur. "Hans is still over there, snooping around."

"That's out of our control," noted Uzi. "Why don't we take a look at what we've got on film?"

Meir snapped off the light, and an instant later there appeared a head-and-shoulders' shot of a man in his mid-thirties in SS regalia: prominent cheekbones, sharp nose, thin lips, impassive eyes peering coolly at the camera from beneath the shiny black visor. The face might have been plucked from central casting, the very image of the Nazi commander, cruel, decisive, utterly sure of himself.

Uzi motioned for the next slide, also taken during the war, but this time unposed, from a distance. The man, wearing a greatcoat and jackboots, holding a riding crop, was looking off to the left.

Behind me the door swung open. I turned. There stood Uzi's pretty secretary, Alona, a cable in her hand, staring.

"Eichmann," she gasped.

Uzi took the cable from her hand. "Yes. But that information stops here." He paused. "You understand?"

She nodded, clearly shaken.

"Good."

"You want me to hold your calls?"

"Please."

As soon as she was gone, Uzi moved on to the next slide: a man of late middle age, balding and hollow-cheeked, a pair of black spectacles perched on his nose above a thick moustache. He was dressed in a neat but obviously cheap suit. Klement, near his San Fernando home.

I leaned intently forward. Could this really be the same man?

"Run the two of them together," I asked.

The first shot reappeared beside this one. I concentrated on the facial features, eyes, ears, shape of nose, angle of chin. It seemed possible Klement's teeth were false. Only the ears and cheekbones of the stooped figure in Buenos Aires bore a clear resemblance to those of the SS man.

"It's not easy to tell, is it?" I murmured.

"These shots have been examined by our best photo ID people," noted Aharon, "and they've conferred with doctors at Tel Hashomer Hospital. They feel good about them."

"Obviously there's some risk," cut in Uzi. "That's a given. We can't be one hundred percent sure until we've got him."

There was a long silence. "Once we're sure," spoke up Meir for the first time, "why don't we kill the bastard on the spot?"

Uzi nodded. "We all share that feeling, I'm sure."

Meir shook his large head bitterly. "What chance did he give those people at the camps?" he demanded. "I *saw* them, the ones that survived. What kind of consideration did he show them?"

The others were more surprised than I was. Not having been with him in Germany, they had never heard Meir speak with anything close to this degree of passion. For a long moment no one made any response.

"Let's never forget," spoke up Uzi finally, "that that's part of the difference between him and us."

And yet, in the couple of days that followed, studying the thick Eichmann file, I increasingly saw Meir's view. Having for so long made a practice of keeping my distance from such material, I found myself repeatedly, unexpectedly shaken. Even more than the broad outlines of the man's career, it was the details that affected me. What kind of mind could have conceived of a conference to set out guidelines as to whether, for example, a quarter Jew should live longer than a three-eighths Jew and by how long? Who, in God's name, could have sat month after month listening to innocent souls plead for their lives—German-Jewish heroes from World War I; people he had known as a child; parents, themselves resigned to their fate, on behalf of their small children—without once being moved to pity? What manner of human being could have dreamed up so many ruses designed, finally, to deny even the doomed a suggestion of dignity?

By the time I laid aside the file, I felt more than just sick to the core; there was also a profound sense of apprehension. Eichmann loomed as a more formidable adversary than anyone I had ever tracked before. By the millions, people just like me had perished at his whim. Fifteen years earlier, Nazi generals in the field—whole armies!—had leapt at his command. If on the page his evil seemed absolutely extraordinary, so did the force of his personality. What stupidity, what *arrogance,* had led me to take sole responsibility for his capture? The possibilities of something going wrong were infinite. A cop could happen by at the wrong moment or someone could look out a window. And afterward all that would be remembered by my colleagues, possibly by the entirety of the Jewish people, was that Adolf Eichmann had been within our grasp, and I had let him get away.

Never before in my career had I been even a little frightened. Now I was terrified of failure. Once, I actually came close to suggesting to Uzi that we work out an alternative plan. But at that instant another part of me took over: "Shut up! What you promised, you are going to do!" I stayed silent.

Reflexively I began to bury myself in work. It has always been my policy to focus entirely on the task at hand. That is why I've never enjoyed dealing with more than one assignment at the same time; it makes me less effective. To be at my best, I must live an assignment twenty-four hours a day, and I have little patience for anyone or anything that distracts me from it. That is the way I now began to feel even about my own self-doubt.

For this misson the physical preparations alone were endless. To start with, since the purchase of certain supplies in Argentina would likely arouse suspicion, Aharon, Meir, and I had to think our way through the operation step by step and day by day, working and reworking the list of what could be safely had there (hammers, nails, saws, wood, and other mundane building materials; ventilation and sanitary equipment) and what would have to be immediately dispatched from Israel. Eventually the following was sent to Buenos Aires, to four different addresses on three different airlines packed in well-lined but innocuous-looking packages:

- Eight French communications units, plus reserve batteries
- Four pairs of British field glasses
- Six pocket flashlights
- A dozen false license plates
- Two kits of miniature electric tools
- Three pairs of handcuffs
- One portable forgery lab
- Burglary tools, including safety locks
- Full makeup kit, including wigs, false teeth, and facial hair

At the same time, I undertook a crash program in the gym emphasizing strength and reaction time. Finding myself obsessed with the need to hone my skills in a more realistic setting, I seized on my reputation for madcap and unpredictable behavior. To the surprise and growing horror of my colleagues, none of whom had the slightest idea what I was doing, I began catching them unawares, leaping at them as they strolled down the hall whistling or rounding the corner reading a memo, and seizing them round the throat. I found women particularly useful as subjects in the development of a grip that was at once strong enough to cut off all sound louder than a gasp, and restrained enough to cause no lasting damage. With men, the larger they were, the better; I needed lots of practice on my hoist technique. My very favorite subject was a guy named Mikael, a mountain of an agent, 260 pounds of muscle, who soon took to fleeing at the very rumor of my presence in the vicinity.

Uzi got a tremendous kick out of my suddenly irrational behavior. Several times I spotted him down the hall, watching me on the prowl, an expectant smile on his lips. But I couldn't help but notice how careful he was to keep his own distance throughout.

Oddly no one ever questioned me about any of this. Ignorant as they were as to what was afoot, everyone on the premises was well aware that anything might be going on at any time, and nothing was necessarily what it seemed; that, by allowing themselves to be victimized, they might be contributing to the success of an operation.

Aside from Isser, the only person in the building safe from attack was internal security chief Amos Manor. This had nothing to do with his prominence. Rather, I was aware of how troubled he was just now. A large and generous-spirited man, Manor had always been very much one of the guys. One of the few nonparticipants fully briefed on Attila, from the beginning he expressed concern about the absence of so many skilled agents at once and the effect that might have on vital operations at home. It was not an easy position to take, and I, for one, admired his guts in holding to it; but, too, it was his disappointment in not being in on the mission himself. Amos had survived Auschwitz, but most of his family had not.

"Peter," he said to me one afternoon, taking my arm as I passed in the hall and leading me into his office, "come talk to me."

We spent a half hour or so discussing domestic security questions, who should assume which of my responsibilities during my absence and which matters deserved most immediate attention. As I got up to leave, he put an arm around my shoulder and looked at me gravely. "Do me one favor. Give his neck an extra little squeeze for me."

There was so little time, and every preparation was so potentially vital! One of the things that seemed to keep falling through the cracks was my plan to create a spare identity for several members of the team. If Eichmann or anyone around him began spotting the same unfamiliar face again and again in their out-of-the-way neighborhood, the operation could be fatally compromised.

Finally it could be put off no longer. Whenever I found a free hour, I would collar someone and, through naked coercion, get him up to my makeshift studio on the fourth floor of headquarters. Becoming a new person takes effort. It's more than simply a matter of different clothes, or hair, or a little makeup. One has to get comfortable in a whole new skin, begin to talk and carry oneself differently, relate to others as this other being might.

With most of our guys, exceptionally casual types, I started with a well-tailored suit. This was a matter of experience. It is startling the impact a couple of hundred bucks of good material can have on the self-image of someone who spends his life looking as if he shops only at thrift stores. Without my having to do a thing further, he begins to walk and sit differently, sometimes even shaving more frequently and cursing less often. Not infrequently, to their astonishment, these people quickly grow to like the feeling. Their new selves are, after all, so much more civilized than the ones they are used to, and seem to be so much more acceptable to so many others. If only this business of keeping up appearances was not so damn much work, which meant shopping for new clothes and keeping them from looking rumpled, conscientiously shaving every morning and getting a haircut every two weeks, they might keep it up even after the assignment was over.

One early evening I managed to get Uzi, Meir, and Aharon all up to the studio at once. It had been another long, tension-filled day, so it seemed like a good idea to work on wigs. After a couple of beers each, everyone began to unwind. As I fitted Uzi for his piece, trying on one after another, the others began nudging each other, pointing, soon unable to contain their laughter. Our friend, with his ruddy, weather-beaten features, looked like an ungainly girl of eighteen trying desperately to be chic.

"I could fall in love with that," noted Meir, laughing.

Uzi launched into his version of a seductive walk. "You've done a lot worse. But first you'll have to do something about *your* hair." He paused. "Like get some."

I was casting about for a new wig when the nearby phone began jangling. Uzi snatched it up, leaving the piece askew atop his head.

"Just the four of us—me, Peter, Aharon, and Meir," he said. Instantly we knew it was Isser. His standard greeting was to ask who else was in the room.

For five minutes Uzi listened without speaking a word.

At last he hung up and turned to us, expressionless. "There is the possibility we will be asked to get Mengele at the same time. Evidently we've had someone trail his wife, and he's convinced he's in Buenos Aires also."

There was a long pause as the startling information began to register.

"What specifics do they have?" spoke up Aharon finally. "Has he been identified on site?"

"It seems to be based on what they've picked up monitoring communications to Germany. Obviously Isser feels the information is good enough to pursue."

I shook my head. This was *insanity*. Of course the prospect was tempting: Mengele—the sadistic doctor whose horrifying pseudo-scientific experiments and pleasure in personally making the selections for the ovens at Auschwitz had earned him the sobriquet "Angel of Death"—was a criminal of epic proportions. He, too, had to be brought to justice. *But now wasn't the time.* Compared with Eichmann, master of the fate of every Jew on the Continent, he was a small fry.

"If we try that," I said aloud, "we'll lose them both."

Aharon concurred with a deep sigh.

"We're not being *asked*, we're being *told*," said Uzi.

But almost immediately he softened. "Look, put it out of your heads. It's not definite. We'll just wait and see what develops on that front."

* * *

There was another task to be performed in the makeup lab, a very personal one that I assigned myself. One afternoon, drawing all the shades and turning off all the lights, I focused a high-intensity lamp on a mannequin head, and over the next three and a half hours, I worked with paints and plaster of paris on the white oval before me. First I sketched in the thin mouth and longish chin, the sharp nose and the prominent cheekbones, then the dark eyes and heavy brows. Now I added flesh tones. Finally I worked up a wig, dark brown, with the hairline slightly receding. At last I picked the thing up and mounted it on a body already in uniform, complete with greatcoat, boots, and peaked cap.

I stepped back to the other side of the room, twenty feet away, and stared. It was startling. The Adolf Eichmann in the photo was staring back at me. I almost expected to see a vein throb, a muscle ripple.

This isn't how he will look, I had to remind myself. The man is fifteen years older. In the photographs Klement looked nearly bald, and his eyes were hidden behind thick lenses. The face is furrowed now; more, in expression it reflects what he has lived through.

Still, the essential character of a face never changes. Before I left for Argentina, I had to know every square inch of this one.

Throughout my career undercover I had taken such measures. They were an essential part of my *emotional* preparation. I needed to visualize an approaching challenge step by step, as an athlete anticipates crucial moments on the playing field, exerting a sense of control over a highly unpredictable situation.

If there was clearly an element of self-delusion in this, that made it no less necessary. To be effective, an agent has to have a lot of gall. He has to approach a mission *certain* that he is going to triumph, focusing not on his own vulnerabilities, but on those of his adversary.

Far more than that, he has to work up a powerful dislike of the target. This is not a parlor game he is engaged in. Motivation has everything to do with gut feelings. The dislike must be intense and, ideally, it should be *personal*.

In this case, of course, it would hardly have seemed to be a problem. Adolf Eichmann was a monster; the whole world knew that. All I had to do was harness the rage within myself.

And yet it was proving to be not so simple after all. Even as I played out the scene in my mind—moving toward him in the dark and slowing down as we came together on the narrow sidewalk, stopping, speaking to him, making my move—something vital wouldn't jell. I felt an odd detachment from it all, as if I were watching someone else in a movie.

Nor was that sense difficult to figure out. Unspeakable horror that it was, I had learned to regard the Holocaust with dispassion. Having for so long refused to acknowledge my own depth of loss and pain, those feelings were almost beyond reach.

For the operation at hand, this definitely presented a problem. Now, for the first time ever, I found myself asking certain questions: *Why* hadn't I listened when they talked about my sister, her children, our village? Just once, why hadn't I been strong enough to stay in the room?

The man who presented himself at my mother's Haifa apartment late on the Friday afternoon before we were to depart was a total stranger to her. Dark, with heavy sideburns and a thick moustache, he explained in bad Yiddish that he was a friend of mine, an American studying at the nearby Technion Institute. He was looking for a room to rent and I had told him that she might have something available.

"A room? Here?" My mother shook her head. "Peter's crazy. I never know what will come out of his mouth next."

She paused. "But come on in. I expect him any minute for the Sabbath."

And so, straight-faced, I stepped inside.

Obviously the disguise I had created for the mission was flawless. Even I hadn't been sure I would be able to fool my own mother.

Familiar Sabbath smells permeated the apartment: roast chicken, gefilte fish, kishke, the challah baking in the oven. The smells of my childhood, the ones that recalled a long-ago sense of utter contentment. For an instant I felt almost guilty.

"So what's your name?" asked my mother.

"Moshe Feldman, Mrs. Malkin."

"All right, Moshe Feldman, sit down, relax. Would you like a little tea? A glass of borscht?"

"Yes, thank you, I would."

"Which? Make yourself clear. Don't you do that in America, or is everyone too polite?"

"Tea, thank you."

My mother.

As she retreated into the kitchen, my eyes wandered to the display of photos on the far wall. They had been there for years, but I had never even once looked at them closely. I walked over now and stood before them. My parents as newlyweds, taken in front of our village synagogue. Me and my brothers standing stiffly in a field, our arms around one another. In his free hand, Jacob, no more than six, held his Bible. A row of photographs featuring my sister, Fruma, starting at age three or four and ending in her early twenties. How pretty she was. Takele, her son, my playmate, as fair as my mother and his mother and me, posed with his tiny violin. In the corner, a shot of his sister, little Bielkede sitting amidst the wildflowers by the river.

Suddenly my mother was back in the room. "That's Peter's sister and her family," she explained. "He never wants to talk about any of that. He heard too much crying as a boy."

"I understand," I offered.

She nodded curtly and set down the tea. "Yes. Come, your tea."

I took a seat on the couch. "What happened? Why did the rest of you come here, but not them?"

"You Americans, you think everything's so simple." She sighed. "I *killed* myself trying to get them the papers. There was nothing to be done. The whole world was against the Jews."

"What about her husband?" I had no recollection at all of my brother-in-law, was quite sure I had never even heard his name spoken. He appeared in none of the photographs.

"Him!" She spat out the word. "He was a man without a brain of his own. He only listened to the rabbi." She rose to her feet, assuming the pose of a religious elder, at once stooped but intensely self-assured. "*Stay,*" she intoned, gesturing dramatically, her voice cracking passionately. "I promise you it will pass. The Lord will provide." She straightened up and, in her own voice, added contemptuously, "The *rabbis*. I always used to tell my husband, Peter's father, never to trust anyone with a beard."

Reflexively I glanced at the large oval photograph hanging with the others of my father, looking unnaturally stern. He had a full beard his whole life.

"Where could Peter be?" she wondered. Moving to the window, she pushed the curtain to peer out.

"Tell me about your daughter," I said, in that other man's gentle voice.

She turned, looking momentarily stricken. "Why? You think I discuss these things just to pass the time of day?"

"I'm sorry. You're right."

But only a moment later, taking a seat beside me on the couch, she launched right in. "Fruma was my firstborn, the only girl. Of all my children, she was the most like me." She went on talking for a full fifteen minutes, recalling my sister's immense charm as a little girl and her curiosity about the world, her courtship, her marriage, her vast joy in being a mother. To my surprise there was not a trace of sadness in any of it. Indeed, the recollections seemed to animate her.

There was a pause. "And she wanted to come here," I said, "despite her husband . . ."

"A bum!" She cut me off with sudden vehemence. "He was almost as bad as the Nazis. When the danger came he ran away and let them die." She paused, collecting herself. "Fruma was desperate to get out. It was all she wanted. Hard as I was trying here, she was trying even harder there. She went all the way to Warsaw, she begged. She worried all the time about her children. Others didn't know what was coming, or wouldn't face it, but Fruma knew. She was my daughter."

For a long moment we sat together in silence, at opposite ends of the couch in the darkening room. "Well"—she clapped her hands suddenly, with exaggerated good cheer—"it's sundown. I have to light the Sabbath candles." She hurried to the table. "I'm very disappointed. Usually he comes every Sabbath when he's in the country. Aside from his brother Yechiel—and he's busy with a family of his own—I'm all he has left in the world."

Funny, I had always thougth it was the other way around.

She lit the candles and, covering her eyes, began gently rocking back and forth in prayer, one of the most beautiful sights I have ever known.

This time, when she uncovered her eyes, I saw they were glistening. "Excuse me," she said, rising, "I'm going to take one last look for Peter."

Walking to the balcony, she peered over the railing, three stories down to the street.

When I sneaked up and grabbed her from behind, her piercing scream startled even me.

"Don't worry," I said in my own voice. Laughing, I pulled off the wig.

She gasped. "Peter! Peter, you're going to kill me!" She was more annoyed than I had expected her to be. "Do you hear, you're going to *kill* me! *Why?* Why do you do these things?"

I was laughing so hard I stumbled back into the living room and collapsed on the couch.

"What is it with you? Everything is just a big joke. Why does a person do this to his own mother?"

But, despite herself, she was starting to laugh now, too.

"I don't know," I said. "For fun."

"You won't tell me?"

"I don't know. I just get these ideas."

Suddenly she was serious again. "So tell me, why did you ask about Fruma?"

"I was just looking at the pictures and I got the idea."

"You never look at those pictures. Where are you going that you wanted to hear about your sister?"

"I got curious, that's all." I paused. "Do you have an extra picture of them?"

"Now you want one."

"Yes, Mama."

She turned and disappeared into the back room. When she returned she was also holding a stack of letters, bound with a brown ribbon. "I brought some of her letters. Maybe you want to see them, too, now that you're suddenly so sentimental."

I took them. "Thank you, Mama."

"Tell me," she repeated, "where are you going?"

"I'm going to Paris," I said, looking her straight in the eye. Technically this was true enough. We were to spend a few days in Paris before heading on to Argentina.

"This is why you wanted to hear about your sister? Because you're going to Paris?"

"Mama, one thing has nothing to do with the other."

"Paris? This is the truth?"

"Yes, I swear."

She knew I couldn't tell her any more, for her own sake even more than for mine. As always, she accepted it in her fashion.

"I suppose that means you won't be here next Friday night, then."

"No, Mama."

She handed me a plate of gefilte fish, served the way I always preferred, like my father before me, with plenty of "yccch," the family term for aspic.

As I reached for the horseradish, my mother took my hand. "Please," she said, "I'm telling you seriously, be careful."

We ate the rest of the meal in silence.

I read the letters in bed that night, the photograph propped up on the bed beside me. They were a revelation. To me Fruma was a grown-up, a mother. Who would have imagined she was so girlish, so full of whimsy, so ready to go for laughs by portraying those in her midst as ridiculous? Who would have imagined that even as the world closed in on her, she had known as much about us as if she were still living next door. I was mentioned in almost every one of those letters. She knew about my life in the streets and my rising sense of independence, and she also knew enough to counsel our mother not to worry about it too much, but at the same time to be concerned herself about what was happening with my schoolwork.

At long last I laid the letters aside and flicked off the light. Tired as I was, I could not sleep.

On the afternoon of April 27, 1960, the team assembled in Isser's office for our final meeting on Israeli soil.

Visitors entering the inner sanctum of Israel's master spy for the first time were generally somewhat taken aback. Sparsely furnished, altogether lacking in distinction, the room might have housed the most aggressively unimaginative middle-management functionary.

Then, again, those who knew Isser even a little found it impossible to conceive of his operating out of the opulent quarters generally reserved for those of his rank. Thrifty beyond reason, ascetic in his personal tastes, his disinterest in traditional comforts (and his aversion to spending the taxpayers' money) was legendary. On one memorable occasion, put up in Paris at our elegant embassy, he shocked and embarrassed the ambassador by requesting a cot in a small back room instead. It was not for nothing that, except when the circumstances of a case dictated otherwise, his agents abroad were resigned to staying at fleabag hotels.

For Isser, almost everything was a matter of principle. As a young man he walked away from the kibbutz where he had spent all thirteen years since his arrival in Palestine when he could not get the apology he wanted for a perceived slight. This was his great strength as a leader. No effort was ever halfhearted, there could be no compromise with what he considered evil—but it could also make working for him a royal pain.

Isser sat now behind his simple wooden desk, as usual almost hidden behind a mound of papers. In a chair to his left sat his secretary Dvora, puffing on one of her trademark cigarillos, the smoke casting a bluish fog over the scene. As we drew close, he came around the desk to greet us, then steered us toward the meeting area, a rickety coffee table by the room's only window.

"So, Peter," he said, taking my elbow and offering a particularly warm smile, "I hear you've been assaulting everyone in the building."

Gazing down at him, I returned the smile. "Right. You might be next."

Isser gave a short, dry laugh and reached up to chuck my cheek like a Jewish uncle. Though he had little sense of humor himself, he understood from experience that *I* was funny; and, more than that, appreciated that a certain degree of kidding around was good for morale.

Taking a seat, I noted that what hair Meir had was still

slick from a shower and that his khaki uniform was unusually well starched. Even Uzi was carefully dressed and groomed for the occasion. It wasn't every day that we met with Isser.

"Okay, everyone, let's talk," he said, taking a seat himself. Dvora, her button nose oddly out of place in a face of otherwise doughy features, seated herself at his left, steno pad at the ready.

For all his pretended calm, Isser was obviously as keyed up as we were, his eyes bright, his every move reflecting suppressed energy.

We waited for him to address the question preying on our minds: the second target, Mengele.

He exhaled deeply. "I want to begin by speaking to you from my heart," he began. "We are about to set out on a historic journey. I do not have to tell you that this is no ordinary mission. We are to capture the man who has the blood of our people on his hands." He paused, looking from face to face. "But we are not moved to this by the spirit of vengeance. We are animated by our deep-seated sense of justice.

"There might well be difficult repercussions. We know this. But the State of Israel is the legitimate representative of the Jewish people. We not only have the right but the moral *duty* to bring this man to trial. You must remember this throughout the weeks ahead. You are guardian angels of justice, the historic emissaries of the Jewish people."

The ethical aspect of the operation—not only the legality but the *morality* of kidnapping a man on the soil of a friendly country and spiriting him abroad without due process—had been a serious source of concern to Isser from the start. Rigorous in his personal integrity, he had had to grapple with these questions on his own, and he considered it imperative that they not weigh on any of us.

I caught Uzi's eye. The two of us had discussed the same issues at length. Isser needn't have worried: Neither of us one moment doubted our moral right, indeed, our moral obligation, to proceed. Of all the world's nations, we alone were willing to risk bringing this man to justice. Almost no one else seemed inclined to hold Nazi criminals accountable for their pasts. And in some places, notably in Latin America, murderers seemed to have achieved the status of honored guests.

But, too, in that glance there was a sense of shared surprise. Neither Uzi nor I had ever seen Isser like this. Normally so brusque and guarded, he was going on movingly, even eloquently, at length.

There would be no talk of Mengele today. Perhaps that scheme had been abandoned.

"We *will* bring Adolf Eichmann to Jerusalem," he continued, slapping the table for emphasis, "and perhaps the world will be reminded of *its* responsibilities. It will be recognized that as a people we never forgot. Our memory reaches back through recorded history. The memory book lies open and the hand still writes . . ."

Suddenly, almost as if he had simply run out of eloquence, he stopped and addressed Uzi. "Are your people ready?"

"All ready," he replied, taken aback.

Now Isser became his old self, running through salient points of the operation, alerting us to new developments, notably, that one safe house had been rented in Buenos Aires, and several others were being considered.

Meir raised a hand. "I hope it has a large cellar or attic for the camouflaged room."

Isser turned to Dvora. "Make a note to put that in a cable to David."

I took his next remark to be directed at me. "I think all in all that Hans has done a good job. That's why I'm keeping him on the project. He'll be the interrogator, but I'll also want him to serve as your guide to the theater of operations."

"Look," I spoke up, "it's important that I check out

Klement's movements myself. I *need* to do that." I hesitated. "Anyway, does it make sense to put Hans back out in the field? He's already been seen so much in that neighborhood."

Isser smiled coolly, his blue eyes boring into me. "You'll have time enough to do what needs to be done." He paused. "Don't worry about Hans, Peter, think about the capture. I'm warning you—no bodily harm. Not a scratch."

The next point on the agenda was the tricky matter of getting Attila—and ourselves—out of the country. It had yet to be resolved. A trip from Buenos Aires to Israel by boat could take as long as two months, with several potentially dangerous stops at foreign ports along the way. And, in any case, with none of our ships due in Argentine waters in the near future, the appearance of one would immediately arouse suspicion.

Getting out by plane was potentially even trickier, since our country had no air service at all to Argentina. But, Isser indicated, clearly pleased to be able to slip into his surreptitious mode, he was working on a plan that seemed promising. He could not, however, needless to say, go into further detail at the moment.

Suddenly he stood up, indicating the discussion was at an end. "I myself will be leaving the day after tomorrow. We'll meet next in Tierra del Fuego."

FIFTEEN

Buenos Aires

THE scene would probably have struck most people as wildly incongruous, but for us it was just business as usual. There the four of us sat, Uzi, Aharon, Meir, and me, in the elegant living room of a sumptuous apartment on one of the most fashionable streets on earth, Paris's Avenue Wagram, hunched over a street map of a drab working-class district half a world away.

By now, we knew the map of San Fernando almost by heart. The Klement house on Calle Garibaldi was marked with a black X; the 80 yards Ricardo Klement walked each morning and evening to and from the bus stop around the corner on Route 202 was denoted by a broken blue line; the route traveled by the bus was in green; streets leading in and out of the area were red. Various observation posts, notably a railway embankment overlooking the house, were also prominently indicated.

The discussion at hand concerned the logistics of the capture. At what point, precisely, should we grab him?

Where should the getaway car be stationed? What about the backup car?

Each of us had an opinion about everything, based on something or other in his own experience.

But we also all realized that at this point the talk would lead nowhere. No final decision on how to proceed could be reached until we had examined the target area at close hand, gotten a sense of its traffic and pedestrian patterns, the sight lines from key buildings and street corners, the attitude of the locals toward outsiders.

In brief, we were in that curious netherworld that precedes many operations. The planning phase behind us, we were primed for action, but still on hold.

"C'mon," said Uzi suddenly, rising to his feet, "let's have a little fun."

That, after all, was part of the point of our being in Paris, with its beautiful surroundings, great food, and freedom from worry. Once we were in Argentina, our lives would no longer be our own. The pressure would be relentless, sometimes second to second. Unable to trust anyone but ourselves, the most innocuous slipup would jeopardize the entire mission.

Heading out into the glorious early May afternoon, we picked up a couple of bottles of wine, some French bread, and an assortment of cheeses and charcuterie, and drove out to the leafy Bois de Boulogne in our rented Citroën.

But soon, locating a reasonably secure patch of ground, we were once again laying preparation for the capture, steeling ourselves, among other things, for the possibility of being sighted in mid-act. Meir, to his consternation, was called upon to play Attila. He emerged from a cluster of trees on a narrow path and walked slowly in my direction. I glanced around, alert to passersby. There were none. Now face-to-face, I saw him flinch and then jumped him. I caught him in a half nelson, hoisted him onto my back, and dragged him toward the Citroën. Putting up only token resistance, he was dead weight. Aharon leapt out, grabbed his legs, and

My father and mother in Palestine in the 1940s.

In Israel, 1960, before I went to Argentina.

The *South American Handbook* in which I drew sketches while watching the prisoner.

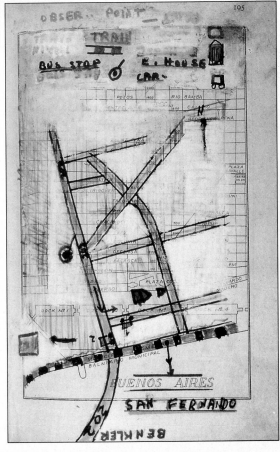

My map of Buenos Aires, pinpointing our surveillance.

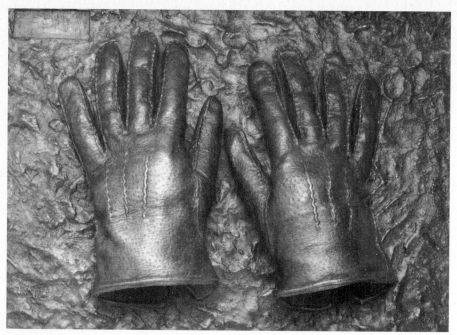

A cast of the gloves I wore that night on Garibaldi Street. They are
now at the Museum of Jewish Heritage in New York City.

The safe house where we kept
Eichmann.

My sister Fruma, who was killed in the Holocaust.

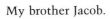

My brother Jacob.

The face of Eichmann over a map of South America.

Eichmann, the trains, Hitler, appropriately like Picasso's *Guernica*.

A study in contrasts: Obersturmführer Adolf Eichmann.

Herr Adolf Eichmann on trial in Jerusalem.

Haasi Eichmann, the little boy I saw sitting on his father's lap. *Francisco Vera,* Life *Magazine © 1960 Time Inc.*

together we stuffed him inside, moved in after him, and slammed the door shut.

An instant later Uzi rapped on the window, holding up his stopwatch for our inspection. "Fifty-two seconds," he pronounced. "Far too long."

We emerged from the car and began running through it again. But just as I was about to take him, there came Uzi's hushed, urgent command. "Wait!"

I stopped in my tracks just in time to spot a group of jodhpur-clad French people on horseback entering a clearing thirty yards away.

"What are you worried about?" I called out, smiling. "You think we look stranger than they do?"

"Just take your places," replied Uzi. "We need to get this down to thirty seconds."

I indicated Meir. "Fine. Just tell him to cooperate. I can't get a decent grip on his neck."

"It's instinct," replied Meir. "Let's see you offer up your neck, knowing it's about to get throttled."

"Fine," sighed Uzi, "okay. Aharon, *you're* Attila."

It proved a sound move. Not only was Aharon a far more reasonable Klement, reacting with simulated panic instead of sullen ill feeling, but Meir's enormous strength helped speed the prisoner into the car. After several tries we were down to thirty-five seconds.

Feeling we had earned a break, we sat on the grass and began preparing our sandwiches.

"Anyone know anything about the food in Argentina?" asked Meir, stuffing a hard-boiled egg in his mouth.

"Don't worry," replied Uzi, "they eat."

"Steak," said Aharon. "Lots of steak. The best in the world."

"What else?"

"What do you mean what else? Don't you like steak?"

"I like it well enough. I just want to know what else."

Aharon sighed. "Look, I've never been there either. Ordinary things. Eggs. Soup. Bread. They're people."

There was a silence as we ate.

"How about tonight?" asked Meir. "What are we having for dinner?"

Now was the time to try to put things in perspective, probably our last chance for a while. "Let me ask you something," Uzi said. "What would you want if you had a choice: $10 million or to be on this mission?"

I returned his smile. "A person can always figure out a way to make $10 million."

He nodded. "You know what I keep thinking about?"

"What?"

"The reaction at home when it's announced we've got him. I visualize the headlines in the papers—'Eichmann in Jerusalem.' I can see people dancing in the streets." He paused. "They will, you know."

"I know."

"It's silly, but that's just the way my mind works."

"It's not silly. I've been imagining exactly the same things."

Aharon left for Buenos Aires two days ahead of the rest of us: As the man chiefly responsible for navigating our way through a large and hitherto completely unknown city, he would need the extra time.

The evening before we were to follow, Uzi, Meir, and I decided to go to one of the better restaurants in town, a place in the old Les Halles district called Pied de Cochon.

Almost as soon as we sat down, Meir began to grouse. "Don't you know what *pied de cochon* means? I really don't think as Jews we should be here at a moment like this. It's *terrible* luck."

"I chose it intentionally," replied Uzi. "A pig's foot happens to be considered *good* luck here."

"What are you, going kosher on us?" I teased. "If you're so set against pork, order the calf brains in black butter instead. That's what I'm having."

From the look on his face, his revulsion was clearly not feigned. "I'll just have a little onion soup and some trout," he grumbled. "But what I'd *really* like is a nice plate of humus and some kebab."

Uzi glanced up from his menu. "Mr. Cosmopolitan." He nodded at Meir. "This one makes *me* feel sophisticated."

As the banter continued apace, a waiter appeared and began pouring the excellent Rhine wine we had ordered. Meir raised his glass. *"Le'chayim!"*

Instantly he realized the magnitude of his mistake. Uzi looked at the waiter, who continued to go about his business in apparent indifference, then turned to Meir, his eyes shooting daggers. "I suggest you get the calf brains," he said in English. "They're probably an improvement over the ones you've got."

The rest of the meal proceeded without incident. Intent on drawing no further attention to himself, poor Meir hardly opened his mouth. When the bill arrived, I took it, leaving a thirty-five percent gratuity. That was *my* superstition, overtipping at the last meal before starting a new assignment. I have always believed you've got to give to get.

The three of us left via Geneva on an old Swissair four-engine prop on the evening of May 3, 1960. I was traveling on a German passport under the name Maxim Nolte. Across the aisle, posing as British businessmen, sat Uzi and Meir.

Always a white-knuckle flyer, Meir seemed even more uncomfortable than usual. During the first couple of hours, face tense, he would lean his huge frame across Uzi's body every five minutes to peer out the window.

"What are you looking at?" his companion demanded finally.

"Nothing," said Meir. "I just want to see what's down there."

"There's clouds down there. Look, you want to switch seats?"

"No!"

"Then look with your eyes, not with your body."

Then, again, even I, who had never minded flying in the least, had a case of nerves. For the first time ever, I found myself reacting to every dip and bump, less anxious for my safety than that of the operation. *Wouldn't it be the supreme irony if we died before we ever reached him?*

Both Meir and I had plenty of cause for anxiety. Almost twenty-two hours long, including a refueling stop in Recife, Brazil, the flight was marked by frequent and severe bouts of turbulence. By the time we landed most of the sickness bags on board were full.

But as soon as we stepped onto the tarmac in Buenos Aires early on the afternoon of May 4, our exhaustion melted away, instantly replaced by an exhilarating sense of expectancy. We faced our first hurdle right away: Passport and customs, those airport conventions, merely inconvenient to the foreign traveler, represent to an undercover agent the baptism of a new operation of foreign soil.

Moving into the drab, single-story terminal (it was much like Tel Aviv's) by prearrangement we made for different control points. Naturally our passports were in perfect order. They had been sent to the Argentine embassy in London weeks earlier and stamped with three-month visas. The young, moustached agent to whom I handed mine leafed through it rapidly, took a quick glance at the photograph and the return ticket, and loudly applied his stamp.

"Have a good time in Buenos Aires," he said in English, his smile showing a couple of rotten teeth. On either side of me Uzi and Meir also breezed through.

As I strolled toward the claim area, waiting for my bags and watching the porters move with almost comical nonchalance, I was surprised to spot a lone figure off to the side sitting on his luggage. It was Danny, the forger. Evidently having arrived on an earlier flight, I supposed he was waiting to rendezvous with another member of the team. I passed him by, avoiding eye contact. There was no reason we should know each other.

It took a good forty minutes for the bags to find their way from the plane to the aluminum rack. I took them off but held back, letting Meir make his way through customs first. Uzi did the same, which is why we exchanged a furtive, concerned look when the customs agent, casually checking the larger of his two bags, pulled out a brown paper parcel, tested it for heft, and asked that the gentleman please open it for his inspection.

Meir calmly undid the string and pulled the paper open. Out rolled some large red apples, several bars of Suchard chocolate, and a thick salami. The agent stared at the contents, looked at Meir, stared some more. Finally he ordered Meir to wrap them back up. Unusual as the items were, they were not illegal.

Taking it in, I gnawed on my lip to keep from breaking up. *Meir!* If someone offered him a nice enough dinner on the night of the capture, he would forget about the whole damn operation.

All at once I was aware of someone standing beside me. I turned and faced Danny. Pale, he was sweating profusely and breathing hard.

"Peter," he said urgently, "will you take my suitcase for me?"

"Danny, what are you doing?"

"Please, I'm begging you."

"I've got my own suitcase," I replied, my voice hard. "We shouldn't even be talking."

"I know," he said. "But please, if you'll just carry it through customs."

There could hardly have been a worse time to argue; besides which, the man seemed to be utterly terrified.

I nodded curtly. "But I won't wait for you. You can pick it up."

With its hidden compartments full of lead printing plates, ink, and every conceivable variety of paper, the damn thing weighed a ton. But to the naked eye it looked like nothing more than standard artist's provisions. Lugging it into line, I passed through without incident. Danny followed and quickly picked up his luggage.

Five minutes later I was waiting with Uzi and Meir at the curb for a taxi. I was surprised by the weather. It was exceedingly cool for May, no more than forty degrees, and a light rain was falling. In my lightweight suit I was chilled to the bone.

"Nice," I said softly, nudging Meir in the ribs. "I'm only surprised the salami wasn't stamped 'Kosher—Made in Israel.' "

He offered his most sheepish grin. "I picked it up at the airport in Geneva. You never know when you'll need something to nosh."

As an ancient cab pulled up, I shook my head. "What a start. First your gourmet feast, then Danny losing it on us. And it's cold as ice here."

Gratefully the three of us piled into the taxi and Uzi handed the driver a piece of paper with a Buenos Aires address. In a few minutes we were speeding along the broad highway leading into the capital. Endless green fields stretched into the horizon. On either side of the road cattle grazed placidly.

"Fine autostrada, no?" spoke up the cabbie in passable English.

Uzi grunted agreement.

"Generalissimo Perón, he builder of this. He do many things. Is a pity he go away."

In fact, we were well aware of the unsettled political scene since Juan Perón's ouster five years before, and somewhat concerned about it. The possibility of armed soldiers in the streets could certainly not make our task any easier.

But none of us answered the driver. We were more interested in the autostrada itself. Having unfolded his map, Uzi periodically checked it for landmarks and side roads. We might have to return this way with Adolf Eichmann.

Still, the driver's next bit of innocuous chatter caught my attention. "Is cold, sirs, in Argentina, no?"

"Colder than I expected," I agreed. "But it will warm up, right?"

He peered around to face me. "Why? Is May."

I nodded, miserable, as it began to sink in. "Ahh."

Of *course*. We were in the southern hemisphere. It was almost winter. Incredibly no one in our crack detachment —perhaps no one in the entire vaunted Mossad—had thought of that.

The address we had been given turned out to be an elegant, four-story apartment building in a wealthy quarter, its facade adorned with sculpted cherubs. In a sprawling, second-floor apartment we found Aharon and a fellow named David. He was serving as the operation's front man.

Short, pink-cheeked, and impressively tailored, with a mane of prematurely white hair to go with his elegant manners and excellent Spanish, the Czech-born David seemed at once wordly and terribly innocent. His baby face and easy, open manner instantly inspired trust. This was the last man in the world anyone would suspect of undercover work.

David had not been with the organization long but I knew that Isser didn't much like him, for precisely the reason that he had now been handed the opportunity of a professional lifetime. By temperament a high liver and free spender, young David was posing as what he fervently wished he really was: the self-indulgent businessman son of an old moneyed European family.

Indeed, never had I seen him look happier. Supposedly looking to invest family money locally, David had passed the previous ten days in an orgy of spending, renting villas and laying out cash deposits of as much as five thousand dollars on cars that barely ran.

Though the relish with which David had taken to the role was surely driving him crazy, Isser could not say a word. The ruse was essential to the plan's success. He himself had decreed that we have at our disposal eight residences and eight vehicles.

Nor, in fact, could David have done things much more cheaply even were he inclined to. We needed safe houses that were large enough to accommodate our entire contingent and suitably laid out to quarter and, if necessary, hide a prisoner; they also had to be secure from prying eyes and afford the possibility of quick escape. Houses fitting such criteria had proven exceedingly hard to come by on short notice. Few owners were willing to lease their properties for less than a year, let alone the couple of months this crazy foreigner had in mind. Even worse, most residences of any size or quality seemed to include on-site employees as part of the package. Indeed, the lobby of the residence in which we found ourselves at that moment was manned by a uniformed concierge, making it useless as a hiding place. Every agent knows how troublesome a concierge can be, even under the best of circumstances, and in an authoritarian state it is safe to assume that most of them report directly to the police.

The automobile situation was almost as desperate. On the trip from the airport, I had noted that most of the cars on the road were at least a decade old, some of them bona fide museum pieces. Even those that looked terrific, their surfaces polished to a high gleam, often chugged along noisily and spewed out black exhaust, seemingly held together by baling wire and luck.

It had quickly been ascertained that in Buenos Aires car rental agencies were small and haphazardly managed. The cars on hand were even junkier than those on the road, and they could be had only at exorbitant rates.

In brief, none of the several vehicles obtained to date was trustworthy. From here on in, David and Aharon would simply have to get what they could, and we would rely on Meir's magic hands.

All of this was communicated in the space of ten minutes. Isser had left word he wanted to see Uzi and me as soon as possible, and before we had time to relax, David put on his fedora and mohair overcoat. "We'd better get moving."

Piling into a '52 Ford jalopy, we puttered our way into traffic, soon finding ourselves on the broadest avenue I had ever seen. "This is the Avenido Nueve de Julio," announced Uzi, studying his map. "Where are we heading?"

"A place called the Ópera Café," said Aharon, behind the wheel. "It's maybe ten minutes from here."

By now it was late afternoon, just before dusk. I had heard it said that Buenos Aires was much like Paris, and it was not hard to see why. Boulevards and fancy grillwork on the balconies were indeed reminiscent of the French capital. Yet, seeing the animation of the people on the teeming sidewalks, and those gesturing dramatically within the glass-walled terraces of the coffee houses, I was reminded more of Italy.

The only jarring note was the presence at key intersections of heavily armed soldiers in jeeps and armored personnel carriers.

The car drew to a halt at the curb of a busy intersection and Aharon pointed. "There, I'll wait for you."

Immense and brightly lit, the Ópera Café was packed, but we spotted Isser right away. Rising from the depths of an armchair against the wall, he strode forward and embraced us like long-lost sons. But once seated, he got right down to business.

"I know you're tired, but I want you to look over the ground tonight. I want plans for the capture finalized in the next couple of days."

We nodded. We were eager to get going ourselves.

He took a sip from the glass of whiskey before him. "One other thing, which is not your concern for the moment. We are still working on taking care of the Doctor at the same time as Attila. We have some addresses that need to be checked out. Any questions on that?"

Oh, no, *no! That* was still cooking! Damn right I had questions! But none that Isser Harel was prepared to hear from a subordinate.

I shook my head. "No questions."

"Good." He glanced down at his watch. "I've got to be off." Then he paused, for the first time seeming to look us over. "Get yourselves overcoats. You can put them on the expense account."

Five minutes later we were back on the road. After dropping David off at the apartment, Uzi, Aharon, and I headed north toward San Fernando. It had begun to drizzle and the night was dark. We were soon aware that the landscape had changed, the large buildings giving way to smaller ones, then to open fields. After a series of quick turns, we were on Route 202, a heavily traveled two-lane road that led straight into San Fernando.

As we approached the district, Uzi, beside me, sat up straight, squinting through his thick lenses. The charts and photos we had studied in our briefings were coming to life. It was almost as if we had been here before.

It was raining steadily now. Aharon eased the car off the main road onto a side street, then made a sharp turn onto a narrow dirt path, weaving his way between the large puddles.

It was a poor area, even more so than the photos had indicated. The houses were small and ramshackle. Few had electricity.

"We're parallel to Garibaldi Street," spoke up Aharon.

We drove a bit farther, slowly wheeled back onto a wider street, and then Aharon slammed on the brakes. Before us in the darkness someone was holding up a red torch. Two figures approached the car. Straining, we could make out that both were armed with pistols and truncheons. We were not armed.

Soldiers. They were very young and probably far more nervous than we were.

Our plan in such a contingency was to pose as woefully lost tourists looking for a hotel in downtown Buenos Aires. But our fractured Spanish was greeted only with silence. One of the soldiers shined a light in Aharon's face; the other examined our license plate. Then, wordlessly, they waved us on.

A few minutes later we turned onto another lane parallel to Garibaldi and Aharon killed the engine. "We'd better leave the car here," he said. "I'd hate for those soldiers to see it again."

So we got out into the rain and, Aharon in the lead, started slogging our way through the thick mud and driving rain. Never had I gotten so thoroughly drenched so quickly. My ridiculous suit was plastered to my body, my shoes began to squeak. The only saving grace, I reflected miserably, was that our footprints would be washed away.

After an interminable ten minutes we made it to the base of a steep hill. Then, on hands and knees, we struggled our way to the top.

Aharon was a genius. We were on the railroad embankment we had noted on the charts. Directly beneath us lay another set of railroad tracks, and just beyond, as in a fairy tale, was spread out the view with which we had become so familiar through the pictures. Off to the left lay Route 202, still heavy with traffic, and directly before us stood the Klement home.

Kneeling on the wooden ties, we rested our elbows on the cold tracks. The only one of us dressed appropriately, Aharon produced two pairs of high-powered Zeiss binoculars from the pocket of his heavy overcoat.

The house was about fifty yards away, but with the field glasses I felt I could touch it. I stared through one of the two front windows, shutters ajar and framed by white curtains, into the dim interior lit by a kerosene lamp; I could make out a table and some chairs, and a door leading into a back room.

Abruptly a woman came into view. Heavyset and deliberate in her movements, she took something from the table—a magazine? a newspaper?—and moved from sight.

It was easier to understand our first investigator's skepticisim. Could the elegant, strutting *Obersturmführer* really be reduced to this? Was it conceivable that a man who had dictated the fate of millions from châteaux and palaces would be living in a colorless little home lacking even the basic amenities? Could this drab and dumpy woman be the companion of the man who courted some of the most glamorous and beautiful women of fascist Europe?

Almost by force of will I pushed the doubt out of mind.

I checked the luminous hands on my watch. Just past 7:15 P.M. According to the reports, Klement usually appeared between 7:20 and 8:00.

I studied the area around the house. The low chain link fence. The small front yard pock-marked with puddles. What looked to be a toolshed just behind, though perhaps it housed a small generator.

I checked my watch: 7:23. A lone bicyclist turned into Garibaldi Street and pedaled through the rain. In the distance a door closed. Once again I turned my glasses toward the bus stop on 202 and the kiosk just opposite.

I nudged Uzi. "Thank God my mother can't see me now. She thinks I'm in Paris."

"So we get double pneumonia," he whispered back, smiling. "The only question is whether it comes before or after."

More silence. The mind continued to race. Then, suddenly, a brightly lit bus detached itself from the highway traffic and squealed to a stop. My watch read 7:35. As the bus pulled away two figures could be seen at the curb.

They crossed the road side by side. One was a woman, bundled up against the wet and cold. The other, a man in hat and light trench coat, seemed almost oblivious to it.

"That's him," hissed Aharon.

On the other side of the road, the two of them separated, the man turning onto Garibaldi Street. My hand was numb, but I held tightly to the glasses. It was too dark to make out his features, only that he wore heavy-rimmed glasses.

But there was the purposeful, measured walk, the erect head, the level gaze.

Instantly the doubt began to melt away.

Eichmann.

SIXTEEN

The Road to Garibaldi Street

THE following morning my surveillance of the target area was to begin in earnest. But en route, Aharon made a detour into another neighborhood, pausing before number 4261 Chucabuco Street.

"That's where he used to live," he noted. "We got lucky."

Neither Meir nor I, beside him in the front seat, both in disguise, had to ask what he meant. This neighborhood of lower-middle-class homes was far livelier than the other, and there was a steady stream of pedestrian traffic before the house itself. A clandestine operation around here would have been impossible.

Ten minutes later Aharon deposited us at a bus stop by the side of Route 202. We waited a quarter of an hour for the arrival of bus 203, the one on which Attila traveled to and from work at a Buenos Aires auto plant.

"Bunkerley," I said, handing the driver a ten-peso note and holding up a pair of fingers to indicate I wanted two tickets. The stop was the one immediately past Garibaldi Street.

The green and yellow bus was half empty. At least twenty years old, it had that odd, depressing feel so common to aging public conveyences in winter, at once cold and stuffy. Steel springs poked through many of the dilapidated leather seats.

From our inconspicuous vantage point in the rear I noted that the other passengers, mainly female in the middle of this weekday morning but including a few farm and factory workers, took pride in their appearance; even the poorest was nicely dressed. But there was little conversation. Staring vacantly ahead or out the window, most seemed lost in their thoughts. Clearly no one was leaving or heading toward anyplace special.

Over the next few days, traveling this same route in both directions aboard several vehicles, those impressions were repeatedly confirmed. The point, of course, was not only to be familiar with Attila's movements but to place myself in his shoes. I wanted to know, as clearly as I possibly could, what he would be experiencing immediately before we met. If the man we were tracking was anything like me—indeed, if he was human at all—he would hardly be at the top of his game. Emerging from that gruesome bus into the chilly winter evening, his mind on nothing in particular, he would be intent only on being inside the warm house just ahead.

We got off the bus near Garibaldi Street on Route 202. As it roared away, Meir cast his eye on the kiosk. "I think I'll get a sandwich," he said, reaching into his pocket.

I stopped him with a hard glance. "Why don't you just attach a sign to your back labeled FOREIGNER IN THE NEIGHBORHOOD?"

Reluctantly he kept pace as I strolled across the highway and turned the corner onto Garibaldi Street. At this time of the morning there was a lot of activity along the street, people moving leisurely along on foot or bicycle, a car passing every twenty or thirty seconds. Then, again, I would have to check it at other times and under different conditions. An environment moves like a clock. I needed to acquaint myself with the mechanism of this one.

As we moved toward the Klement house the woman suddenly appeared in the yard from around the corner. We maintained our even pace, strollers on a crisp winter morning, but my heart was thumping. Up close, she was even portlier than she had seemed the night before, with unkempt, dirty blond hair and the heavy, nondescript features of a Brueghel peasant.

When we were about twenty paces from the house, a boy of about five or six, in brown jacket and tattered corduroys, came running out after her.

The woman picked up a large washing tub full of laundry and, just as we drew even, lugged it into the house, the boy trailing after.

Meir and I had seen enough; or, more to the point, had been seen enough ourselves. Due in less than an hour to rendezvous with Aharon at the spot where he had deposited us earlier, we circled back to the bus stop and caught the return bus toward Buenos Aires.

When we reached the designated place, our friend was nowhere in evidence. We stood there, irritation warring with concern. It had started to rain again, and we still had no winter clothes. After half an hour we gave up, making our way back to the safe house by taxi.

We didn't have to wait long.

Aharon, accompanied by Uzi, straggled in soon after we did, their clothes not only sopping but smeared with grease. The car had broken down. Uzi, cursing his luck and Argentina in general, ordered Meir to go back out with him and put the damn thing in running order, the first in what would be a series of such episodes. Eventually, to save time, Meir would simply rebuild the engine of every car we rented as soon as we got our hands on it.

That evening I returned to San Fernando on my own.

When I arrived, shortly after 6:00, it was already dark. I took my place lying prone atop the railroad embankment and waited. Though I was dressed reasonably this time, having bought a raincoat and gloves, it was still far from comfortable. No matter which way I turned or twisted, part of me ended up in a puddle.

Still, I was almost able to forget all about that. The interior of the house was well lit, and there, playing on the living room floor, dressed only in his underpants, was the little boy. I watched him in rapt fascination. He seemed a happy child, jumping around and full of fun. The mother, wandering in and out of view, seemed indulgent with him, giving him the run of the place, laughing at his antics.

A little after 7:00 a motorcycle pulled up to the house, and a moment later those inside were joined by a young blond man in his early twenties. It was probably Dieter, one of the older sons; we had reports that he owned a motorcycle.

Now the boy stopped playing to lean to the windowsill and gaze out at the rain.

For, yes, dammit all, it was raining again.

Still, it was the best look I had at him yet. He was an extraordinarily beautiful child, the sort certain Renaissance artists used to use as models for angels. He reminded me of my murdered cousin, Takele.

But what was he staring at? Could he be waiting for his father?

Sure enough, a little past 7:30 the 203 bus pulled up to the stop and Klement got off. He was dressed exactly as he had been the evening before, and he moved toward the house with the same purposeful stride, his hands at his sides.

This last observation was vital. Even if he was armed, he would not have ready access to the weapon.

He could hardly have been better suited to our purposes: a man of absolutely rigid habits. At Nuremberg the commandant of Auschwitz had reported that every incoming trainload of Jews was preceded by a telegram from Eichmann bearing the identical words: "To be treated according to the directives for 'special treatment'—the code for gassing," a horrific bit of information, that, however, bode well for us. On the crucial night, any spontaneity on his part could cause trouble.

The pattern continued when the light in the house got brighter as soon as he stepped through the door. The same thing had happened the night before, as, I would learn, it did every night. It was another piece of Klement routine to be filed away for possible use.

Now, his hat and coat off, Klement was at the boy's side. He lifted him in the air and spun him around, then got on the floor beside him and began crawling around on all fours, both of them laughing.

On any other occasion such a scene would have had me smiling also. It reminded me of my father with me at the same age. More, it was the kind of father I hoped someday to be myself.

Now they moved to the window. The boy sat on the man's lap, both of them gazing out.

They stayed that way, just staring out, for a long time, seeming to daydream in unison. Then, off to my right, there came a rumbling noise. Slowly it began to grow louder. Now the man stirred and pointed. A moment later a freight train appeared, roaring by on the tracks directly below me.

All at once I was hit by an almost indescribable sense of revulsion.

The father was smiling slightly, and his lips were moving. Finger extended, he was helping the child count.

"You bastard," I thought, "still with the trains!"

SEVENTEEN

Safe House

THE safe house was getting crowded. When I returned after that second nocturnal visit to San Fernando, I discovered that, in addition to David, Aharon, Uzi, Meir, and myself, Danny had moved in.

We never exchanged a word about the queer episode at the airport. It might as well never have happened.

When I came upon him that night as he worked on a false passport, hunched over his worktable in a back room like some clerk out of Dickens, a magnifying glass in one hand, a stiletto-pointed pen in the other, he looked up with moist, expectant eyes and greeted me with a nod.

"When did you get here?" I asked.

"A couple of hours ago. You saw him?"

I nodded. "He was playing with his little boy in the house. It looked like a picture on a Papa's Day card. It was us with our fathers."

While he offered a smile, I realized at once that the remark had been thoughtless. Or, who knows, maybe I was

evening the score for what he had put me through at the
airport. Either way, I regretted it. Born in Hungary, the site
of Eichmann's most unspeakabale achievements on behalf
of the Reich, Danny was unable even to bring himself to
speak the man's name. He had lost his father to Bergen-
Belsen.

I looked over the vast array of supplies carefully arranged on the large table beside the one at which he
worked—brushes, pencils, magnifying glasses, X-acto
knives, seals, chunks of wax and burners to melt it down;
cameras, film, developing chemicals and trays; reams and
reams of paper, in different colors and of various stocks—
and thought wistfully of how much it had weighed.

"Did you bring your art supplies?" he asked. As he
knew, usually I was never without them.

"Just a few." I paused. "It didn't seem important."

"I know. I know."

Eager to avoid arousing suspicions, we began taking
ludicrous precautions with our comings and goings, making
sure to be out of the house prior to the 8:30 A.M. arrival of
the concierge at his post by the front entrance and not returning until after 6:00 in the evening, when he left. Clearly
it was an untenable situation, and there was general relief
when David announced on the morning of the third day
that he had rented exactly the villa we needed in a wealthy
suburb, an hour and a quarter from San Fernando. On Isser's
orders Meir and I were to take up residence there immediately and begin getting the place in shape.

Driving onto the grounds through an entranceway in a
high stone wall, David could scarcely keep his eyes off our
faces as we took it all in.

"I didn't exaggerate, did I?" he asked, beaming. "Pretty
nice place, wouldn't you say?"

"No, David," I allowed, "you didn't exaggerate."

The broad expanse of lawn was framed by a beautifully
tended garden. To the left, there was also a babbling brook,

and beside it a rock garden that might have been imported from Japan. To the right, a tiled footpath ascended a grassy hill and disappeared beyond. The house itself, fronted by Moorish arches, was immense, something out of a Hollywood fantasy.

"How in the world did you find this palace?" I asked, as we strode toward the front door. "This must run at least five thousand dollars a month."

"Don't ask," he replied with evident satisfaction. "But double it and you're still not there."

Inside, opulent chandeliers were suspended from the high ceilings and plush Chinese carpets swallowed our steps. The rooms were huge, the furnishings antique Spanish.

All of which, of course, was merely a bonus. Quickly Meir and I mounted the polished wooden stairs, past the bedrooms and study on the second floor to the attic. At the head of the stairs was a small wooden door; beyond it, crisscrossing beams supported the roof. We detached a beam and moved it forward a couple of feet. Perfect. A hinged, false wall could be installed, leaving enough room to hide a man.

The materials we needed were already in the car, purchased at a lumberyard en route. As we descended the steps, we were surprised to see a fellow in workclothes standing with David in the entryway.

"We've got a problem," said David sourly in German. "The landlord neglected to tell me we have a caretaker."

The man, knowing we were discussing him, nodded and smiled our way.

I smiled back. "Can't we get rid of him?"

David shrugged. "He lives in a hut out back. He has orders to hang around and make himself useful."

It fell to me to break the news to Isser. Three hours later I was sitting at a window table in a bar on Avenida Corrientes, the latest addition to our leader's ever-changing list of rendezvous locales, when a tiny figure strode in wearing a heavy fur overcoat and a huge fur hat. It was its size that gave him away, and the distinctive ears protruding from the furry mass on top. And the fact that the figure was trailed by Hans, the interrogator.

It was the first time I had seen Hans in months, but we greeted one another with only the most perfunctory of nods. I never liked the man, finding him arrogant and overbearing, someone of little flexibility and even less humor. Nor did I care at all that he regarded me with equal contempt. In general, I kept quiet around him, more in self-defense than anything else. Hans was the sort of man who files away everything everyone says in his presence, even in jest, in case it should prove useful to him later on.

"Excellent choice," he said to Isser crisply, the ultimate brownnose, "I know this place well. It's first-rate."

"Isser," I spoke up, ignoring him, "there's a problem with the villa." And I told him about the caretaker.

For a long moment he said nothing. "Tell David to rent the other villa. It's not perfect, but it will have to do."

For all his practiced calm, I knew the news had ruined Isser's day. In his universe everything went as he intended.

A couple of minutes later the frustration began to show. "Peter," he said, nodding after the waiter who had just taken our drink orders, "you're not drinking. Order something."

I had never been much of a drinker. "But I ordered a Coke."

"Something hard. Owners of these places expect people to drink whiskey."

"Isser's right," said Hans.

I cast him a withering glance. "Isser," I said softly, "I don't *like* whiskey."

"I don't want you calling attention to yourself." He signaled the waiter and ordered me one.

"Just do it," he said. "Let them see you drinking like everyone else."

"That's crazy. Who gives a damn?"

"Peter," he said wearily, as if I was the one with the insane fixation, "just do it for me, will you?"

I was sipping the whiskey when he got down to business. "We don't have much time. I've decided to make a concerted effort, involving all possible resources, to locate the Doctor."

I nodded, not betraying my considerable distress. "I'll let the others know. It should be realized, of course, that things remain to be worked out on Attila."

In fact, I had pretty well settled on the precise plan of capture, but I certainly didn't want Eichmann to become even momentarily anything but everyone's first priority.

"No," interrupted Hans. "In the matter of Attila, the plan has already been designed. Your function merely will be to carry it out."

I was stunned, flabbergasted. Such chutzpah was unheard-of! And right in front of Isser. I looked to the Old Man for a reaction. He said not a word.

Still, I managed to hold my tongue. I had occasionally known Isser to encourage competition among his men, even a certain degree of animosity. But he had no use at all for hotheads. For all Hans's high-handedness, I simply could not conceive of the possibility that he might win such a struggle. Isser's baffling hesitancy now could only be a reflection of the extraordinary pressure he was under. Never in his life, either, had the stakes been so high. But certainly, in the end, this most respected professional of the clandestine world could be counted on to make the right judgment. Couldn't he?

David signed the lease for the new villa that afternoon. An hour and a half later Meir and I were inside the place, setting up. It was hoped that by the middle of the following day, May 7, Danny would be the sole remaining occupant of the original apartment. As a painter of still lifes (his cover), he rarely left the building and so was unlikely to arouse the interest of even the nosiest of busybodies. Still, just to be sure, Meir rigged up a cache in the fireplace for his forgeries. If necessary, a touch of a match and the phony documents would go up in smoke.

The latest villa, code-named Tira by the ever-inventive Isser, was hardly the equal of its predecessor. A rambling affair of no distinctive style located in a resort district an hour north of the capital, it was normally used as a summer home. There was no heat. The thick walls, so useful in keeping the place cool in hot weather, turned it into an icebox now. Moreover, it had no attic or basement, so there was no obvious place in which to construct a hiding niche.

On the other hand, the district was reasonably isolated, the house was surrounded by a wall of perhaps eight feet, and it came entirely free of staff. Inside, on the first floor, there was a vast and comfortably appointed living room, a modern, well-equipped kitchen, three small bedrooms, and, through sliding glass doors off a short hallway, a veranda, its wooden enclosing wall covered by dense foliage. The second-floor rooms were in storage, their contents draped in sheets and tarpaulins. They were even colder than those on the first.

Meir proposed that the small bedroom adjacent to the kitchen be set up for the prisoner. It was the warmest spot on the premises, had only one tiny window, and offered easy access to the veranda through which, in the event of trouble, he could be spirited from the villa. Or where, Meir determined after some study, he could be hidden in a pinch.

As earlier, our first job was the construction of the hiding place. After removing from the veranda floor the plank nearest the yard, we fashioned it with grooves so it could slide in and out easily. There were sixteen inches beneath to the concrete foundation, more than enough space for a man, bound and gagged, to be placed temporarily. Above, hidden in the surrounding foliage, we built the attachments for a sort of dumbwaiter. In an emergency it could be quickly fitted with a wooden slab upon which our man could be lowered into place, not only making our job easier but protecting his back from the cold concrete.

Next, we rigged up a bell in the prisoner's room with connections to the front gate and the living room. With a discreet touch, those on the outside would be able to alert his guards of approaching danger.

Finally we set about the task of covering over the windows to shield the house from prying eyes. It was particularly melancholy work. By now it was late afternoon and even colder. The blankets David had brought for the purpose, at seventy dollars apiece, were pure wool from Scotland. As we pounded them into the walls with inch-long nails we longed for nothing so much as to throw them around ourselves.

Finished at last, sitting in absolute blackness, chewing on cold, dry sandwiches, we passed the time by making a mental list of items that sonofabitch David had better provide by the next day: blankets for *us* and several heating stoves, lamps and flashlights, a couple of packs of playing cards and a chess set, a few more blankets for good measure.

The following day, as planned, the others moved in, followed that evening by another operations man, my old colleague Jack. It had quite properly been determined that, with the hunt for Mengele still alive, additional hands might well be needed.

The day after that, our contingent grew larger still, with the arrival of a tall, nattily dressed stranger of about forty. Uzi introduced him as Dr. Maurice Klein. It turned out the two of them had known each other for years. The leading anesthetist at a major Tel Aviv hospital, Klein was one of the numerous doctors my friend had encountered during treatment of his various war wounds.

"We're glad you're here," I observed to Klein. "I hope you've had some experience treating double pneumonia."

He smiled good-naturedly. "Ah, but I understood this to be a vacation. I thought I had only one patient to worry about."

As I was to learn, the doctor's even manner hid a steel constitution. A Holocaust survivor with no previous undercover experience, he had leapt at Uzi's offer to participate in the mission.

The move to the new villa was already proving useful on the automobile front, since its courtyard provided an ideal spot for Meir to tinker with engines unobserved. Even we were amazed by the cars that David kept coming up with. Each had its own distinctive, infuriating personality. One had bald tires and front windows that would not close; another refused to shift out of first; the one after that, in need of a new gearbox, stalled at every other intersection.

Any one of them would have been grist for a classic Laurel and Hardy sketch. But for us the implications were the opposite of comic. Already, after two more had had to be abandoned on the road, Isser had ordered that henceforth, whenever possible, we would travel in mini-convoys.

Meir was not even bothering with most of them. Since only a few days remained until the capture, he concentrated on the two cars that would see action that night: a gray Chrysler and a black Mercedes.

Especially the Mercedes. It was the vehicle in which Attila would travel to captivity.

To the untutored eye—mine, for instance—the Mercedes seemed fine. But the more deeply Meir probed, the more concerned he became, and finally he enlisted David's service full-time to run around the city and find replacements for worn parts. Even the light bulbs had to go. Satisfied at last, Meir fitted the restored car with one of his own inventions, a spring device that enabled us to change license plates in seconds.

Shortly after dawn on the morning of the ninth, I was jolted out of a deep sleep by a prolonged jangling of the front doorbell. Exhausted from the latest surveillance in San Fernando the night before—assorted pieces of my disguise still lay on a couple of chairs, where I had haphazardly discarded them in my rush to bed—I walked groggily into the living room, nearly stumbling over Uzi, asleep on the carpet under a great coat, and pulled open the front door.

"What's wrong with you people?" demanded Hans, brushing by me and into the living room. "Are you deaf?"

Spotting our commanding officer's foot sticking out from beneath the coat, half covered by a torn sock, he strode over and nudged him with the toe of his boot. "Uzi, wake up."

Uzi's eyes fluttered open and he looked about, disoriented.

"The Old Man wants an all-out effort to locate Mengele," said Hans sharply. "I have a list of addresses. They have to be checked out right away."

Uzi sat up, feeling for his glasses. "What do you mean? What addresses?"

Hans reached into his inside jacket pocket and pulled out a sheaf of papers. "It's in this report. You're to check out the locale marked in red. We have to know by tonight whether to continue this aspect of the operation."

As Uzi peered at the top page, trying to make sense of the handwritten notations—a record of Mengele's suspected recent movements, based primarily on intercepted correspondence and other second-hand data—our visitor turned and headed toward the door. "I've got other business. I'll be back late this afternoon to discuss the plan of operations regarding Attila."

Half an hour later I found myself behind the wheel of a fifteen-year-old Buick, the first time I had driven since our arrival. With Uzi navigating, we located the house around 7:15. It was a rambling, three-story structure in the Vicente López district, one of Buenos Aires' wealthiest. Parking the car around the corner, about a hundred yards away, we sat and watched.

After a short time the front door opened and a youngish woman in sports clothes emerged, followed by three young children carrying school bags. Fifteen minutes later she returned alone. Another half hour and a youngish man emerged, got a kiss on the forehead from the woman, and drove off.

"You know what this is?" observed Uzi. "It's like one of those comedies on American television."

"I'm going to pay her a visit," he decided a few minutes later. He copied the number of a nearby house into his notebook and ripped out the page. He would pretend to be looking for it. "Wait for me here."

Uzi walked up the pathway and rang the bell. The woman answered, they exchanged a few words, and he disappeared inside. A half hour passed before the door opened again and, waving good-bye, he strode out.

"Guess what," he said when he reached the car, "they *are* American. She even served me some American coffee."

"And the doctor?"

He shook his head. "No good. He used to live there, but we missed him by a month. She's still getting German-language newspapers from Switzerland."

"Who are they?"

"They're from Philadelphia. They just got here, never even met him. All they know is what the landlord told them."

"No forwarding address?"

"Of course not. He hasn't been in touch since he left."

Neither of us had to state the obvious: His vanishing act coincided exactly with Hans's investigation of Eichmann.

At noon we rendezvoused with Aharon in front of a movie theater downtown and Uzi switched cars. Since the strategy meeting the two of them had scheduled for this morning had been put on hold, they would talk now, en route to the villa. I, unfamiliar with the city, would follow close behind.

It sounded reasonable enough. What I had not counted on was that Aharon, lost in conversation, might forget I was there. Soon he began to pick up speed, after a while moving so fast that I found myself having to labor to stay near him, weaving through traffic on narrow, unfamiliar streets. I honked my horn to get his attention, but either he didn't hear or he failed to distinguish it from all the other cars honking. Suddenly, without warning, he made a sharp turn. Probably his turn signal wasn't working. I wheeled around the turn just in time to see him shoot up the crest of a hill and vanish down the other side.

I was growing desperate.

Pedal to the floor, I was just beginning to make up ground when, fifty yards ahead, he shot through a yellow light and disappeared around another curve. Pausing only momentarily at the intersection, I zoomed after him, then slammed on the brakes. Thirty yards ahead, five or six army and police vehicles were moving into position. A roadblock!

Oh, God, came the first, harrowing thought, *they've got us all!*

The grim-faced young soldiers approached me, rifles at the ready.

I took a deep breath and smiled. This is what we were trained for.

"What's the problem?" I asked in English, pulling out my passport.

They made no reply, just ordered me out of the car with a movement of their rifles.

But already I was aware that other cars were being stopped as well, and that their drivers were also being made to step onto the street. In a couple of minutes there were over twenty of us. Formed into a line, we were ordered up a hill and across a damp, grassy field. On the other side stood a small concrete police station.

Five tables had been set up in the entryway. Behind each sat an officer, fingerprint sheets and ink before him. I eyed those around me desperately, searching for a European or American to help me out. Under no circumstances could I leave my fingerprints.

And what, I wondered, as I stood in one of the lines, about the car? Who knew what might have been stashed in the trunk? A piece of building material that no legitimate tourist would ever need? Maybe even a phony license plate.

The wait to reach the head of the line was at least half an hour. By the time I sat down before the young officer, my stomach was in knots. When I made it clear I spoke no Spanish, he summoned a second officer.

"No good," said the second man when I produced my driver's license. He made a tearing motion, indicating I had the wrong half of the document.

Uzi, damn him, had inadvertently kept the right half.

I smiled and shrugged, pulling out a sheaf of other forged documents: my passport, my medical forms, the car's registration. Beside them I placed the pack of unopened Kents I always carried with me.

Instantly the officer's manner changed. "Are a tourist?"

"Yes, an artist. You have a beautiful country."

He scribbled a few words into a loose-leaf notebook, firmly applied a large rubber stamp to the page, ripped it out, and handed it to me. "Okay," he said, "show this to policeman on the road." With his other hand he slipped the cigarettes into his pocket.

At the bottom of the hill a new group of motorists was being rounded up for questioning. Only now did I finally begin to understand what was going on: the Perónists, as part of their campaign to disrupt Argentina's approaching 150th anniversary festivities, had planted a bomb at a nearby military base.

The question now was how to find my way back to the villa. I had made the trip only a couple of times, but never on my own. And I had no street address. I thus amazed myself when after an hour, operating on instinct, I found myself in territory that looked increasingly familiar; and then, incredibly, spotted the villa itself.

I burst into the house, elated, and spilled out my story. I was feeling so good, so heroic, that I couldn't even bring myself to be annoyed with Aharon.

But Hans, present for the meeting, almost instantly wiped the moment away.

"I don't believe it," he cut me off. "I drove down that road myself and nothing happened. So did Aharon and Uzi."

I gazed at him with cold fury. "What, you think I'm lying? Obviously you passed through before the road was blocked. Look, here's the pass the cop gave me."

Uzi took the paper and looked it over. "Maybe I'll send this over to Danny," he observed with a small smile. "It wouldn't hurt for each one of us to have one of these, just in case."

Even then Hans refused to accept it. It was a disease with him: He had to be the final authority on absolutely every subject.

Nor did this bode well for what was to come next, the meeting to finalize the plan for the capture. I had dreaded it for days, but also planned for it.

"Listen," he began, utterly confident, "there's nothing to discuss. Isser has already approved my plan."

"And what is your plan, exactly?" asked Uzi, with the appearance of real interest. Reflexively mindful of others' feelings, Uzi was physically incapable of treating Hans with the contempt he deserved and so sometimes seemed almost cowed by him.

Hans spread a map of the target area on the table before us. "Peter, you'll wait for him here"—he pointed at Garibaldi Street, just before the house—"and jump him here, on the path. You will wrestle him to the ground and hold him there. Meir, you will have been hiding nearby, and now you will appear to help Peter. I and the rest of the team will be waiting around the corner on 202 in the two cars." He indicated a couple of small rectangles on the map, on the highway shoulder. "As soon as we see you've secured him, we'll swing around the corner, pick you up, and take off."

He continued in this vein for perhaps five minutes, pointing out things on the map, then stood back, fingertips pressed together, looking from face to face in expectation. "Fast and simple," he concluded. "No problem."

No problem. Way back in the army, I had learned that whenever someone said those words, it was time to start worrying.

But I was not about to give Hans the satisfaction of seeing me lose my temper.

"Isser has approved this plan?" I asked coolly.

"In every detail."

"Let me see if I understand you." I paused. "Meir and I are to remain exposed until you decide to arrive with the car?" Again I paused. "A question. What if a policeman happens by, or even an ordinary pedestrian?"

He pursed his lips. "That won't happen. We will act with all due speed."

"But let me just pose it as a theoretical proposition," I pressed on. "I'm sure you've considered it. What happens *if* we're taken during the abduction?"

"Certainly I've thought about it." He paused meaningfully. "Under no circumstances will you let go of Attila. You are to identify him and let it be known that you are Israelis, emissaries of the Jewish people on a mission aimed at righting a historic wrong. But I repeat"—he was actually wagging a finger at me now—"you are not to let go of him."

This would have tried the patience of a saint. The man was unaware of the most basic rule of the business: to anticipate the unexpected and leave oneself options.

"You moron!" I exploded. "You amateur! That's the worst plan I ever heard. You think we came here to be Jewish heroes?"

His face went white with anger. "That is the plan and you are to follow it. It's Isser's order."

"Follow it yourself. This isn't a plan to get Eichmann

into a Jerusalem courtroom, it's a plan to get Meir and me into a Buenos Aires jail!"

"All plans involve calculated risk," he said coldly, as if he had invented the cliché. "All of them."

"Right, Hans—and those are the *only* ones I'm prepared to take."

"It's not your choice," he repeated, "it's an order."

"Go fuck yourself! We're not in the German army here. If you and Isser are so in love with your plan, let you two do it yourselves. *I'm* Hamlet here; I'll play it my own way."

Hans paused. Something was going on in his head. It only occurred to me later that he was afraid. He was a novice. Aside from its other virtues, notably that he could take credit for it, his plan kept him far from the scene. "It's not open for discussion," was all he could find to say. "It's been decided."

"We've heard enough," interrupted Uzi decisively. "Peter happens to know a little more about operations than you do. And he happens to be right." He paused. "We'll talk to Isser and get it changed. Isser's not God. He makes mistakes, too."

The next day at 10:00 A.M. we gathered in the living room of Danny's apartment downtown. Isser sat deep in an easy chair facing the rest of us. His eyes were bloodshot and his skin slack. He had been working nonstop, especially on the escape plan. It was masterful. Working with top El Al officials, he had arranged an unprecedented special flight to carry the Israeli delegation from Tel Aviv to Buenos Aires for the 150th anniversary celebration. However, between their complicated regulations and even more complex personalities, the Argentine bureaucrats involved were not making it easy on him.

It was Thursday, May 10. Originally this was to have been D-day. The change had been made partly to allow Meir more time with the cars, still our most likely Achilles' heel.

The second car to be used in the capture, the Chrysler, still needed work. But it was also the case that, eager as we were to be under way, most of us were desperately in need of some rest.

It fell to Uzi to describe the conflict between Hans and me. He laid out the opposing plans fairly, without any hint of personal preference. Mine differed from the scheme to which I so violently objected in several ways, but one was most essential: I wanted one of the cars, the Mercedes, positioned *on* Garibaldi Street, hood up as if disabled, so that Attila would pass directly by it en route home. Meir was to be on the street side of the car, hidden by the raised hood, pretending to tinker with the engine, while Hans and Uzi stayed out of sight within. Strolling in the opposite direction, toward Attila, I would have no apparent connection to the seemingly empty vehicle. But after we met and I had subdued him, Meir would appear and together we would get him into the car and take off. The other car, driven by Aharon, would join us moments later, turning onto Garibaldi from 202 and taking the lead position. They would secure us in case of a blockade. If there was pursuit of any kind we would try to evade the pursuers long enough to switch Attila to the other car, then reappear to lead them astray.

Now it was my turn to speak. I had not only to argue the strengths of my plan, playing up its speed and simplicity, but to lay out my objections to its alternative. In Hans's plan, I noted, there were simply too many imponderables. Aside from our being exposed with the captive to passersby, what of the possibility that those waiting in the cars on 202, blinded by oncoming headlights, might be unable to make out what was happening? What of the even greater likelihood that a cop, spotting two cars on the shoulder of the highway, might stop by to investigate? What if one of the giant rigs that traveled 202 pulled off at just the wrong place at just the wrong moment, blocking access to Garibaldi entirely? During our surveillance of the house, we had seen that happen once before.

Isser studied me intently for a long moment. He knew me well, knew, above all, that to be effective I couldn't be kept on too short a leash.

"I understand, Peter," he said, "why you need to feel comfortable with the plan. My question is this: What happens if Attila sees the car waiting before him in the road and panics? What if he leaves the sidewalk and cuts through the adjacent field to reach his house?"

It was a legitimate apprehension. From the start, the only seeming advantage of the other proposal had been that it served to minimize our man's suspicion. I had given the matter a great deal of thought.

"He will continue straight ahead," I said. "I'm sure of it."

Hans, sitting beside Isser, began shaking his head furiously.

"Look," I said, "imagine you're Attila. You get off the bus, cross the highway, start walking up Garibaldi Street. Now you see a car with its hood up. It's maybe thirty yards to your house. What do you do? Do you turn and go back to the street?" I paused. "I'll tell you what happens. You're a proud German officer, a creature of habit and routine. A little dialogue goes on in your head. You're a little ashamed of yourself even to be feeling such fears. After all, it has been fifteen years. You can't run away from every single suggestion of the unknown. It's impossible to live life that way. The house is closer now, and very welcoming. You continue on."

"You don't think he'll cut through the field? That will get him home just as well."

I shook my head. "I've spent a lot of time in Germany, and I've seen a lot of Germans in shiny boots. They will not walk through the mud if they don't absolutely have to." I paused. "There's something else. If Hans's plan fails—if the police come, or I'm interrupted during the capture and he gets away—that's it. We'll never have another shot at him. With my plan, even if his suspicions *are* aroused and he avoids us, we simply continue to work on the engine, slam down the hood, and drive away. In all likelihood, he figures he was paranoid and we try again later."

Isser pulled himself out of the chair, walked over to me, and placed his hands on my shoulders. It was both a benediction and a warning. "All right. I agree. But, Peter, it's on your head."

EIGHTEEN

"Un Momentito, Señor"

ON May 11 Meir and Uzi were up at dawn to test the cars. When they returned an hour later, Uzi was soaring.

"Like new," he announced. "Like we just drove them out of the showroom!"

But Meir kept whatever enthusiasm he may have been feeling in check. He knew even better than the rest of us that with these cars, nothing was certain and that he was on the line every bit as much as I was. Throughout the rest of the day, he kept returning to the courtyard to tinker with the engines.

At least he had something to keep him busy. For the rest of us, there was only waiting. We talked absently, we played chess and gin rummy. Most useless of all, we lay down and tried to get some rest. Alone with our thoughts, we usually emerged jumpier than we had been before.

My sole responsibility of the day was to prepare the prisoner's room for his arrival. That took no more than twenty minutes. After putting fresh sheets and blankets on the bed, which was iron, with low, curving side rails, I placed a pair of striped pajamas, a towel, a large black cotton handkerchief, and a pair of dark motorcycle goggles on top. The handkerchief would serve as a blindfold, the goggles would secure it in place. Next, I filled a white enamel jug with water and put it on the night table with an empty glass. These would be beyond the prisoner's reach. In the drawer went a toilet kit containing a toothbrush and toothpaste, a comb and brush, mouthwash, nail clippers, everything generally found in such a thing except razor blades.

To one of the side rails, I fastened a pair of handcuffs.

The room was tiny, no more than ten by twelve, but it felt larger because it was so sparsely furnished. The only other piece of furniture was a high wooden stool. A plain mirror hung on the wall opposite the bed. The only window was covered by one of David's blankets.

An hour before we were due to leave, I returned to my own room across the hall, pulled off my clothes, and lay down in my underwear, trying to relax. I tried to think about Gila, about my mother, but nothing worked. Everything else was crowded aside by a vivid and persistent image: Klement coming toward me in the darkness.

I breathed deeply, rhythmically. I had to keep the doubts at bay, but they kept intruding: He was a trained soldier; a man who had survived on instinct for fifteen years. The slightest mistake on my part—a sudden quickening of my pace, an inadvertent glance in the direction of the car —and he could be off. Or he could simply take off for no reason at all.

Klement. It was, I recognized, in self-protection that I refused to use the other name. In some unspoken way, the figure mentioned so often in the Nuremberg transcripts remained a larger-than-life adversary, and I *had* to anticipate only a man.

And, too, there remained the terrible question: Was it really him?

Certainly the evidence had continued to mount that the older sons were Eichmann's and that the woman was the same Vera Lieble to whom he had been married during his murderous career. But we could never entirely dismiss the possibility that the man was a stepfather and second husband; that, indeed, Ricardo Klement was not an alias at all.

In fact, in recent days a plan had been formulated to meet that possibility. If that was the case, Meir and I were to take him to a remote area several hundred miles to the north, and after giving him money and warning him to keep his mouth shut, disappear across the border to Brazil.

I went to the bathroom, splashed cold water on my face, studied it in the mirror. What does a kidnapper look like? A moment later I pulled on my wig and carefully combed it into place. Back in my room, I dressed in dark clothes, a deep blue wool sweater, and a pair of black pants I had bought locally. Though it was as cold as ever outside, I decided to leave my heavy coat behind. I stuffed a pair of fur-lined leather gloves into the pants pockets. The gloves would of course help with the cold, but that is not the main reason I bought them. The thought of placing my bare hand over the mouth that had ordered the death of millions, of feeling the hot breath and the saliva on my skin, filled me with an overwhelming sense of revulsion.

Now it was 6:40 P.M., five minutes to go. In the living room Meir was wearing a bulky overcoat that added pounds to his frame. Beneath it, in the event he needed a quick change, he wore a sleek and incongruously sporty suit.

Dr. Klein was off to one side, his medical bag beside him, his face betraying nothing. As he waited he absently moved chess pieces about the board.

It was time. In the courtyard Aharon, Jack, and the doctor got into the Chrysler. Since they would not be in the open none was disguised. David swung open the front gate. Uzi gave them a thumbs-up as they pulled into the street.

The gate closed behind them. It was cold and it seemed about to rain. Rubbing his hands together, trying to make himself useful, David was the very picture of anxiety. If there was a screwup, he would be the one to contact Isser, who was waiting impatiently for news in another villa. Undoubtedly he would also be the one to get us a lawyer.

Hans was already behind the wheel of the Mercedes and Meir waited in the back seat. The phony plates had been splattered with mud, making them impossible to read. As I got into the back Uzi stepped into the passenger side. Hans started the engine. We were off.

We were intentionally cutting it close. The thirty-to-thirty-five-minute ride to San Fernando would leave us approximately fifteen minutes before the usual arrival of Attila's bus, not long enough for a broken car to arouse any serious suspicions.

We drove in silence, first through the ever more desolate outskirts of the city, then on to the rush of the highway. There was thunder now and an occasional bolt of lightning, but still no rain. Uzi and Meir both stared straight ahead, the oncoming headlights periodically illuminating their features. Watching them I felt a sudden surge of warmth. Already I owed these men more than I could ever tell them; and now, again, I was placing my life in their hands. Indeed, in this odd mood, I was even feeling charitable toward Hans, who was peering ahead through the windshield, his jaw muscle working furiously. Maybe he wasn't so bad after all. He only wanted the same thing we all did; and if he was intent on doing things his own way, well, which of us didn't have ego invested in this project?

We arrived in San Fernando a little past 7:15. Swinging onto Garibaldi Street, we eased to a stop twenty yards before the house. Ahead, on the shoulder of the highway, we could make out the Chrysler, its headlights dark.

The street was deserted. There was still no rain, but the wind had picked up and every minute or two there was a flash of lightning. I got out, stretched my legs. The lightning was worrisome; in my dark clothes, only partially obscured by bushes and trees, I might be visible from the house.

Within just a couple of minutes, the bolts were coming more frequently, and the thunder was far louder, but still it was dry. Indeed, everything had taken on an almost surreal quality, like a scene from a biblical epic by Cecil B. De Mille.

I walked back forty paces, measuring the distance to the spot where I intended to meet him. Then I waited. Buffeted by the wind, I tried to stay warm. Ten minutes went by. Fifteen. Twenty.

I wandered back to the car. The windows were so foggy it was impossible to see inside. I tapped lightly on the front window. Uzi's head popped up. A lightning bolt flashed, eerily illuminating his face.

"It's getting late. What do we do?" I asked.

"Maybe we missed him." It was Hans answering. "Maybe he came earlier."

I shook my head. "No. He's not there yet. You can tell from the light in the house."

To my surprise, he accepted this without argument.

"We stay," decided Uzi. "I don't want to have to do this again. Give him fifteen more minutes."

For the time being, I stayed by the car. If someone came by, I would pretend to be helping out with the engine.

Just then, off to the left, heading north on 202 from Buenos Aires, at once familiar and startling, the 203 bus came into view.

Literally at that instant, a young man turned up Garibaldi Street on a bicycle, his overcoat whipping behind him like a cape. Spotting us, he yelled a friendly something in Spanish and started peddling our way.

Leave us the hell alone, the words rang out within. *Get away, you goddamn Good Samaritan.*

Smiling at his approach, Meir simply shook his head and slammed down the hood, giving it an affectionate pat for good measure.

Waving, the guy passed by and continued around the corner. Instantly Meir reopened the hood.

I began to retreat, measuring out the steps. Fifteen. Twenty. Thirty.

The bus was at the stop now. I froze, watching, the wind in my face. When it pulled away, there, framed in silhouette by the oncoming headlights, stood Attila. Beside him was a stocky woman. For several agonizing seconds, as they crossed the highway, it appeared they were together. But on the other side, she veered off to the left, and he went to the right.

As he turned onto Garibaldi, I began my leisurely stroll toward him. There was still no rain, but the lightning was flashing, the thunder boomed.

It was Judgment Day.

I had made up my mind minutes before: If he darted into the field I would go after him. But, burrowed within his coat, his collar upturned, hands in his pockets, leaning into the wind, he continued steadily toward me.

I was passing the car now. He was no more than twenty yards away. "Watch his hands!" hissed Hans suddenly from within. "I think he has a gun."

"Oh, God," I wanted to shout at him, "*don't talk to me. Not now!*"

But the words stayed with me. He could be right. I would have to take that into account and go for the right hand.

We were fifteen yards apart. I could hear his footfalls, regular as ticks on a clock. Would he pause at the sight of the car? No. He didn't even hesitate. Twenty-five feet between us. Fifteen.

"*Un momentito, senõr.*" The simple sentence I had been practicing for weeks.

He stopped. Behind black-rimmed glasses, his eyes met

mine. He took a step backward. I leapt at him, grabbing for his right hand.

We fell hard to the ground and tumbled into the shallow ditch alongside the walkway. I was on my back in a couple of inches of mud, holding him with all my strength, one hand around his throat, the other restraining his right hand. He was making gurgling noises. As I struggled to my feet, hoisting him with me, I eased the pressure on his throat.

Suddenly, shockingly, he let out a piercing scream. It was the primal cry of a cornered animal.

Tightening my grip, I abruptly cut it off.

Momentarily shaken, I quickly recovered. *It will do you no good, you bastard,* I told myself as I dragged him toward the car. *This is the end for you!* Suddenly Meir appeared. He lifted the prisoner's feet, and I kept hold of his shoulders and head. We were at the car. The back door swung open and we stuffed him inside.

I slid in after, still holding fast, my hand hard over his mouth. Meir ran around to the front passenger seat. Hans shifted the car into gear. As we lurched forward, we gagged him and covered his eyes with the goggles. Meir produced a blanket from the front, and we threw it over Attila. Fully covered now, he lay absolutely still on the back floor.

"*Ein Laut und du bist tot,*" spoke up Hans. (One sound and you are dead!)

My hand still covering his mouth beneath the blanket, Klement nodded in assent.

Following orders, we drove in silence. Suddenly I was exhausted. Now that we had actually done it, more than anything else I felt profound relief, freedom from a crushing weight.

It was several minutes before I was aware that we were alone. The Chrysler was nowhere in sight. Evidently Hans became aware of it at almost the same moment.

"Where are they?" he suddenly spoke up in English.

"Where do you think?" I hissed. "Still on 202!"

But this was hardly the time for recriminations. We

were all too aware of being unprotected and of the possibility of roadblocks.

Agonizing minutes later we spotted the Chrysler's distinctive headlights moving up on us from behind. Slowing to allow Aharon to pull alongside, we offered relieved smiles and vigorous thumbs-up signs, wiping the obvious concern from our colleagues' faces. Moments later they had assumed their assigned place, a hundred or so yards ahead of us.

Now, at long last, I removed my gloved hand from the man's mouth. It was soaked through with his spittle. I stared down at the bony figure beneath the blanket. *Could this really be the monster responsible for such horror? Could HE have evoked such dread?*

Fifteen minutes later the two cars pulled into the courtyard of the villa.

"Did you do it?" cried David, breathless, slamming the gate behind us and rushing to the Mercedes. He peered within. "You did it!"

I stepped out and he grabbed me in a bear hug, covering my face with kisses.

"Stop it, will you?" I said, wiping my face with my sleeve.

Now Aharon, Jack, and the doctor joined us, vastly relieved, explaining at the same time that not only had they been unable to see the capture but our car pulling away as well. But they fell silent as they watched Uzi remove the prisoner from the car and tie a blindfold over his eyes. Wordlessly, one by one, they clapped me on the shoulder.

Trailed by Hans, Uzi and I led Attila to his room. Shutting the door behind us, we studied the prisoner for the first time. He stood in the center of the room, still in his overcoat, his eyes obscured by the goggles. He was utterly rigid, except for hands that kept opening and closing spasmodically. The man was terrified.

Months before, Fritz Bauer had forwarded to Tel Aviv a list of Eichmann's identifying characteristics obtained from the SS files. Hans, whose primary responsibility as interrogator was to make a positive identification, knew it by heart.

- A scar of three centimeters beneath left brow
- Two gold bridges in upper jaw
- A scar of one centimeter on left tenth rib
- Tattoo under left armpit listing blood type
- Height: 5'8½"–5'10"
- Weight: 154 lbs. (in 1934)
- Circumference of head: 22"
- Hair: Dark blond
- Eyes: Blue-gray
- Shape of head: Elongated and narrow
- Shoe size: 8½
- SS nos.: 45326 and 63752
- Nazi party membership no.: 889895.

At Hans's direction we lay him down on the bed, still fully clothed.

"Was ist dein Name?" demanded Hans sharply, a master addressing a disobedient dog. (What is your name?)

"Ich bin Ricardo Klement," came the trembling reply. His voice was weak and very raspy.

"Was ist dein Name?!"

"Ich bin Ricardo Klement."

Four times the question was asked and the answer repeated.

"Take off his coat and shirt," snapped Hans in English finally, with sharp contempt.

I could see why he was known around headquarters as "the Spanish Inquisitor." To a man in the prisoner's position, the tone must have been extraordinarily menacing, indeed, harrowingly familiar.

As we pulled the prisoner to his feet, it suddenly struck me: He's not wearing his glasses. My God! What happened to his glasses?

I didn't say a word. What was I going to do, tell Hans I had lost his glasses?

We removed the coat, his jacket, white shirt, tie, and shoes. He stood before us in trousers and socks, his hands still working. At Hans's direction I lifted his left arm. Where the tattoo with his blood type should have been was a small scar. Something had been removed.

The scar on the chest was just where it should have been.

Silently we began to take his measurements. His height, the circumference of his head. His shoe size. All three of us buzzed around him with measuring tapes like so many tailors fitting a gentleman for a fine suit.

Everything matched perfectly except the dental information. The man before us wore dentures.

"*Was ist dein Name?*" demanded Hans again.

"Otto Heninger," he said now. It was the one he had used all those years before, as a forest ranger.

We looked at each other. It meant nothing to us.

"Your SS number," spoke up Hans sharply, "was 45526."

There was a pause. "No," he corrected, "45326."

"Good. Now—*Was ist dein Name?*"

"*Ich bin Adolf Eichmann.*"

NINETEEN

The Ideal
Prisoner

SSER had been sitting alone in a hotel room all evening, waiting. Now Aharon quietly left the room to deliver the news.

Dr. Klein was called in for a preliminary physical. He checked Eichmann's blood pressure and pulse. Both were higher than normal, but under the circumstances not alarmingly so. Then he probed his mouth and ears and hit him with that little metal hammer.

Meanwhile I silently searched his clothes. He had been carrying no papers and very little else. The only object of any significance was in the pocket which Hans had been so alarmed to see him reach into. It held a small flashlight.

I had been somewhat concerned that his body might give out under the stress. So was Uzi.

"Don't worry," reassured the doctor in English, "he's strong as a horse."

Eichmann, expressionless, spoke not a word throughout, standing or sitting as he was told.

It now fell to me to finish undressing him and prepare him for bed. When the others left I washed his face, secured the blindfold, and fixed the goggles in place above it. After refusing the use of the toilet with a shake of his head, he allowed me to help him into pajamas and obediently assumed his place on the bed. His only reaction was a faint start when I snapped a metal cuff on his ankle; he seemed to have expected it. The light in his room continued to shine brightly. Our orders were that it was never to be turned off.

Throughout I was intensely preoccupied. When a few minutes later Meir appeared to take up guard duty, I quickly made my way out to the courtyard for a thorough search of the Mercedes. The glasses weren't there.

The thought was more insistent than ever: *What if the family finds them in that ditch?*

With a rising sense of panic I knocked on Uzi's door and poured it all out. "I'm going back," I told him.

He thought it over briefly, calm as ever. "I'm not sure you should."

"Listen, let me take care of it. You know I won't do anything dangerous."

I returned to San Fernando alone on the 203 bus and walked up Garibaldi Street. It was close to midnight now and freezing cold. All was silent. With a tiny flashlight I found the spot where we had grappled in the mud. After several minutes of searching I found a few pieces of broken glass but no frames. Nor was there anything to be found along the path we had taken to the car.

Enough, I decided finally. There was nothing more to be done. Slowly I began retreating toward Route 202.

To this day, I have no idea what became of those glasses.

As I made my way in the direction of the bus stop, I glanced one last time over my shoulder. The light was on in the house. They were still waiting.

* * *

I was back in Eichmann's room very early the following morning, sitting on the stool at the foot of the bed. He was awake. Indeed, he had slept only briefly. Nor, since his arrival, had he accepted anything to eat.

We did not speak—strict orders had been issued in that regard also—but I could not take my eyes off that blindfolded face. It was impossible to imagine anyone less at peace. His expression kept changing, his lips, jaw, brow continually working, apparently beyond his control. Fear seemed to give way to defiance, then to rage, and then, just as quickly, melt into helpless submission. Every so often he would shudder spasmodically, his leg jerking, rattling the chain.

Somewhat rested, more my old self than I'd been since my arrival in Argentina, I was seized by powerful feelings of deep loathing and contempt. I had expected more of this most honored representative of the master race. At the very least I thought there would be bearing, dignity, pride. Stripped of power, Eichmann seemed a classic weakling, lacking the character even to accept his fate.

But, oddly, for the same reason, he engaged my curiosity far more than I expected. After all, Adolf Eichmann was a human being, someone who walked and talked and breathed exactly as I did. After seeing him with his child, I even thought it likely he felt some of the things I did.

For years the question had plagued me, a challenge to my very worldview: How had it happened? How had supposedly civilized people descended to such depths of barbarism?

The great frustration, of course, was that I couldn't speak.

Shortly before dawn I was relieved by Uzi. Returning to my room, I got in a few more hours of sleep before abruptly sitting up, wide awake again. Hans was due this morning to begin formal interrogation of the prisoner. This I did not want to miss.

For the first time, Eichmann's blindfold was removed. To our surprise he kept his eyes tightly closed until Hans ordered him to open them. Then he squinted, lids fluttering as he adjusted to the light, and looked quickly at each of us in turn. I noticed that he avoided our eyes. He was calmer now. It flashed through my mind that on some level he, too, was relieved it was finally over.

"*Jetzt habe ich ein paar einfache Fragen,*" began Hans. (I just have a few simple questions for you.) "Answer them for me, and we won't have any problems." Obviously in his element, confident to the point of arrogance, Hans's customarily flat voice had taken on a hard edge.

Eichmann nodded quickly. "*Jawohl, mein Herr.*"

"First, we're interested in finding out where Mengele lives. Can you tell us?"

Clearly the Old Man was calling the shots here.

He shook his head. "*Nein, ich weisse nicht.*" (No, I don't know about that.)

"I suppose you don't even know if he's in Argentina?"

"I don't know," came the immediate response.

"And Martin Bormann? Do you know anything about his whereabouts?"

"No. I have no idea."

"But wasn't it your friends who helped you with false papers and to reach Argentina?"

He hesitated. "That was a long time ago."

"Would you like something to drink?" A nice change of pace.

"No," he replied quickly.

"Do you want us to help your family?"

For a long time he made no response. He gnawed on his lower lip. "Have you done anything to them?"

"They're fine." He paused. "Let's talk about your wife. We'll get back to the matter of your SS comrades later. What do you think she's done about your not having returned?"

"Nothing. She's frightened. She doesn't understand."

"What about your sons Nicolas and Dieter?"

"They will know something has happened. Perhaps an accident. They'll check where I work, with the driver of my bus, maybe at the hospitals."

"Will they go to the police?"

"I don't know. I don't think so."

"What is your connection with the parties of the Right here in Argentina?"

"*Wir sind Deutsche. Wir verkehren mit Deutschen.*" (We are Germans. We keep company with Germans.)

"Do you know who we are?"

There was a long silence.

"Do you know who we are?" he asked again.

"You are Israelis. I knew immediately."

For most of us in the villa the questions about the reaction of the Eichmann family to the disappearance were more significant at this point than those about Mengele. Had the authorities been alerted? Even if they hadn't been, would Eichmann's friends—and we had no doubt that there were many—risk a move on his behalf? That was key to what would happen next. Or, as we hoped, fail to happen.

In our small group there were two schools of thought. On the one hand, the theory was advanced hopefully that Eichmann's very notoriety might place him beyond help. After all, the most fervent desire of many of those who might otherwise want to aid him was to avoid attracting attention to themselves, and any rescue attempt would make headlines worldwide.

However, others in our party were convinced that we could be attacked at any time. Especially Uzi. As a precaution he had a sentry posted by the entrance at all times. More than once in the course of that first week, shaken by some premonition, he roused me in the middle of the night to help him patrol the perimeter.

We were, in brief, totally isolated, and so even more

subject than usual in undercover situations to wild speculation and outright paranoia. Living behind blackout curtains in our sprawling, out-of-season villa, the mind played
tricks. Who was out there hunting for us? Were they getting
closer? How in hell were we ever going to get out?

Above all, it was the sense of powerlessness, the in-
ability to take constructive action, that was so unsettling.

Our only contact with the world outside was a portable
radio. Though only Jack could understand Spanish, we all
spent a large part of the day waiting for the news reports
sandwiched between the soap operas and the salsa music,
listening intently for the word "Eichmann." But there was
nothing. The news, so we were led to understand, was dominated by the impending national celebrations and mounting local labor unrest. Occasionally there was a report on
the American presidential primaries, where someone named
John F. Kennedy was doing surprisingly well.

Not that lack of news about Eichmann necessarily
meant anything, of course. Even the most naively optimistic
among us realized that, had his disappearance been reported
to the government, the subsequent investigation would
likely be conducted in extreme secrecy, regarded as a matter
of state security. For highly placed Argentines, the affair
stood as a potential double embarrassment of incalculable
proportions. They had not only sheltered the world's leading
Nazi fugitive for more than a decade, they had now permitted foreign agents to snatch him from under their noses.

Repeatedly we hashed over the various options: boat or
plane, a train or some manner of truck or car to a neigh-
boring country, and then taking it from there. There seemed
to be problems with each. Not that it would be our decision
anyway. We could only hope that Isser's vaunted plan was
for real and that it was proceeding without hitch.

The assorted uncertainties hardly made the hours pass
any more quickly in the villa. Endlessly leafing through my
guidebook, reading for the third time descriptions of mu-

seums and public monuments I would never have the chance to see, I took to making notations in the margins about which sites might provide refuge in case of trouble. I starred certain churches, circled the synagogues. I underlined the address of the American embassy in red, the same with the Canadian embassy. The British embassy I passed right by. If they got the chance, they would find some way to screw us.

The fact of being caged under the same roof with a man whom we all despised—indeed, whom several among us would have loved to kill with their bare hands—contributed immeasurably to the low morale. Meir, serving as one of his guards, made so many unfunny jokes in those first days that badly masked genuine feelings that I finally felt compelled to set him straight in the same spirit. "That's fine. Isser will see to it that there's a show trial in Jerusalem anyway. Yours." Others, though somewhat more subtle, were no less obviously depressed.

Spirits rose with word of the impending arrival of the next and final member of our party: the female agent, designated by Isser to act as David's wife. We all knew from experience how dramatically the right woman could alter the chemistry on a team and make even the most tedious operation suddenly more livable.

Which is why we were so taken aback, late that day, to find the new operative at the door: Rosa.

"This must be the Old Man's idea of a joke," muttered Uzi under his breath, pulling off the tie he had been wearing since learning she was due.

It was not merely that Rosa was hardly the most attractive of Israel's agents. In fact, with brown eyes made enormous by thick lenses and a somewhat awkward physical manner, she was a distaff version of Uzi himself. The problem was *who* she was. Extremely religious—she even wore a white *tichel*, or kerchief, around her head in the Orthodox style—and known for an air of moral rectitude, Rosa was sometimes impossible to take even in normal times. Most of her family had been wiped out in Europe. This was hardly someone whose presence was going to make the atmosphere in the villa any less oppressive.

When she stepped into the living room she was flushed with excitement. Having been ordered to Argentina just days before, she had not learned the purpose of the mission until her arrival in Buenos Aires.

"Peter," she gushed, running over to me, "I know everything. It's so wonderful. I'm so grateful for the chance to help."

Yet, to no one's surprise, within a day she was as grim as anyone on the premises. Indeed, after one brief visit to the room to stare at the once-powerful *Obersturmführer*, she made it clear she was sorry she had gotten involved. "The thought of cooking or washing up for him makes me sick to my stomach. I shudder even to think of touching anything that he's touched."

Bad as things were for us, Eichmann's emotional state was an ever greater source of concern, at least for me. Responsible for helping to meet the prisoner's basic needs, I became more and more worried that he might not make it through the ordeal of captivity.

His sessions with Hans, in particular, seemed to send his anxiety level soaring. Little wonder. Hans's style, his clipped, precise German, his obvious impatience with much of what he heard, his none-too-subtle air of menace, must have given Eichmann a powerful sense of déjà vu.

This is not to suggest the technique was ineffective. Eichmann was as cooperative as could be expected, answering all questions put to him with great diffidence, taking to his role as helpless victim as naturally as Hans assumed that of high-handed inquisitor.

But in the most essential areas—the whereabouts of other Nazis, his willingness to discuss his own crimes openly—the bullying might well have been counterproductive. The prisoner knew as well as anyone what tended to happen to the subject of such interviews after his questioner was done with him.

Toward the close of their first prolonged session, Eichmann asked, the first of many times, whether we were going to kill him, and quite obviously, he did not buy Hans's insistent reassurances to the contrary. I wouldn't have either.

For a full day afterward, lying chained to his bed, the left side of his face twitching, he continued not only to refuse food and drink but even use of the toilet. Aside from considerations of his well-being, there was a clear danger of subtle loss of control. We could not let the prisoner dictate the terms of his imprisonment.

At the start of my first three-hour shift that day, I once again sat quietly on my stool, watching. But then I went across the hall to my room and got some oil-based sketch pencils from my makeup kit. Back in his room, I began drawing him on the only paper I had handy, the pages of my guidebook.

The first sketch, in brown on a page bearing a map of Argentina, was of his face. Working quickly, I concentrated on the thin mouth and sunken cheeks, filling in the blindfolded eyes from memory. Then I flipped the page and did him in his SS regalia. Alert to the sound of someone approaching (surely this was in violation of regulations), I continued drawing in a kind of frenzy. Now I had him watching a railroad train, counting the cars; now in abstract, lying prone atop a flatcar, bearing a machine gun; now, on facing pages, appeared Hitler and Mussolini; now my parents and, in muted pastels, her eyes immense and brooding, my sister Fruma. By the time Uzi relieved me at dusk, I had filled a dozen pages. As always, the lights were on in the room. But, for the first time since his capture, Eichmann seemed to be sleeping peacefully.

The following morning I decided to try a new tack. Carrying in his breakfast of orange juice, a hard-boiled egg, and crackers on a tray, I *ordered* him to eat. I placed the

mug of juice in his hand. Instantly he complied. Then he
wordlessly allowed me to spoon-feed him the egg and place
the crackers, one by one, between his lips.

I gave him a shave next and, putting on his bathrobe
and slippers, led him, still blindfolded, out to the veranda.

"Now," I commanded, "it is time for your exercises.
You are going to do deep knee bends. Do you understand?"

"*Jawohl.*"

"*'Rauf. 'Runter. 'Rauf. 'Runter.*" (Up, down. Up,
down.)

At first he seemed hesitant, perhaps even self-con-
scious, since his pajama pants kept slipping down. But after
a minute or so, he was going about it with real enthusiasm.
Indeed, suddenly he joined me in the count. "*Unten, oben.
Unten, oben.*" Now Uzi appeared at the veranda, smiling
broadly.

I ordered Eichmann to stop. He did so instantly. "Now,"
I said, "I want you to use the toilet."

He nodded crisply. "*Jawohl, mein Herr. Danke schön.*"

Leading him to the toilet, perhaps twenty feet away, I
pulled down his pajama bottoms and helped him to sit
down. I left the door ajar and walked a few feet away.

A minute passed. Then another.

"*Darf Ich anfangen?*" called Eichmann. (May I begin?)

I caught Uzi's eye and had to make a physical effort to
keep from breaking up.

"*Jawohl!*" I commanded. "*Sie können anfangen!*" (Begin!)

The man's system must have been in desperate straits.
There followed a collection of bathroom noises that defied
imagination. And after every fart and protracted gurgle,
every grunt and torturous wheeze, he would say he was
sorry, the apologies growing ever louder to match the noises,
until he sounded as if he were addressing a full battalion.

"*Entschuldigen Sie.*" (Excuse me.)

Watching it unfold—fart, "*Entschuldigen Sie*"; fart,
"*Entschuldigen Sie*"; fart, "*Entschuldigen Sie*"—Uzi and I

could restrain ourselves no longer. My friend, doubled over, the tears streaming down his face, staggered backward into the living room. I, trying to be discreet if I could not be polite, actually gnawed a gash in my lower lip in a failed effort to keep from exploding in laughter.

But if Eichmann was aware of it, if he even understood that anyone might have reason to find the scene amusing, he never let on. For another ten minutes he continued, until he at last announced he was finished and requested permission to wipe.

That night, while the rest of the house slept, I once again sat silently on my stool, sketching in my guidebook.

Suddenly, out of the blue, he addressed me.

"*Sind Sie der Mann der mich gefangen nahm?*" (Are you the man who captured me?)

I hesitated a long moment. "Yes. How did you know?"

"I recognized your voice."

Un momentito, señor.

What was I going to do, refuse to answer? What difference did it make anyway? Indeed, I was secretly grateful he had created the opening.

Regulations or no regulations, it was something I *had* to do.

"Yes," I answered, "I'm the one. My name is Maxim."

It was the one on my passport. Though Eichmann had his name back, I was far from reclaiming mine.

TWENTY

Eichmann in My Hands

ONCE we got started, it didn't take long to get down to the very heart of the matter.

"How did it happen?" I asked. "How did you come to do what you did?"

Eichmann didn't seem taken aback in the least. "*Es war den Auftrag den ich hatte,*" he said evenly. "*Ich hatte den Auftrag zu erfüllen.*" (It was a job I had. I had a job to do.)

"Just a *job?*"

He hestitated, perhaps surprised by the vehemence of the reaction. "You must believe me, it wasn't something I planned, nor anything I'd have chosen."

"But why you? Tell me exactly how it happened."

So he went on to relate the story of his early rise within the SS, describing how at first he was assigned deadly boring clerical tasks, and so leapt at the chance for a position at the new "Jewish Museum" being set up at headquarters.

It did not take long to see that Eichmann loved talking,

particularly about himself, and that he had a sharp mind. Though his tone was respectful, sometimes frankly obsequious, the obedient child eager to please, he was also canny. He knew exactly what he was doing. Here I was, likely the first soul he had ever encountered—certainly the first Jew—to whom he felt obliged to defend himself, yet he was going about it with cool aplomb. Apparently straightforward, yet subtly shading things to his advantage, he distanced himself from real responsibility, even as he confirmed the record in every particular.

Yes, he acknowledged, matters had gotten out of control. But that hadn't been the intention at the beginning, not his immediate superiors' and certainly not his. Working from within, he had always argued for moderation. But he was a soldier—in this he took enormous pride—and a soldier is never entirely his own man. When decisions were made by those above, and orders issued, they had to be obeyed. This was duty. For him, *this* was a matter of moral responsibility.

Listening, it was not quite so easy as I had supposed it would be to frame cogent replies. I had imagined he would be defensive, that he would express at least token remorse. Instead he talked as if he had spent those years working as a grocery clerk.

As he put it, "I thought to myself 'Why not?' I'd have done anything to get away from those files."

When he finished I made no reply.

"You must believe me," he added suddenly. "I had nothing against the Jews."

"Then what were you doing in the SS in the first place? The ideology was not exactly a secret."

"But it wasn't only me. Everyone knew a change was necessary in Germany; it was only a question of what form it would take. Times were terrible. I had a job myself, selling gasoline products in Upper Austria, and for me things were not so bad. It was one of the most beautiful places on earth. I was moved and inspired every day by its glorious mountain forests. But a man does not live only for himself. Hitler was the only one who could rally the people against the Communists. He brought hope of jobs and bread. I freely admit it; I was inspired as much as anyone."

We conversed with surprising ease. If we had met, say, as seat mates on a long plane ride, we'd certainly have found enough in common—a shared love of nature and the wild, a common appreciation of certain kinds of music, a similar interest in world events—to make the trip pass more quickly. Both of us were social by nature and gave every appearance of accessibility.

Already, though, I was seeing in him qualities that I would have found oppressive even in an ordinary man: an utter lack of humor and an even more striking inflexibility of mind. Indeed, as time went on, it would become more and more apparent that not only was the man incapable of viewing the world from any perspective but his own, but he was impatient with the notion that any reasonable soul should expect him to do so.

But there was something else. Though I did not yet have access to the complete record of his duplicities (the tapes he had made with Sassen had yet to come to light and witnesses at his trial would further confirm his extraordinary talent for deception), I sensed he was being less than entirely straightforward. That, indeed, the very appearance of candor—his seeming vulnerability, the strategic admissions of error, even his refusal to back away from what he regarded as principle—might be aspects of a calculated self-presentation for my benefit. This was, after all, a man who had risen to immense power on the underestimation of others.

"As time passed," I asked now, "did your opinion of the Führer change? What did you think of him?"

"*Der Führer war unfehlbar*," he answered instantly. (The Führer was infallible.) "My oath as an SS officer was to Adolf Hitler personally. And I was not released from that oath until May 1945."

"You both came from Austria," I observed. "In fact, I understand you attended the same high school."

He allowed himself a small smile. "*Ja.* That is true."

"You even shared the same first name."

"*Ja.*" He paused. "But he was the leader of the Reich. I was only a functionary."

"Tell me, did you come from a political family? Tell me about your father."

He shook his head. "He was a very strong personality, my father. But his energies went toward religion."

"And you?"

I had meant the question to be about the strength of his own religious conviction (later I would learn it was limited), but he took it entirely otherwise. "I was a good son. It was not my place to question him." He went on to note that for a time he worked for his father in a mining enterprise. "I was treated no better or worse than the others."

"Did that bother you?" I asked.

Momentarily he seemed genuinely baffled by this. "I was a young man. I was accustomed to being led."

In the years after, I would more than occasionally think back on that response. And, by extension, to the larger question of what it is that molds an individual's sense of moral responsibility. Why is it that one person comes of age profoundly humane while someone else, of the same culture and social background, is seemingly impervious to the needs of others?

The conclusion I reached, though hardly original, nonetheless still seems far too little appreciated. It has everything to do with how one is regarded as a child. Those who as children are valued and nurtured, loved without expectation and listened to and heard, are likely to become compassionate adults who think for themselves and make moral choices. Those many others around whom regimentation is the norm and unconventionality is taken as aberrant are quickly made to understand—by parents, by teachers, by almost everyone in their universe—that they are of worth only as part of the larger whole. As second nature they learn passivity and obedience, not conscience.

Such an insight would prove useful in my work, helping me understand those whose behavior sometimes seemed unfathomable. It would come in even handier later, in my own life, when I became a father.

The first soul in whom I confided about my new relationship with Eichmann, oddly enough, was Rosa.

Then, again, it wasn't so strange at all. She was my roommate, assigned the other single bed in my room. Though at first I chafed at the arrangement, a consequence of the room's proximity to the kitchen (as the only woman on the premises, Rosa had assigned herself the task of keeping us all fed), in the intensity of the atmosphere an odd thing happened: I almost immediately discovered in her a warmth and gentle humor that I had never noticed in years of casual acquaintance. I even began to find her attractive.

It was late at night, two days after that first conversation with Eichmann, and neither of us could sleep. We were talking softly, in our beds, when I let it slip.

I didn't have to see her face to know I had made a mistake. She was horrified.

"You *talk* to him? You're becoming his *friend*? What's wrong with you!"

"Look, it's not that. How often does a person have an opportunity like this?"

"It's against regulations. Peter, how can you do this?"

"So, it's against regulations. I can't help that."

"But it doesn't make sense. What do you have to talk with him about?" She paused. "This is criminal. I should report you!"

I was starting to get irritated. "You want to report me? Go ahead! What makes sense? Does it make sense that you keep kosher for Adolf Eichmann?" I stopped. "You know, you really shouldn't be so hard on him. He's the only one around here who never complains about the food."

There was a long silence. I listened to her breathing.

"Tell me," she said finally, "what's he like?"

"Are you really interested?"

"I asked you, didn't I?"

I told her I was very much confused on the subject myself. He was a paradox, apparently reasonable one moment, a man capable of normal give-and-take, yet a stone wall the next. He was pitiless, seemingly unaware anything wrong had been done at all, certainly taking no responsibility for it. I had never been through anything more frustrating, more infuriating . . .

"How can you even do it?" she interrupted. "Such a monster!"

"Look, it's all in the hands of God anyway."

"Don't you dare link Eichmann and God! You disgust me!"

"If God hadn't allowed it, it wouldn't have happened."

I did not say this just to irritate her, nor even only to win the point. I also more or less believed it. The Holocaust had much to do with why I, like so many others, had moved away from religion.

"But you do believe in God, then," she observed. "You believe He exists."

"When I'm in a jam, I believe. But if He does exist, He has a logic all his own. Haven't you ever questioned how He could let it happen?"

"God is not like us, flesh and blood. You can't relate to Him that way. He was testing us as a people, as He tested Abraham and Job."

For a long time I said nothing. "Let me ask you a question," I said at last. "What are you doing in the Mossad?"

"It isn't difficult. At the beginning I went to my rabbi and asked him about the work. He gave me a release. He said, 'Whatever is done out of love can only cause pleasure.' "

"Would you eat pork if the assignment demanded it?" I asked.

"No. Of course not. Jews have been burned alive rather than eat the flesh of a pig."

"Would you sleep with a strange man?"

There was another silence. "I don't know. It would depend . . ."

"You *would*?"

She laughed. "I don't recall that any Jew was ever burned at the stake for that." Then I heard her roll over heavily in bed, signaling an end to the discussion. "Good night, Peter."

It was no exaggeration about Rosa's cooking. The woman was more inept in the kitchen than anyone I had ever encountered. She couldn't even fry an egg. When she tried, she would emerge from the kitchen bearing a plate with a large yellow stain. Yet, because of her adherence to Orthodox dietary rules, she refused to hear of anyone taking her place, even for one meal.

Boredom and paranoia, an awful mix to start with, are only heightened by this sort of thing. Even Isser was aware that morale in the safe house was becoming a serious problem. Four days into Eichmann's internment, he decreed that we would be allowed time away from the villa, singly and in pairs.

Anointed first to leave, I was absolutely delighted. Except, like a convict suddenly sprung from a life sentence, I had no idea what to do with the freedom. Where to go? Should I visit one of the sights I had read about twelve times in my guidebook? See the famous harbor? Go to a movie?

Thinking it through, carefully weighing priorities, I ended up at a restaurant downtown. In English I ordered their most expensive steak. Still, when the waiter brought it, I was sure a mistake had been made. "I'm sorry," I said, pointing to the enormous slab of meat before me, "I ordered for one person."

He nodded and smiled. "*Sí, sí.*" Then, in English, "Eat."

Departing an hour later, two thirds of a cow still on my plate, I headed for Danny's place. As ever, he was hard at work on a set of documents in the name of Zichroni. The alias had been designated for Eichmann for the trip back to Israel.

In addition to the standard forms—passport, visa, health certificates, driver's license and the rest—Zichroni needed a documented medical history. Whether he would eventually be spirited onto the El Al flight or, as was being considered as an alternative, smuggled out of the country in an ambulance, he would have to be temporarily incapacitated. Reasons would be needed. Indeed, at that moment, one of our agents lay in a local hospital, with symptoms for what, after coaching from Dr. Klein, passed for a mild concussion suffered in a car accident. The man had been admitted under the name Zichroni. Danny would make the appropriate adjustments for age, height, and weight on the discharge papers. In the event of a call to the hospital later from a suspicious authority, the doctors, in all innocence, would confirm everything.

I could never get enough of watching Danny work. Once I had seen him produce freehand a near-perfect replica of a birth certificate on a moving bus. In a situation like this, stooped over his worktable, his pen in one hand, a magnifying glass in the other, with time to labor over the tiniest detail, his work was nothing short of genius, utterly impossible to distinguish from the real thing. The man could even reproduce lengthy documents and complex seals in languages like Arabic, Japanese, and Urdu, which employed alphabets with which he was totally unfamiliar.

Danny clearly welcomed the intrusion. If the rest of us had been too long marooned with one another, he had been passing his days entirely by himself, alone with thoughts which, evidently, had been eating at him ceaselessly.

After a few minutes of small talk, it began to come out.

"Why couldn't I have taken part in the capture?" he put it to me. "My only function is to sit scribbling."

"Danny," I said softly, amazed that the obvious had to be stated, "without you this whole operation would have been impossible. Of all of us, you're the only one who is irreplaceable."

He shook his head. "I've got a score to settle, that's why I came. I want to face him. I want to tell him what I think of him!"

"Don't you know what you're doing here? You're making it possible to get him out of the country. You're sitting here writing his death sentence."

"I know, Peter. I do. Thank you. It's just . . ." Suddenly he was crying. Taking off his glasses, he buried his head in his arms upon the table. For a full thirty seconds, as I stood awkwardly by, his body was racked by sobs.

"Please, Danny," I said, laying a hand on his bony shoulder, "Danny, forgive me. But if you've got to cry, could you please not do it on the documents."

Looking up with wet, red eyes, he broke into a smile.

"Don't worry, I had them covered with my arms. I'm the one who'd have to redo them."

At the beginning Hans had come by every afternoon for the interrogation sessions. Each lasted an hour or so. Having elicited the background information, he was basically after two things: anything he could get on the whereabouts of other war criminals, notably Mengele, and persuading Eichmann to sign a document prepared by Isser saying that he was going to Jerusalem willingly, of his own accord.

He made little headway. In the meek and correct tone from which he never deviated with Hans, German prisoner to German jailer, Eichmann was unmovable on both counts.

He promised, swore, that he knew nothing about anyone else. He had been alone all those years in Argentina, left to fend for himself. As for signing the document, Eichmann was terrified by the very sound of the word "Jerusalem." He was willing to stand trial in Argentina, he offered, or even better, in Germany. But what chance would he possibly have in Israel?

Eventually, after four or five days, Hans tired of asking the questions. His visits to the villa became infrequent, the sessions almost perfunctory.

My own conversations with Eichmann, meanwhile, had become an almost nightly routine, one that, although increasingly trying for me, he soon came to anticipate as his only chance for comparatively normal discourse. Since we were now removing his blindfold at mealtimes, and when he used the toilet (Eichmann always kept his unbound eyes tightly closed until someone remembered to give him the order to open them), it struck me as pointless that he should have to wear it with me.

In brief, we found ourselves co-conspirators of a sort. He knew as well as I did to fall silent at the sound of approaching footsteps.

What Eichmann enjoyed talking about most was his children. His greatest fear, the one that periodically reduced him to paroxysms of anguish and desperation, was that we might do something to them. He simply could not bring himself to believe our repeated reassurances, finding it beyond comprehension that anyone with the power to take such an action would not use it.

He had particularly strong feelings for his little boy, the only one of his sons whose childhood years he had been around to share, and whose presence had clearly made his exile infinitely easier to bear.

"*Ich liebe Kinder,*" he put it to me one night early on, smiling almost dreamily. (I love children.)

"*Sie lieben Kinder?*" I shot back, unable to help myself. "You must mean *some* children."

"*Nein, ich liebe alle Kinder.*" (I love all children.)

"Do you?" Once again, I found myself struggling for self-control in his presence.

"Look," he replied evenly, daring to broach the subject himself, "perhaps to you it seems as if I hate Jews. I don't. I was never an anti-Semite. I was always repulsed by Streicher and the *Sturmer* crowd."

The reference was to the most primitive racist ideologue at the top echelons of Nazism and his venomous magazine.

In fact, he continued, "*Ich war den Juden immer zugeneigt.*" (I have always been fond of Jews.) "I had Jewish friends. When I was touring Haifa, I made a point of finding Jewish taxi drivers. I always liked the Jews better than the Arabs."

I said nothing, just stared at him. He pressed on, apparently taking my silence as approval.

"Perhaps you won't believe it, but I read Theodore Herzl's book *Der Judenstaat* about the dream of a Jewish homeland. In connection with my work, I read a wide variety of Jewish newspapers and periodicals. I fully understood the aspirations of the Jews. I can't tell you how much I loved studying Zionism."

"What were you doing in Palestine anyway?" I cut in, shifting the subject.

"It was a study tour, to see the Jews in Palestine. It was necessary for my work." He paused. "Haifa. *Ach*, the view from Mt. Carmel is enchanting." He stopped again. "You must believe me, I was always an idealist. Had I been born Jewish, I'd have been the most fervent Zionist!"

"I was there then," I noted, "as a Polish refugee. Otherwise I wouldn't be here now."

He caught the tenor of the comment. "You must understand," he said, "it wasn't the same then as it is now. I was a soldier. Like you, I had orders to follow." He paused. "You know, I even studied Hebrew with a rabbi in Berlin. Unfortunately I have forgotten most of what I learned."

"Why? Most European Jews spoke Yiddish."

"Yes. But, you see, language is mentality. One cannot understand the problem of the Jewish people without understanding its original language." He stopped, smiling slightly. Something had occurred to him. "I do remember one prayer that the rabbi taught me." And tilting back his head, he began to intone: *"Shma Yisrael, adonai elohenu, adonai echad."*

The most sacred prayer of our people, the deathbed profession of faith of every pious Jew: "Hear, O Israel, the Lord our God, the Lord is One."

I felt myself beginning to shake with rage. "Eichmann, do you have any idea of the meaning of those words?"

"Ja," he replied genially, and proceeded to offer an accurate translation in German.

"Perhaps you're familiar with some other words," I said. *"Aba. Ima.* Do those ring a bell?"

"Aba, Ima," he mused, trying hard to recall. "I don't really remember. What do they mean?"

"Daddy, Mommy. It's what Jewish children scream when they're torn from their parents' arms." I paused, almost unable to contain myself. "My sister's boy, my favorite playmate, he was just your son's age. Also blond and blue-eyed, just like your son. And you killed him."

Genuinely perplexed by the observation, he actually waited a moment to see if I would clarify it. "Yes," he said finally, "but he was Jewish, wasn't he?"

TWENTY-ONE

The Mind of a Murderer

I knew that sooner or later I would have to tell Uzi, not only because he was my superior but, even more vitally, because he was my friend.

Once I had done it, I couldn't figure out why I had waited so long. Being Uzi, he wasn't upset about my transgression in the least. In fact, he conveyed the impression that as long as it didn't interfere with prospects of getting Eichmann back to Jerusalem, he wouldn't give a damn if I went out and got the prisoner a couple of hookers to brighten up his nights.

"So," he asked, puffing on one of the cigars he had purchased on a foray to the outside world, "what does he say?" Oddly, typically, in his other hand, he held a raw carrot. Just watching him go unselfconsciously from one to the other brightened my day.

"He says he likes the Jews."

Uzi's look of incredulity almost immediately turned to laughter. In a moment I was laughing, too.

"How could he say this?" he asked finally. "What does he say?"

I shrugged. "Haven't you ever heard of the love-hate complex?"

Still, there was no way to truly share the burden. Even with Uzi it was impossible to express what I was feeling, how, after each conversation with Eichmann, listening to him discuss what he had done without even the remotest sense of its horror, I was unable to sleep, my stomach in knots, my head about to explode.

I had dealt with criminals all of my adult life, including some whose crimes were shockingly brutal, Mafia hit men and terrorists who had calmly shot down small children. Yet always I had been able to find common human ground. But with Eichmann it just did not seem to be there. So often he seemed so reasonable that I would feel we were approaching a genuine basis of understanding. And then, abruptly, that impenetrable wall once again loomed between us.

What was I hoping to hear? Even I didn't know. Maybe a trace of real sorrow, a sense that he felt something about it beyond regret at getting caught. Perhaps something as simple as an admission that maybe the Führer wasn't infallible after all.

But, never, not once, did the man convey anything but the feeling that everything he had done was absolutely appropriate. Not nice necessarily, or even reasonable, but absolutely correct in context. There was a job to do and he did it.

"Aren't you a soldier?" he once again put it to me one night. "Don't you follow orders? Who told you to come here and get me? What's the difference?"

How does one even begin to tell someone who has to ask? "What we are doing isn't the same," I said. "The reasons we're doing it are different. We didn't come here to kill you. We came to bring you to justice."

He listened impassively, a barely perceptible smile

seeming to play on his lips. I felt a sudden rush of fury. "You never gave a chance to anyone. You never even offered your victims the respect of telling them the truth. My sister probably never even had a chance to say good-bye to her children."

That wiped away his smile. Whenever I showed even a little anger, he fell silent. Then, like a dog in abject terror, he showed me his neck.

For five minutes there was silence.

"*Werden Sie mich töten?*" he said finally, voice quaking.

"No, I'm not going to kill you. If I'd wanted to kill you, I could've shot you through the window of your home that night I watched you with your little boy."

He stiffened. "You're going to hurt the child!"

"I keep telling you, we've got nothing against your family. We just want you in Jerusalem." I paused. "Look, I understand how you feel. He looks like a lovely child." I paused. "I told you how much he reminds me of my sister's little boy."

Not that Eichmann made no effort at self-explanation. To the contrary, he argued his position—that he would have personally preferred to resettle Jews rather than eradicate them—as vigorously as I argued mine. "The idea," as he explained it to me one night, with undisguised pride, "was *judenrein*, a Jew-free Reich. Madagascar was discussed, as well as a number of other remote places. In fact, before the war, it was policy to encourage Jews to leave. But there was no country that would take them all." He paused. "I ask you, who was at fault, Germany or the rest of the world?"

There was, of course, more than a grain of truth to such an assertion, as I knew so well. Even many Jews who recognized what was coming long before the war had been unable to escape. But it was a delusion to equate the policies of other nations with those of the Third Reich.

More to the point, his explanations were studded with half-truths and outright fabrications. Either Eichmann was unaware that we had access to internal SS documents proving, for instance, that Madagascar was essentially a ploy to concentrate the victims for easy extermination later on and that Eichmann himself took a personal and very active role in designing the death machine, or he had actually come to believe his own rationales. To my mind this last was preferable. It at least offered the possibility of a conscience.

"Let me ask you this," I said. "When it was determined that the policy was not to be resettlement but death, how did you feel about it?"

"There was nothing to be done," he replied evenly. "The order came down from the Führer himself."

"But how did you *feel*."

"There was nothing to be done."

"I see. So you turned into a killer."

"No, that's not true. I never killed anyone. When I would have to visit those sites, I would always make a point of avoiding the worst of it." He paused. "Besides, I must remind you, we did it to our own people also. The first concentration camp"—I was struck by how casually the term fell from his lips—"was Dachau. Most of those inside were German."

"You freely admit you knew what was going on inside the camps."

"*Ja.* But that was not my field of competence. I was involved in collection and transport."

His answer, finally, was that there was no blame to be assessed, no responsibility to be assumed. What had happened was somehow inevitable, not the doing of men, but of circumstances.

Since I made no reply, he must have felt he was beginning to make his point, for he kept on in the same vein for a good while. I could read sharp disappointment on his face when I at last cut in.

"You do realize we are talking about innocent people here? Small children. Old men and women . . ."

For, indeed, that was the irony: He was as frustrated as

I was. Eichmann could not understand why I, as a fellow professional, seemed so reluctant to give him credit for having done his job so well.

More than once, it was as if he totally forgot to whom he was speaking. He would actually start boasting, describing how he sometimes had to take on the Wehrmacht to get the job done properly—they wanted to take his trains to move troops—and even, on occasion, find ways to circumvent the wishes of his superiors. Others may have been faint-hearted, but no matter what it took, he made certain those boxcars were full, rolling into the camps on schedule. "Near the end," he told me one night, "Himmler himself wanted me to stop. He thought we could save our skins. But I pressed on. If a man has an assignment to perform, he does not stop until it is done."

And he sat there beaming, knowing that members of my own family had been massacred, waiting for me to exclaim, "God, that's admirable!" I swear, if I had been killed myself and come back as a ghost, even then he would have looked to me for praise. His only sorrow was that he had not had the time to complete his mission.

Still I refused to accept it. There is a human being here, I would tell myself, he can be reached. I can make him see.

After each such session, I would replay the dialogue in my mind, furious at him and at myself; obsessively replaying what I had said and casting desperately about for ways of saying it better the next time.

And the next day I would try again.

Thinking it over, I was quite certain Eichmann meant what he said: He had never hated the Jews, not in the same sense as his more stridently racist colleagues. Indeed, he only began to hate us after the capture, for questioning his right to do what he had done. *That* turned his world upside down. How dare we question his authority? He had his orders, it was all legal. How dare we presume to judge him?

In the end it was not Eichmann who was changed by those conversations, but me. Afterward, I would never again be so unshakable an optimist about humankind. I would face the fact that perfectly normal-seeming individuals, products of conventional homes, can be so emotionally dead as to find themselves beyond the reach of human feeling. It was a powerful revelation, and a desperately sad one.

But, too, those sessions caused me to reflect on my own actions in ways I never had before. I realized that in the course of my career I had participated in actions that were unjust, perhaps even criminal. Always I had followed my superiors' orders absolutely, most of the time for what seemed noble reasons—because we all loved Israel, because I honestly believed they loved humanity and justice—yet also because it was a matter of habit.

I would never be that easy on myself again, or find excuses to deny the hard evidence of my eyes, and ears, and heart.

For the fact is as simple as it is inescapable: If the conscience stops functioning, even occasionally, one is in mortal danger of losing oneself.

Now, at long last, we received word that the escape plan had gotten the go-ahead. For the first time an El Al flight was to land on Argentine soil, bearing Israel's delegation to the 150th anniversary festivities. In coordination with El Al's management, Isser had arranged the recruitment of a special crew and mechanics for the flight. A vast array of special permits and clearances had been obtained. Permission had been granted for the plane to be parked in a remote part of the airport, for it to taxi to the tarmac instead of being towed, for the crew to board in the maintenance area rather than from the terminal. Above all, airport security was to be augmented by our own people. If word of Eichmann's disappearance had indeed been put out among his friends, there was the very real possibility that someone would put two and two together and move to sabotage the plane.

So long caught between the sense that we were about

to be discovered at any moment and the sinking feeling that we would be stuck there forever, those of us in the villa took the news as a relief of immense proportions. Immediately I stepped up work on my own role in the escape, the creation of Eichmann's disguise.

Already I had done three or four studies on him, using different glasses, clothes, varieties of facial hair. He was a willing subject, taking to it as a kind of parlor game, and days before I had reached a couple of conclusions. If we went with the escape by ambulance I would make him an elderly American, probably bundling him up for the journey in a shapeless overcoat buttoned to the chin, and obscuring his creviced face and shaggy gray moustache with a heavy scarf. If we went with the plane, he would be an El Al employee, probably a steward.

But now it was time to get the details nailed down. The day we got the news, I sat him down in a chair after lunch, gave him a close shave so the makeup would adhere to the skin, and set about making him twenty years younger. Erasing the lines on the forehead and beneath the eyes, I built up the cheekbones, then made the hair fuller and touched up the gray.

Even as I worked, I sensed that the transformation was succeeding beyond my expectations. I was working from the photo of Eichmann in his SS heyday. All that remained was to dress him in the El Al uniform that had been delivered that morning. After removing the insignia, I did, as a final touch pulling on a pair of highly polished boots.

The effect was staggering.

"You may look in the mirror," I said.

He walked slowly toward it, then froze, staring. Then a remarkable thing began to happen. Straightening up, throwing his shoulders back, he actually seemed to grow taller.

"*Ist gut!*" he exclaimed. "Nice uniform!"

He adjusted the peak cap, reproducing exactly the angle in the photograph. "*Ist wunderbar!*"

Without any word of command from me, he turned and started walking around the room, regaining more of the old arrogance with every step, until he was fairly strutting, back straight, chin out, eyes narrowed almost to slits. All he needed was his riding crop, and he might have been on an inspection of Auschwitz.

If there had been so much as a trace of doubt in my mind about this man, it was gone. Now I had seen the real Eichmann in the flesh.

He was back in front of the mirror, admiring the braid and the brass buttons, when there was a knock on the door. I ordered Eichmann to sit down on the bed and shut his eyes. The obedient soldier, he did so instantly

I opened the door and there stood Hans, accompanied by David.

"Gentlemen," I intoned, "allow me to present Obersturmführer Adolf Eichmann."

As Eichmann pulled himself erect they stared in frank horror.

"Peter," said Hans finally, in a tone I had never before heard from him, "you're an artist."

But once he regained his bearings he was his old self. The youthful Eichmann, he informed me half an hour later, was interesting, but unsatisfactory for our purposes. Far from obscuring our man's identity, it made it obvious to anyone who had encountered him during the years when he was most visible. Who knew—we might even be tripped up by one of his former victims.

Irritated as I was by the familiar high-handedness, I had to agree that he had a point. It would undoubtedly be safer, if less dramatic, to *add* years to his face.

In fact, from a technical standpoint it was considerably easier. When I set about it the next morning, in forty-five minutes I was facing a tired old man.

Eichmann himself was deflated. But he expressed the rather startling conviction that such a disguise would succeed well.

Again I put on his uniform, this time, though Eichmann didn't know it, with a cap bearing the El Al insignia. Danny had arrived to take photos for Zichroni's passport. At long last the forger had the chance to confront the murderer.

But when he entered the room Danny could scarcely bring himself even to look at him. Ghost-pale, he went about his work quickly and in silence, except for an occasional terse command—"Head up," "Look to the left"—to which Eichmann would respond instantly. In fifteen minutes he was done and gone.

But, then, of course, it wasn't really surprising. "I hadn't expected the feelings to be so overwhelming," he told me afterward, still shaken by the experience. "To be in the same room with him I had to force myself not to feel anything." He paused. "That's a different kind of craziness."

He had no idea how fully I understood. That very evening Uzi and I found ourselves in a popular Buenos Aires café called Pallo Borracho, literally the Drunken Sailor, once again trying to distance ourselves from the day we had just lived. We were doing quite well. The food was excellent and plentiful, the crowd around us in excellent humor. On a raised dais a trio of guitar players added to the din, strumming a vigorous tango as they stamped their gaucho boots. We joined enthusiastically in the applause of the locals.

When the guitarists took a break the atmosphere was momentarily calm. Then, abruptly, from a table nearby, a large contingent of middle-aged men broke into raucous song in German. Singing ever louder as they clinked foaming steins of beer, swaying in unison, oblivious to those around them—indeed, to the culture itself—within seconds they had totally altered the feeling in the room.

"It's no wonder he felt so at home here," observed Uzi mildly.

For a moment I made no reply. Then the words seemed to come out of their own volition, surprising even me. "I should have killed him."

TWENTY-TWO

The Statement

ATE on the afternoon of May 19, Uzi and I left the villa on an assignment as pleasant as any either of us had ever undertaken. Its supposed purpose was a surveillance of the route from our hideout to the airport; but the El Al Bristol Britannia bearing the Israeli delegation was due to land at 5:00 P.M.

As we drove through Buenos Aires all appeared in order. For once the sun had broken through the thick, low-lying clouds. Houses draped in bunting and Argentine flags gave the city a wonderfully festive air. Crowds were everywhere. Band music drifted from public squares.

It was not until we hit the highway, and especially as we drew closer to the airport, that it became apparent how extraordinarily tight security had become. With foreign dignitaries streaming in from around the world, command cars stood at almost every intersection, supported by heavily armed soldiers.

For us there was nothing particularly alarming in this.

Our party, with Eichmann in its midst, would be official, with the papers to prove it. Indeed, the heightened security could even work to our advantage, considering the workings of the military mind. In the event of a hitch—a problem with airport personnel or a last-minute challenge from Eichmann's allies—a sharp reference to our diplomatic status might be enough to enlist an officer and his men to our aid.

Though it was something I would not admit, I was as excited as a little kid. The first landing ever of an Israeli airliner on Argentine soil! Yet more evidence that our young country was assuming its full place among the nations of the world! Hardened as we often liked to pretend we were, I was stirred to my very depths. It was even possible to forget that, thanks to us, it might also be the *last* Israeli plane to be welcomed here.

Making our way to the observation deck, we noted several of our security people positioned strategically in the crowd. There were a great many other Israelis also, presumably attached to our embassy. All around us people talked animatedly in Hebrew. Uzi nudged me. Below and off to the left, at a table in a restaurant with a clear view of the runways, sat Aharon and Hans with the Old Man. He wasn't about to miss this either.

We waited. Soon word came that the takeoff from Recife had been delayed. What was this? Could there be a problem? No, that was impossible. At this stage the flight was entirely legitimate.

At last, a little past 6:00 P.M., the familiar blue and white colors came into view. Easing down to a perfect landing, the big plane taxied toward us.

In fact, we later learned that an overzealous Brazilian air controller had delayed the plane, at worst, no more than a run-of-the-mill anti-Semite making mischief. He had insisted that, while the aircraft had authorization to fly in Brazilian airspace, and to land, it had none to take off again.

Now, as the door swung open, those around me burst

into cheers and wild applause. The noise grew even louder as the tall, portly figure of Abba Eban, former ambassador to the United States, appeared in a tailored black overcoat and began making his way down the steps. The consummate diplomat, a longtime adversary of the blunt and egomaniacal Isser, Eban had never looked more distinguished. He was followed off the plane by the diminutive Major General Meir Zorea, one of Israel's most renowned military men.

On the red carpet at the foot of the steps, they embraced their Argentine hosts, then snapped to attention as a military band struck up the national anthems.

So, at the same moment, did those of us on the observation deck. As the strains of "Hatikva" filled the Argentine evening, I glanced over at Uzi. He, too, was blinking back tears.

Now, his glasses reflecting the surrounding spotlights, Eban stepped up to the microphone. To our astonishment, instead of Hebrew or his familiar Oxford-accented English, he began talking in seemingly flawless Spanish. Though we, of course, understood little, the import was clear. We were, he maintained, witnessing the beginning of a shining new era in Israeli-Argentine relations.

I glanced across the way at Isser, taking it in with equanimity, then at Uzi. "My God," I whispered, "he doesn't know!"

We made it back to the villa by 9:00 P.M. A couple of hours later I was again with the prisoner. We started talking about Dr. Rezso Kastner, a notorious name in Israel. A leader of the Hungarian Jewish community during the war, Kastner, in an effort to save some Jewish lives (including, not incidentally, his own), had cooperated extensively with Eichmann in the destruction of hundreds of thousands of others. To my mind he was evil personified; to Eichmann's he was one of the good Jews, a man who, were he still alive, would have been ready to vouch that he had played

by the rules. Though Eichmann knew exactly how Kastner had died, shot down in a Tel Aviv street in 1955 when
his wartime history came to light, and knew, too, that the
Kastner revelations had launched a spate of trials of other
Jews who had collaborated to save themselves, none of
this seemed to figure at all in his estimation of the man's
credibility.

Partly in self-protection, I had been sketching throughout. I had learned, by now, how to hear the words while
refusing to absorb their full meaning.

"Look," I said finally, more sharply than usual, "you
can believe whatever you like. I'm not your judge."

The silence that followed was broken only by the
scratching of my pen.

"I just thought it was something you might want to
know," he spoke up. "After all, we have been together a
long time."

I made no reply.

"Please, may I see what you are drawing?"

It was another portrait of him, with special attention
this time to his long, bony hands. I turned the guidebook
toward him. He was still the only one on the premises who
had seen it.

He studied the sketch briefly, then responded as he
always did. *"Schön, sehr schön."* (Nice. Very nice.)

Indeed, he, too, suddenly seemed tired of a battle that
neither of us could win. Before long, he forgot Kastner and
started reminiscing about the culture he had left behind.

"Waren Sie mal in Deutschland?" he asked, almost
dreamily. (Have you been in Germany?)

"Yes. Many times."

"Tell me about it."

"What's there to tell? The scenery is still beautiful.
They're still drinking the same beer."

"Ah, our German beer is wonderful, don't you agree?"

"I agree. It is the best in the world."

"But I'll confess something I probably shouldn't. I'm a wine drinker myself."

"Oh, yes? I prefer wine, too."

"Good red wine. In the whole world there's nothing like it."

Suddenly I had an inspiration. "You know what, I'm going to get you some." I stood up.

"What?"

"Right now."

Quickly stealing up to the second floor, in the hall closet I found the bottle of expensive French red wine David had bought for the Sabbath. Then, as an afterthought, I eased into his room next door and snatched up the old windup record player he kept by the door, as well as the record most immediately at hand.

When I returned, Eichmann was sitting up in the bed, eyes alive with anticipation. I opened the wine, then got out a pack of cigarettes.

"Here," I offered, "have one."

He hesitated. "Really?"

"Sure. Go ahead."

I lit it for him and placed it between his lips. He sucked in the smoke gratefully.

"Now, here," I said, pouring a glass of wine, "take this."

He held the glass gingerly, by his fingertips, as if afraid it would come to pieces in his hand.

"Skoal," he said finally, and took a long sip. "Ahh. That's so good. Thank you. Thank you for doing this for me." He started to hand back both the cigarette and the wine.

"No, finish them."

"Really?"

"What's wrong with you? Of course."

Visibly he seemed to relax. "Why are you doing this for me?"

"It's a small thing. You told me you liked wine."

There was a long moment of silence.

"Eichmann," I said, "I think it's about time you sign that paper."

He stiffened. "I don't want to go to Jerusalem," he repeated. *"Warum kann es nicht in Deutschland sein?"* (Why can't I go to Germany?)

"I'm not going to try to force you, but I want you to think seriously about it. Signing that statement will be your declaration to the world that you are prepared to defend your behavior, as you've defended it to me."

"But it's impossible. What chance will I have?"

The old thought flashed to mind—What chance did your victims have?—but I held my tongue. "All I can guarantee is that you'll have a fair and open trial. You can have the lawyer of your choice. Your family will be free to visit you."

He shook his head. "No. It's something I have to think over."

"Fine. Like I say, I'm not going to force you."

We smoked and drank for a couple of minutes. Then I rose and placed the record on the machine. It was a flamenco, even at low volume, an aggressively annoying one.

He smiled. "Oh, that's nice. Thank you."

"I'm sorry I couldn't find you a Viennese waltz."

"Have you been to Vienna recently?"

"Yes."

"Are they still waltzing?"

"Of course. Nothing ever changes in Vienna."

He offered a wistful smile. "You know what—get me the paper."

"I don't know where it is."

He pointed. "It's there, by the mirror."

I handed it to him. Carefully he read over the words Isser had dictated.

I, the undersigned, Adolf Eichmann, hereby declare of my own free will that, since my true identity has become known, I realize the futility of trying to continue to flee justice. I declare myself ready to travel to Israel and to stand trial before a competent court. It is clearly understood that I shall be provided with legal counsel, and I myself will endeavor to clarify the facts of my years of service in Germany so that future generations may receive a true picture of those events. I am making this statement of my own free will. I have been promised nothing and no threats have been made against me. I desire at long last to find repose for my soul.

He looked up with a quizzical expression. "May I make an addition?"

"Of course."

"May I use your pen?"

I handed it to him, then unfastened his leg iron.

Moving to the edge of the bed, he lay the paper down on the night table and began writing in a tidy hand: "Since I can no longer remember all the details, and sometimes confuse certain events, I hereby request assistance in my effort to reach the truth by being given access to pertinent documents and depositions."

He looked up. "All right, I'll sign now." He paused. "What it says is right. It will be good to be able to explain myself."

Standing above him, heart leaping, I watched as he wrote, "Adolf Eichmann, Buenos Aires, May 1960."

I think that in the end, Eichmann on some level truly had come to accept the premises implicit in the document. Realizing he was doomed, for him a show trial in Jerusalem represented an irresistible opportunity, not only to once again be a figure of renown but to get some credit for what he had done, as he had so persistently sought credit from me. If he had to die, why not as a martyr to the cause, leaving a public legacy for his children and Nazi sympathizers everywhere?

"You will be with me in Israel, too?" he asked now.

"No. But I will come and see you."

"Really, you mean it?"

"Yes."

I rose and turned the record over. A tango.

He nodded appreciatively. "Ahhh, *wunderbar*. Could I, perhaps, have a little more wine?"

It was the first time he had ever asked me for anything. At bit startled, I poured him another glass.

"Now," I said a moment later, "you know there is one other thing we have to discuss."

Instantly the tension was back in his face.

"No," he said, shaking his head, "I'm sorry. I cannot help you with that."

"But surely you've had contact with others in Buenos Aires. It's very hard to believe otherwise."

"No." He shook his head violently. "I've already explained; to them I was a leper. They all stayed away from me."

"We have information that Dr. Mengele lives here."

"I don't know, I don't know anything about that."

This was, I still believe, primarily a matter of loyalty; though doomed himself, he was unwilling to desert the cause. But, too, as always, he was concerned about his family.

I paused a long time, gazing at him evenly. Maybe that could be played upon. "I know you're not a liar, Eichmann. But what you're telling me just doesn't make sense. Your sons are involved with the local Nazi party. Do you mean to tell me that they don't know anything either? Or that they never bothered to tell you?"

Perhaps it was the wine, but at the very mention of his family his lower lip began to quiver and tears welled in his eyes. "They never told me!" he insisted.

"You say you hate the sight of blood. Josef Mengele, he gloried in it. Why shouldn't such a man be brought to justice?"

"I know nothing about him!"

"We don't want to ask your children, but if it comes to that, we will."

"They don't know anything! None of them ever hurt a fly." He was crying in earnest now. "Please, why do you want to involve them?"

Watching him, I felt nothing but contempt. If this was not a performance, if he felt as deeply as he seemed to, then the distance he had traveled in the service of Nazism from his best self was even greater than I had imagined.

I fell silent, sipping my wine. Perhaps, sensing the worst was over, he began to relax. A moment later he took a tentative sip of his. Turning the record over, I played the first side again.

Suddenly, frighteningly, there came the sound of someone rapidly descending the stairs. I barely had time to redo his blindfold before the door was flung open. There stood David, barefoot in a pair of gray pajamas, eyes wide as he took in the scene.

"What the hell are you doing," he said incredulously, "throwing a party for this murderer? Have you taken leave of your senses?"

"It's not a party," I started to explain. "I was just . . ."

"And with *my* music?!" he interrupted. Striding over to the record player, he jerked the needle off the record. His face was red now and he was shouting. "You amuse *him* with my music? This butcher of my family?!"

Eichmann, sightless, could not have known for sure who was speaking, but it was not hard to guess at what he was saying. He shrank back, as if trying to burrow into the bed.

Now Uzi appeared at the door, bleary eyes working to adjust to the light behind thick lenses. He was followed almost immediately by Meir, Rosa, and Jack. "All right," said Uzi calmly, clasping his hands on David's shoulders to calm him down, "what's going on?"

"He"—he pointed at me—"this man is holding a concert for Eichmann!"

At the sound of his name the prisoner seemed to grow even smaller.

"Look," I offered, "there was a point to it. I . . ."

"My God, the Sabbath wine! He gave him the Sabbath wine!" gasped David, pointing. He picked up the bottle and cradled it.

"My God!" echoed Rosa. "How low can you sink?"

"You'll pay for this," said David, actually trembling with rage. "I'll make sure there's an official inquiry."

"Look," I said, "will you just listen?" I held the statement aloft. "He's signed it. He's agreed to go to Jerusalem."

Somehow the announcement had less impact than I had supposed it would.

"What business was that of yours in the first place?" It was Jack, as angry as the others. "We're under orders not even to speak to him. Who are you to disobey?"

Uzi took the document from my hand and looked it over.

"All right," I admitted, "maybe it was a mistake. But it was no party. It seemed to make sense at the time."

"Never mind," said Meir. He threw a protective arm around my shoulder. "Go to bed. It's almost time for me to relieve you anyway."

Glancing at my watch, I saw he was right. It was just a few minutes before 3:00 A.M.

"All right," agreed Uzi, "it's time for everyone to go back to sleep. We'll deal with it in the morning."

He ushered us all out of the room, then, hanging back, caught me by the elbow. "Good work," he whispered. "I'd have done the same thing."

When I walked into my room, Rosa was in bed, turned toward the wall, refusing even to acknowledge my presence. Slowly, by the light of a small table lamp, I prepared for bed.

"What did I do?" I asked. "Are a little wine and some music so important?"

"I don't want to talk to you," she hissed. "That wine was for the Sabbath!"

"If he'd told me where Mengele is, would you complain then?"

She turned to face me. "There's something wrong with you. You're crazy. You act like you're in love with him."

"It's cold," I said, getting into bed. "I don't want to talk to you either. Good night."

She said nothing. I lay there for ten minutes. Thousands of miles from my loved ones, from any human connection, I had never felt so terribly alone.

Finally, quietly, I got out of bed and walked across the room. "Could you move over a little?" I asked softly.

We fell asleep in one another's arms, holding tight for dear life.

Isser arrived the following day precisely as scheduled, at 10:00 A.M., accompanied by Aharon. The atmosphere in the villa remained tense. David and I had not exchanged a word all morning.

"Let's have a look at the prisoner," demanded the Old Man.

Uzi and I led him to Eichmann's room. Jack, standing guard, rose from the stool at his appearance. For a couple of minutes the Old Man stared at the blindfolded figure dozing fitfully on the bed, then wheeled and returned to the living room.

Now Uzi handed him the signed statement. His eyes widened in pleased surprise as he looked it over. "How did this happen?"

"Peter got it."

He turned to me, smiling. "Good. Excellent work. This is vitally important."

None of the others, arrayed about the room, said a word.

"What about Mengele? Did you ask him again about Mengele?"

I nodded. "He wouldn't say a word. I honestly think he'd make us kill him first."

He then gave us a brief status report on preparations for the escape. Things at the airport were proceeding well. The plane was in excellent condition. Though most of those manning the aircraft had no idea what was up, they were following the instructions they had been given to the letter, moving past the Argentines guarding the plane at all hours of the day and night, often joyously raucous, as if having done too much celebrating in town.

Despite myself I grinned. No one I knew back in Israel would buy such a ruse for a minute. In general, Jews tend to be moderate drinkers. In some families a single bottle of after-dinner liqueur, purchased in case of guests, remains intact for decades. The notion of an entire crew of an important El Al flight staggering around for days in their cups struck me as hilarious.

Thank goodness the Argentines knew as little about us as we did about them.

Now Isser scanned the room, his gaze moving from face to face. "I know what you've all been through. All you have to do is hang on for a couple of days longer." He focused on Uzi. "I want security intensified. This will be the most nervewracking part, the final act. I just have a feeling they're drawing close."

He rose to his feet, began putting on his overcoat.

"What about Eichmann's family?" spoke up Uzi suddenly.

"What do you mean?"

"What happens to them?"

"When the time comes, they'll certainly be permitted to visit him in Jerusalem."

"I mean who will provide for them?" He got to his feet also. Though short himself, he towered over Isser. "They have no other source of income. I say the State of Israel ought to help."

The Old Man's face reddened. "That's outrageous. There is no law on the books requiring such a thing. No one provides for the family of an ordinary criminal sent to prison. The head of a family ought to think about that before he commits a crime." He paused, thinking it over, angrier by the second. "Don't you think for a moment that Eichmann's family was unaware of what he was doing!"

The subject was closed. He strode to the door and slammed it behind him.

Isser was right, of course. We owed Eichmann nothing, were, indeed, already giving him far more than he deserved.

Yet never had I been more impressed with Uzi. In the end it was he who understood best of all of us what this whole thing was about: the need to hold on to one's humanity even if, all around, others have surrendered theirs.

TWENTY-THREE

Escape

F OR at least a day Eichmann had known that something was up. Even when blindfolded, he was alert to shifts in the atmosphere, and it had not been hard to pick up the increased activity around the villa.

The front door could be heard opening and closing far more regularly than at any time since his arrival as David and Rosa, singly or as a couple, continually strolled the neighborhood looking for suspicious movement. Once again preoccupied with the condition of the cars, one of his guards (Meir) had all but disappeared. The rest of us were obviously on edge, even the unflappable Dr. Klein.

When Klein had come by his room to conduct his nightly examination, it had not escaped Eichmann's attention that this time the talkative doctor had gone about his work in total silence.

I understood what Klein was feeling. At long last, his moment on center stage was near. He was to incapacitate the prisoner long enough to get him on the plane, evidently a delicate procedure. Too low a dosage of the sedative and Eichmann, within full view of airport security personnel, would surely sound the alarm. Too much, and he would seem in such precarious health that, written guarantees from the local hospital notwithstanding, someone might question his fitness for such an arduous journey.

When I relieved Uzi at dawn on May 20, Eichmann was wide awake. He had gotten even less sleep than the rest of us. I led him through what had become a routine, walking him across the veranda to the toilet, shaving him before the mirror, leading him back out to the veranda for his exercises. I was helping him with his deep knee bends, holding his outstretched hands, when he paused in mid-bend. *"Werden Sie mich heute töten?"*

"No, we're not going to kill you." I paused. *"Heute werden Sie nach Jerusalem gebracht."* (Today is the day you're going to Jerusalem.)

I literally felt the shudder run through him. But almost instantly he pulled himself together, the good soldier. *"Ja,"* he said with a crisp nod.

Then, "Are you going with me?"

"No. In a little while I'm going to make up your face."

It wasn't absolutely necessary; he wouldn't be leaving for the airport until nine that evening. But I had no other responsibilities to attend to, and as obsessed as everyone else by the possibility of some kind of last-minute screwups, I felt we needed a dress rehearsal. Adolf Eichmann was being sent into the world. There was no such thing as over-preparation.

An hour later, a towel around his neck, I was well into it: graying the hair, accentuating the facial lines and the bags beneath his eyes, adding the unkempt moustache. Then came the uniform, the starched white shirt and tie, the blue pants and jacket, the pair of freshly polished shoes, and, finally, the cap.

Only this time, when I led him to the mirror, it bore the El Al insignia, a blue Star of David at its center.

Seeing it, he recoiled. "Oh," he said softly, "I understand."

"You're to be one of the El Al crew."

He kept staring into the mirror, clearly shaken. "You have nice uniforms."

"You recognize the star?" I goaded, unable to help myself.

"*Ja*," he nodded. "Of course."

Leading him back to the bed, I took off the uniform and began removing the makeup. "I'm going to want you to get some rest," I said. "It's going to be a long day."

Even by the standard to which we had grown accustomed, the hours that followed dragged on endlessly. We played game after game of chess. We read magazines we had already read five and six times before. When in mid-afternoon David asked me into his room and offered his heartfelt apologies, even giving me the flamenco record as a souvenir, my gratitude was genuine; but I was even more grateful for the diversion. To the end, David was in character. In his room he served the best cognac to be had in Buenos Aires. The suitcases lying open on his bed were full of silk shirts and exquisitely tailored suits. I could not help but sense that he was as wistful about the approaching end of the mission as the rest of us were grateful.

Only Eichmann seemed to use these hours well. When I returned to his room late in the afternoon to begin preparing him for the journey in earnest, I was struck by the change in his demeanor. He was as calm as I had ever seen him, evidently reconciled to whatever was ahead.

By 7:30 P.M. his makeup was back in place. Putting on his sunglasses—even at night, an old guy trying to recover from a final fling on the town would hardly want to deal with bright light—I allowed him a last look at himself in the mirror. He used it to adjust the cap slightly, then turned to me.

"Thank you. You have been very correct with me. I thank you."

I answered only with a nod.

Now it was time for Dr. Klein. Entering with his bag, he had Eichmann remove his jacket and roll up his right sleeve. He rubbed a bit of alcohol-soaked cotton on his arm.

Momentarily Eichmann panicked. "It isn't necessary to give me an injection," he pleaded. "I won't utter a sound, I promise!"

"Don't worry," the doctor reassured, "it's nothing, just something to control your excitement."

"No, no, no. I'm not excited."

"Please," I said, "we have to. We have orders."

This he understood, and he fell silent.

Quickly the doctor inserted the needle, taped it in place, and ran a connecting tube down his arm. With a trigger mechanism in his hand, Klein was able now to administer small doses of the sedative as needed.

As a test he gave it a squeeze. Almost instantly Eichmann began to nod out. Then, less than a minute later, he suddenly revived. "No, no," he slurred, "I don't need it."

"Good," pronounced the doctor, putting on his own El Al jacket, "Let's get him into the car."

I fetched Uzi. Taking Eichmann under the armpits, the two of us lifted him to his feet and draped his arms over our shoulders. He shuffled along, swaying slightly but basically moving under his own power.

"No," he slurred, his voice dull and thick, "I'm all right. I can do it myself."

When we got him out to the courtyard it pierced his consciousness that he did not quite fit with the doctor and Jack, also in unform. "I don't look right," he said in agitation. "I have to put on the jacket!"

Indeed, it was as if he was taking a rooting interest in the mission's success.

Of course he was right about the jacket. As soon as he was in the back seat, slumped between the other two, Klein carefully draped it over his shoulders.

Now Aharon took his place at the wheel, and Uzi slid in beside him.

"Don't worry," slurred Eichmann, just before I slammed the back door shut, "you can rely on me. I don't need any more injections."

The engine started. I ran to open the gate, and a moment later the car swung into the quiet street. It was followed a moment later by one driven by Hans, Meir beside him.

Alone now, Rosa and I walked back into the house. Suddenly the place was silent. It felt astonishingly empty. There was much to be done—the house would have to be made precisely as it had been ten days before—but we would get to that later.

For now, we just sat and waited, only occasionally bothering to make small talk. We were both wondering the same thing, silently making the same calculations. It's 9:15 now, they should be on the highway. It's 9:45; almost there. Had they run into any roadblocks? What was going on at the airport? Ten o'clock! What was happening?

"Would you like some Sabbath wine?" I asked.

"Yes. Thank you."

So I poured out what wine Eichmann and I had left in the bottle. It was indeed a Friday night. With desperate good cheer, we began singing Sabbath songs.

It was not until two in the morning that Uzi and Aharon returned. All it took was a look at Uzi's face as he bounded out of the car. "They're off?" I said.

"They're off! He's on his way to Israel!"

As exhilarated as they were frozen (halfway back, the car's heating system had given out), they could hardly get the story out fast enough. Eichmann had been no problem at all. Eased along by the medication, he had continued to behave like a very pleasant drunk. When they arrived at the airport, the guards at the control point, noting that all three passengers in the back seat were apparently sleeping off a binge, had laughingly waved the car through without checking anyone's papers. *Just a few more drunken Jews.* The car drew as close as possible to the plane. When it was time to board, the real crew members surrounded the fake ones, helping the doctor and Jack ease him inside.

Eichmann, semiconscious, was seated in the left forward window seat of first class, with the doctor in the aisle seat beside him. The other six first-class seats were immediately occupied by legitimate uniformed crew, under orders to pretend to sleep. The lights in the first section were extinguished, not to be turned back on until the plane was airborne.

A couple of other precautionary measures were being taken. Recife was to be avoided this time. The plane was charting a more difficult course directly across the South Atlantic to Dakar, Senegal. Moreover, the takeoff time had been listed as 2:00 A.M., two hours after its actual departure.

This last proved crucial. Eichmann's son Nicolas would subsequently reveal that a week before, having checked morgues and local hospitals, the family had guessed the truth, and as many as three hundred local fascists were involved in a desperate search. Finally someone had thought of the plane that had brought the Israeli delegation to Buenos Aires. "We found out about it half an hour too late," noted young Eichmann. "Had we known a little earlier we could have prevented the plane from taking off."

It might have been exaggeration for dramatic effect, of course, or an outright fabrication. But hearing it, even long afterward, I shuddered slightly. It was precisely what we had been fearing all along.

"Do the others on board know who he is?" I asked.

Uzi glanced at his watch. "They do now. They were to be told once the plane was out of Argentine airspace."

In fact, we would soon learn that the disclosure had prompted one profoundly moving scene. In the excitement that followed the disclosure, one crewman, El Al's chief mechanic, moved off by himself and quietly went to pieces. A Polish-born veteran of the camps, he remained captive to the experience, haunted, above all, by the memory of having to stand helplessly by as an SS man dragged his beloved six-year-old brother, screaming and crying, to his death. At last regaining control, he received permission to have a closer look at the prisoner. Eichmann, awake now but sightless behind dark goggles, was aware of the shift in the atmosphere. He began fidgeting and moving uncomfortably in his seat. Meanwhile, five feet away, the other man grew visibly calmer with the passing minutes, a victim suddenly turned accuser, beginning to find a measure of peace for the first time in his adult life.

We four, plus Danny, were the only members of the team still on Argentine soil. Isser, Jack and the doctor, Hans, David, and Meir were all on the plane. Our instructions now were simple: Straighten up and get the hell out.

Early the next morning we set feverishly to work. Half a dozen cars had to be returned, the house put in order, hiding spaces dismantled, blankets removed from windows, and nail holes filled in. It took the five of us the better part of a day.

Danny and Rosa left together early that evening on a plane bound for Montevideo, Uruguay. It would be up to them to make their way home from there. But they were the lucky ones. Uzi, Aharon, and I hadn't given more than perfunctory consideration to how we were going to get out of the country. And because of the ongoing anniversary celebrations, we were unable to book any flight out at all.

Instead, we ended up on a train bound for Santiago,

Chile, and a grueling, thirty-hour journey through the Andes. Arriving there in the dead of night, we were lucky to find a room in a shabby hotel. But the next morning we discovered that there were no flights out of Santiago either, for at least a week.

Unfamiliar with the city and at a loss as to how to proceed, we made contact with the only soul any of us knew in the region, a young Israeli, with whom Uzi had once been infatuated, who worked in Santiago as a translator. She was almost as happy to see us as the other way around and immediately took it upon herself to show us the town. Since we were pretending to be tourists it was hard to put her off.

All that day and into the next we looked at sights: churches and plazas and Spanish haciendas, museums and ruins and more churches. This person was so intent on our not missing anything that Aharon had to contrive an elaborate story just to escape for an hour to send a coded cable home as to our whereabouts.

At the end of the second day, heading back to the hotel on a public bus, I happened to glance across the aisle toward a man reading the evening paper. It had the boldest, blackest headline I had ever seen. One word leapt out at me: **EICH-MANN.**

As soon as we got off we bought a copy of every paper in sight. Beside herself with excitement as she read, Uzi's friend filled us in on the remarkable news: Israeli agents had captured Adolf Eichmann and spirited him to Israel! Prime Minister David Ben-Gurion had himself made the announcement before a startled Knesset. In Israel there was jubilation in the streets.

We stood there with silly smiles on our faces, our feigned joy no match for the elation of our companion. In fact, we felt a certain ambivalence. We had been assured that the announcement would be delayed until all members of the team were safe.

"Where?" I asked. "Does it say where they got him?"

"No. There's speculation about Kuwait. Also Argentina." She grinned. "Who knows? Maybe *you* captured him."

We had made vague plans to head to Valparaiso the next moring. What the hell, we figured, as long as we were stuck, we might as well see South America. However, that very evening an earthquake devastated much of southern Chile. We were thus obliged to spend several more days in Santiago before at last we got hold of three airline tickets out, two to Montevideo, one to Rio.

Aharon and I took the two. What we didn't know is that the plane to Uruguay made a stop in Buenos Aires. The normally cool Aharon, having been seen at the airport with the Israeli delegation the night Eichmann was smuggled out, was a wreck for the entire hour and a quarter we were on the ground, not only refusing to leave his seat but to even momentarily lower the newspaper he was pretending to read. But the flight took off without incident.

From Montevideo we caught another plane to Rio, where, two days later, we secured a flight to Paris, and then an Air France flight home. It had been almost three weeks since the completion of the mission.

TWENTY-FOUR

Back in Jerusalem

ON our return, Israel was still in an uproar. The reaction to the capture had far exceeded even my wildest imaginings; there was nothing less than an explosion of national pride. It dominated the headlines, the airwaves, casual conversations. Flags and banners were everywhere. *We had struck back!* ran the unspoken theme. *For the first time since the days of the Old Testament, we had risen in righteous fury!*

When I joined my mother and brother at her apartment the first Sabbath after my return, Yechiel flatly declared that this was the best thing that had ever happened to the Jews. "I wish I could have been part of it," he said. "I'd give my right arm to have been one of those people."

I, of course, played dumb. I asked a lot of questions. Having been in Paris throughout, I didn't have all the details.

"What," said my mother, eyeing me closely, "they don't have newspapers in Paris?"

"Mama, it isn't quite as big a story there."

She leaned forward. "Where were you really?"

"Look, didn't you get my letters?"

"I did. They were like all your letters. They could have been written last year or tomorrow." She paused. "Tell me the truth, were you involved in this?"

For just a quarter of a second I felt an overwhelming urge to tell them.

But, no, such a breach of national security was out of the question.

"Please, Mama," I said, "enough. I was in Paris."

She nodded. "Well, if you weren't there, it's a pity you weren't here." And together they went on and on about all that had gone on in Israel since the capture and all I had missed, above all marveling at the brilliance of Isser Harel, who had made a rare public appearance with Ben-Gurion in the Knesset, acknowledging the gratitude of the nation.

When I reached Gila, her suspicions were even more pointed. "How was it in South America?" she asked, as soon as she heard my voice.

"I was in Paris," I offered. "I'll tell you all about it over dinner."

"No," she said, uneasy, "no. It's not a good idea." She said her life was just getting back on track; the last thing she needed was to throw herself back into an emotional maelstrom.

She didn't say so, but I had the impression she was seeing someone else.

I didn't argue with her; that had never been my style. But what she didn't know is how much I had begun to change in our time apart. If she had agreed to see me, I probably would have asked her to marry me.

The capture provoked an even more intense diplomatic fire storm than we had anticipated. The initial Israeli stance that, as a matter of national security, no details about the case would be made public had set off an astonishing round of speculation. Press reports had the operation taking place everywhere from Germany to Kuwait. One Viennese paper reported that Eichmann had been brought to Israel on a submarine; a Cairo daily had information that he had been located by Communists in Iraq. The vaunted *New York Times* noted that "one of his many mistresses is reported to have put Israeli agents on his trail."

However, within seventy-two hours of Ben-Gurion's appearance before the Knesset, an Argentine afternoon daily, acting on sources within the Argentine government and military who had been aware of Eichmann's presence in the country, authoritatively announced that he had been abducted in Buenos Aires.

In a nation where public debate had long been characterized by emotionalism and macho posturing, the revelation was a national scandal. Newspapers competed in the ferocity of their denunciations of what all agreed was a clear violation of international law and Argentine sovereignty. Politicians across the Argentine ideological spectrum demanded the facts and talked ominously of sanctions against Israel.

For a time, hoping to contain the damage to relations with a friendly government, Israel continued to maintain a discreet silence. But in the first week of June, when Argentine Foreign Minister Diogenes Taboada publicly demanded from Israeli Ambassador Aryeh Levavi a full response to the charges, adding that, if proven, Argentina would take unspecified "appropriate measures," Israel was forced to change course. Levavi soon produced a carefully worded and less than wholly persuasive reply: The criminal had indeed been discovered in Argentina, by "volunteers," and he had agreed of his own free will to stand trial in Israel. The note in Eichmann's hand was produced as evidence.

Far from defusing the crisis, the Israeli response only heightened it. On June 8, under mounting pressure from the Right, the Argentine government demanded Eichmann's immediate return and punishment of the individuals responsible for his abduction. Prime Minister Ben-Gurion, shocked by the demands, now sat down and wrote Argentine president Arturo Frondizi a long personal letter, attempting to explain what he considered obvious: that, for Israel, Eichmann was a special case. No harm was intended to Argentina, he wrote, and if any had been done, he was grievously sorry. But "6 million of our people were murdered . . . and it was Eichmann who organized this mass murder, on a gigantic and unprecedented scale throughout Europe."

The Argentine response was frosty: The Israeli ambassador was expelled from the country and a resolution condemning Israel lodged before the Security Council of the United Nations. It maintained that the "illicit transfer of Adolf Eichmann to Israel from Argentina created an atmosphere of insecurity and mistrust incompatible with the preservation of international laws."

Most other nations agreed, at least on the record. The resolution was fiercely debated for two days. Israel was represented by foreign minister Golda Meir, Argentina by, among others, Dr. Mario Amadeo who, it would shortly be revealed, had himself been labeled by the U.S. State Department a onetime "trusted collaborator" of the SS. In the end it passed 8–0, with the United States, Britain, and France voting in favor and the Soviet Union abstaining.

But the U.N. vote was widely recognized as merely the face-saving device it was. On August 3 Israel and Argentina issued a joint statement affirming that the matter was closed.

In fact, as soon as the capture was announced, Israeli representatives in capitals the world over had been privately congratulated. In a world governed by *realpolitik* few failed to recognize that Israel's action had been of compelling national and moral interest. Indeed, in many quarters we suddenly found ourselves looked upon as the world's conscience.

For their part, Austria and Germany, which had the most to lose through the revived attention to the Nazi past, took pains not even to appear to question the Israeli action, and both moved to distance themselves from Eichmann. The Austrian minister of the interior announced that, while Eichmann's father had obtained Austrian citizenship, it had never been extended to the son. German chancellor Konrad Adenauer made the stunning claim on nationwide television that Nazi sentiment "no longer exists among the German people."

Even the expected worldwide surge of anti-Semitism— the rumors of plans among neo-Nazis to avenge themselves against the Jewish communities of Latin America, the talk in the newspapers about the possibility of reprisals against Israel itself—was of a different variety than any we had known before. It was more tentative, far more respectful. Nicolas Eichmann himself later admitted in an article in the West German magazine *Quick* that in the wake of the capture "Nazi friends of my father just melted away. Most of them went to Uruguay for safety. We never heard from them again." Notice had been served that no ex-Nazi was safe anywhere around the world. Now, fifteen years after the war, they cringed in fear of us.

This was an unexpected and most welcome repercussion of the capture. In too many places around the world, Jews themselves were, as they remain today, quietly accepting of the anti-Semitism in their midst, conditioned, after lifetimes of acquiescence, to something other than first-class status. On assignment abroad I have seen countless individuals living with the same kind of fear my parents had known in Poland before the war, often reluctant even to be heard speaking Yiddish or Hebrew. To the extent that the operation endowed these people with a greater measure of courage and self-respect, it remains a source of enormous pride.

But, too, where once I would have returned from such a mission feeling only pride, the lessons I had learned during this one were troubling and complex. Foremost among them was that self-certainty born of strength alone is extraordinarily dangerous; that, to wield power without a clear set of governing ideals is always to risk becoming what one claims to despise.

That understanding has informed my outlook, personal and political, through all the years since. Above all, character is a matter of vigilance. In small ways, all of us are tested constantly, and we deserve to be measured by how we respond.

More than occasionally afterward in the course of a normal day—in an office, in a store, sitting in a restaurant—I would be watching someone and it would suddenly hit me: This guy is a small Eichmann, he thrives on the same sense of absolute power over others.

Not long after my return from Argentina I was called upon to spend most of an afternoon with such a man, the head of a large company. The way he made people wait outside his office to see him, even if he had nothing to do; the way he humiliated his employees, evidently just for the satisfaction of watching them cower; even the way he talked about his children was chilling. "My three-year-old will be a bank chairman," he told me, "and my six-year-old will be foreign minister. They understand this. Anything is achievable if one has the will."

I pitied those children. But, even more, I shuddered to think what they would be like in twenty years.

It didn't bother me at first that those of us who had actually carried out the Eichmann operation received no recognition, nor even that the Israeli papers kept running "exclusive reports" and "secret diaries" supposedly written by the agents who had pulled off the capture. It was enough that we were fully appreciated at work, stars in a hidden firmament. None of us had done it for personal glory anyway. It seemed to me that as head of the secret services, Isser deserved ultimate credit. And, as he himself so persuasively maintained, any attention we drew stood to compromise our future effectiveness.

Still, it did strike me as curious when I learned that

the Old Man had tried to block a private, behind-the-scenes reception for the team with the prime minister where it would be acknowledged at the very highest level that we had done something special for our people and our country. The meeting came about, finally, only through the intercession of Amos Manor, our internal security chief.

Meanwhile, as preparations for the trial continued apace, with investigators fanning out around the world to interview as potential witnesses hundreds of survivors of Nazi atrocities, and searching the world's archives for documents that would link them to the defendant, curiosity about Eichmann himself only increased. One heard variations on the questions everywhere: What kind of man was he? Would he even try to justify what he had done?

And I would sit there like a dummy, offering my opinion like everyone else.

"My God," some blowhard spoke up one night at a dinner party, "the ones I can't understand are the people who spent all those days with him. They must be made of stone."

"They're professionals," I pointed out. "They're trained for those situations."

"I say if they had real fire inside, they wouldn't have been able to keep themselves from killing him."

"Oh, no? That's what you think?"

"I know some of those people. They're automatons."

It was hard not to take at least a passing exception to that. "Maybe they're a little smarter than you. Maybe they realized the best revenge was getting him here." I paused. "Maybe they realized that the point of this thing wasn't just an eye for an eye but justice."

He glanced at his neighbors with a thin smile. "Suddenly," he said sarcastically, "everyone's an expert."

The trial lasted more than four months. It was followed by nearly four months more of deliberations by the three-judge tribunal. Their verdict was at last delivered on December 10, 1961: guilty on all counts of crimes against humanity and the Jewish people. Eichmann sat stiffly as the verdict was read, betraying nothing.

After my single brief excursion to the courtroom, I never tried to see Eichmann again. Perhaps that was a character failing on my part, a betrayal of whatever relationship we had forged. Uzi not only visited him several times in Ramle Prison but was actually present in the death chamber as a witness on May 31, 1962, when he was hanged, the only man ever executed in the State of Israel.

Unyielding to the end, he rejected an appeal by a Protestant minister that he repent. Refusing a hood, he spoke his last words in German: ". . . Long live Germany. Long live Argentina. Long live Austria. These are the countries with which I have been most closely associated and I shall not forget them.

"I greet my wife, my family and friends. I had to obey the rules of war and my flag. I am ready."

Eichmann's remains were cremated two hours later aboard an Israeli police boat, the ashes scattered over the Mediterranean outside Israeli waters. There would be no grave for Nazis to turn into a shrine.

The night Eichmann died, I slept every bit as well as I normally do. The fact is, I did not want to keep dwelling on him. I was busy getting on with my life. Four months after my return to Israel, I had started seeing a woman I had known slightly as a young man in Haifa. Soon we were serious in a way that for me was new and quite remarkable. By the time of Eichmann's death, we were married.

As time passed, my role in the capture was something I occasionally reflected upon as a source of professional pride, but it fairly quickly receded from daily consciousness. It was one more page in a thick mental scrapbook. Yet, prompted by particular events, memories of that time could return with a rush.

One afternoon at work, just three years after the mission, I received the crushing news that Danny had died of heart failure. He was only thirty-five. What none of us had known—what he had successfully hidden from a bureau itself dedicated to the keeping of secrets, by forging the appropriate medical documents—was that his heart had been bad for years. Suddenly there was an answer to what for me had remained one of the great mysteries of the operation: Danny's behavior that day at the airport.

Four years after that, in the spring of 1967, I was on assignment in Athens when I was awakened by a midnight call from Aharon.

"Your mother is ill," he told me. "She broke her hip and is in the hospital."

I was all she had left. Yechiel had died the year before.

"Is it serious?" I asked.

"Peter, at this age you never know."

I rushed out to the airport. At that hour there were no commercial flights, but I discovered a British Airways cargo plane due to leave shortly for Jerusalem and hastily explained the situation to the captain. He was apologetic but firm: It was strictly forbidden to carry an unauthorized passenger.

I was in a frenzy.

"Please," he said, "try to understand, I could lose my license."

"I promise you, you won't have any problems. Call the head of El Al in Tel Aviv. Call the secretary to the prime minister. You'll get the necessary waivers."

He eyed me with obvious curiosity, then disappeared to look for a phone. "Who are you?" he asked when he returned.

"Somebody who knows these people."

He nodded. "Get in."

My wife was waiting for me at Lod Airport and we raced to the hospital. It was just after dawn, hours before visiting time, and they wouldn't let me in. Retreating outside, I climbed up to the second story, entered through a hallway window, and located her room.

Instantly I knew that Aharon had been right. She was dying. Her color was bad, her breathing labored.

I knelt beside her bed and took her hand. "Mama," I whispered. "Mama, it's me. Peter."

The elderly lady in the next bed turned toward me. "She doesn't talk," she spoke up loudly in Yiddish.

"Mama, I want to tell you something. What I promised, I have done. I captured Eichmann."

There was no response.

"Mama, Fruma was avenged. It was her brother who captured Adolf Eichmann."

I repeated it.

"Quiet," said the other lady, "she doesn't hear."

But suddenly her hand began to squeeze mine.

"Do you understand, Mama? I captured Eichmann."

Her eyes were open now. "Yes," she managed in a whisper. "I understand."

For fifteen years that was the only time I violated Isser's gag order. My son and daughter, born in the midsixties, never even heard the name Eichmann spoken in our home. Believing as they did that I worked as a government clerk, they were stunned when an elementary school classmate passed on the story that their father had helped kidnap the most notorious Nazi of the postwar era. I could not help but note their deep disappointment when I told them he was mistaken.

In fact, by then it was not entirely surprising that a sharp ten-year-old should suspect the truth. Articles had been written and roundabout acknowledgments made. But my training on the point had been explicit. When national security was held to be at risk, one damn well kept his mouth shut.

Even when I retired from the secret services in 1976, I

adhered to that credo. By now all of my friends had come to know of my involvement, and Isser himself had written a book on the subject. Yet the order we had been given had never been formally lifted.

The irony was that my very adherence to that order made the task of finding other work infinitely harder. Ending my secret services career as head of the Department of Operations, I found myself having to explain away to prospective employers a twenty-seven-year gap in my résumé. In a very real sense I was a victim of my own success. In my business, only the failures became known.

I was still feeling young, but increasingly I was aware that I no longer seemed that way to others. Sometimes, despite myself, I had trouble keeping the questions at bay. In the end what had been the point?

Finally, because I had always liked the place and there was no reason not to, I decided to move to New York. I would paint and write.

Thus it was that one frigid winter morning in 1981, an Israeli friend and I stood bundled up on Third Avenue, scanning the street for a cab. We were in a rush to get to LaGuardia Airport. We were due at a conference on airline security in Washington.

Finally we got one. Staring out the window at the Manhattan streets, my mind was a blank. My friend began chatting with the cabbie. Hearing a familiar accent, I glanced at his hack license.

"Are you Polish?" I asked in English.

"Yeah."

"Jewish?"

"Yeah."

"Where are you from?" I asked, switching to Yiddish. He answered in kind. "A little place you never heard of."

"What's it called?"

"I told you, you never heard of it."

Definitely a Polish Jew.

"What's the name?"

He threw up a hand in exasperation. "Żołkiewka. Satisfied?"

I was dumbstruck. Things like this just didn't happen.

"Did you," I asked, as calmly as I could, "by any chance know a family called Milchman?" It was our former name.

There was a long pause. "Who are you?"

"They are my family. My name is Peter."

He glanced at me in the mirror. "Sure, I know them."

And one by one he started reeling off the names. Duorale, Chava, Reuven, Yiłzchak. My parents, my aunts and uncles, everyone. He even know vaguely of me, one of the few in the village who had escaped.

It was not a very long ride; already we were approaching the Triboro Bridge. "Do you know how it was for Fruma?" I asked.

He knew, and in greater detail than I was prepared to hear.

Early one pretty spring morning in 1941, a year and a half into the German occupation of Poland, the Jews of the village were roused from their beds by SS men and gathered in the central square.

"I know that place," I said. "By the pump." One of my earliest memories was of my mother allowing me to help her work the handle. It was where Piatnik had died.

He turned his head and glanced at me. "Yes. By the pump."

He said the children were taken that first morning. They were sent to a small camp outside Lublin. It was later learned that they were shot upon arrival and tossed into mass graves. The women followed a few days later, and also were killed immediately. He did not specifically recall seeing Fruma or the children, but there was no question that this is when they died, and how. His own mother and three younger siblings had died at the same time.

Of the entire *shtetl*, only a handful of men had been temporarily spared, himself included. Removed from the final transport out of town, they were instead sent to Auschwitz as slave laborers.

Now it was as if he went on automatic pilot. Like so many survivors, he had told the story so often that he related it almost without expression, speaking about his movement from camp to camp, things he had seen and heard, the varieties of suffering and degradation. Once, he said, he had actually seen Eichmann himself on one of his inspection tours of Auschwitz. He remembered his bearing, his arrogance, his air of absolute authority.

"You survived four years in the camps?" I asked.

"No. I escaped in 1944. I was being transported to the extermination camp at Treblinka, and there was a loose panel on the car. A few of us got away, and I managed to join the partisans."

"Did you ever go back to Żołkiewka?"

"Not to the village itself. I didn't want to." He paused. "But near the end of the war we came to the camp where my family had died. It was deserted, just a few small buildings surrounded by barbed wire. In one of them, under a wooden plank, I found a message in Yiddish, written in charcoal: 'We know we are about to die. We leave in your hands our last testament. Avenge us.' It was signed by three girls, with their ages. Two were eleven, one was ten."

The driver didn't say anything for a while. We were on the Grand Central Parkway, approaching the airport. "For years that weighed on me. I felt a responsibility. But what could I do? I was only one man." He stopped again. "It was only when the Israelis captured Eichmann that I began to feel better. I felt that at last those girls were avenged. The victims could not sit in judgment!"

I was aware that my friend was staring at me hard. "Tell him!" he whispered.

I stared ahead, saying nothing.

When we pulled up to the curb before the Eastern Shuttle, I handed my friend a twenty-dollar bill, then got out of the cab and started moving toward the terminal. We were late. Turning, I was surprised to see that he was still inside, talking animatedly with the driver. Suddenly he pointed my way.

Now he got out and motioned. "Peter, come back. He wants to talk to you."

I shook my head. "Come on, we'll miss the plane."

"He won't take the money!"

"I don't want to talk to him. Tell him I'm sorry." I turned and continued toward the gate.

"Please, sir!"

It was the cabbie. He was on the curb now, waving frantically, eyes glistening. "Please. Is it true?"

"Yes," I called back.

A minute later, pausing to wait for my friend, I caught sight of the cabbie again. He had not moved. He was just standing there on the curb, staring after me.

AFTERWORD

I am quite often asked: Could it happen again?

Almost always, the questioner expects to be reassured. The prevailing view is that the events of the war years left so indelible a mark upon humankind that civilized opinion will never again allow such things to occur.

I say look around. Look at Cambodia. Look at Uganda. Look, too, at events far closer to home. For decades, innumerable Nazis—not only the Mengeles and Müllers, but former camp guards and *Einsatzgruppen*—have lived openly in dozens of communities, surrounded by men and women who knew precisely who they were and what they had done. Yet painfully few have come forward in shock and horror to bring them to justice. That today so much of the world views the Holocaust with frank dispassion, or even indifference, as nothing more than part of the historical record, is evidence of how dramatically, their defeat notwithstanding, the Nazis succeeded in imposing part of their vision on mankind, deadening us to the value of human life.

Evil does not exist in isolation. It is a product of amorality by consensus.

Could it happen again? Who can say?

I only know it is a question we must never stop asking.

BIBLIOGRAPHY

Arendt, Hannah. *Eichmann in Jerusalem.* New York: Viking Press, 1963.

Ashman, Charles, and Robert J. Wagman. *The Nazi Hunters.* New York: Pharos Books, 1988.

Conot, Robert E. *Justice at Nuremberg.* New York: Harper & Row, 1947.

Dawidowicz, Lucy S. *The War Against the Jews.* New York: Holt, Rinehart, & Winston, 1975.

Eisenberg, Dennis, Uri Dan, and Eli Landau. *The Mossad —Inside Stories: Israel's Secret Intelligence Service.* New York: Paddington Press, 1978.

Elon, Amos. *The Israelis.* New York: Holt, Rinehart, & Winston, 1971.

Gilbert, Martin. *Atlas of the Holocaust.* London: Michael Joseph Ltd., 1982.

Harel, Isser. *The House on Garibaldi Street.* New York: Viking Press, 1975.

Hausner, Gideon. *Justice in Jerusalem*. New York: Harper & Row, 1966.

Heydecker, Joe J., and Johannes Leet. *The Nuremberg Trial*. Winter Park, Fla.: World Publishing Co., 1961.

Infield, Glenn B. *Secrets of the SS*. Briarcliff Manor, N.Y.: Stein & Day, 1981.

Katz, Samuel. *Days of Fire*. London: W. H. Allen & Co., 1968.

Klarsfeld, Serge, ed. *The Holocaust and the Neo-Nazi Mythomania*. New York: The Beate Klarsfeld Foundation, 1978.

Musmanno, Michael A. *The Eichmann Kommandos*. Philadelphia: Macrae Smith Co., 1961.

Reitlinger, Gerald. *The Final Solution: The Attempt to Exterminate the Jews of Europe, 1939–45*. Northvale, N.J.: Aronson, 1987. (Reprint of 1953 edition.)

Samuel, Maurice. *Light on Israel*. New York: Alfred A. Knopf, 1968.

Schleunes, Karl A. *The Twisted Road to Auschwitz*. Champaign, Ill.: University of Illinois Press, 1970.

Smolen, Kazimierz. *Auschwitz*. Krakow: Krajowa Agencja Wydawnicza, 1981.

Steven, Stewart. *The Spymasters of Israel*. New York: Macmillan, 1980.

Stevenson, William. *The Bormann Brotherhood*. Orlando, Fla.: Harcourt, Brace, Jovanovich, 1973.

Von Lang, Jochen, ed. *Eichmann Interrogated*. New York: Farrar, Straus & Giroux, 1983.

Wyman, David S. *Abandonment of the Jews*. New York: Pantheon, 1984.

INDEX